BORDERLAND

Volume III of
The Wormingford Trilogy

Ronald Blythe

With illustrations by
Mary Newcomb

BLACK DOG BOOKS

First published in England 2005
by Black Dog Books
104 Trinity Street, Norwich, Norfolk, NR2 2BJ.

Copyright © Ronald Blythe 2005

A CIP record of this book is available from the British Library.

ISBN 0-9549286-0-1

Typeset in 11.5 point Times

Printed in Great Britain
by Biddles Ltd., *www.biddles.co.uk.*

In memoriam
R.S.Thomas

Reflections of a white bridge
(a fish has risen in the centre of the river) 1982

Mary Newcomb

Artists and writers swiftly recognize a shared vision. It is not that they think or see things the same way, but that they find themselves capturing in their work certain minutiae and essentials which do not appear elsewhere. They possess a shared eye but a different medium. Mary Newcomb and myself are East Anglian contemporaries, she on the Suffolk-Norfolk border, myself on the Suffolk-Essex border. The light-drenched buildings, the glimpse of the locals in the lanes and the busy-ness of nature runs between us. I could ask for no greater compliment than her pleasure in giving me permission to have her work reproduced for *Borderland*. Those who want to know her work more should read *Mary Newcomb* by Christopher Andreae, published by Lund Humphries (1996), a collection of her paintings, plus extracts from her delightful diary.

R.B.

Introduction

Borderland completes the weekly Journal I have kept for the years 1992-2004 whilst living in the Stour Valley. It marks below its quiet surface the stirrings of agricultural change, the disaster of foot-and-mouth and many developments of religious thought and social behaviour. Wormingford, Little Horkesley and Mount Bures have their feet in the Stone Age and have grown out of immensely ancient settlements above two little rivers, the Colne and the Stour. The scenery is modest but famous, due to Thomas Gainsborough and John Constable, and latterly John Nash. The farming is nearly all out to contract and what would have been a strange quietness to even our grandparents prevails. On the exciting side there is the planting of a new 500 acre wood at Fordham, just up the road, and a gradual return of plants and birds which the intensive farming of the Sixties onwards looked like destroying for ever. My neighbours mostly work in nearby old market towns or in London. The three parish churches are loved and cared for all the year but are only full on great occasions. But who is counting! I am more interested in what is *happening*.

R.B.

January

The Oilman Cometh - Two Thousand A.D. - The Prospect
Before Us - Richard Mabey's Wetlands Walk - All Snug
Within - Winter Wild - And the Waters Covered the Earth -
On the Eve of the Epiphany - Pictures - Dirty Weather - Fine
Tuning - Priests and Gentlemen - Human Incense -
Unsearchable Riches - Sylvia Dies - Translator's Day -
Please May I Leave the Room? - Bell Cage - Fellows' Gate -
Snowfall - Gallanthus - Taking Notes

The Oilman Cometh

There is an oil fright and a piteous call to Castle Fuels. Would they have me perish? We might, they reply, used to my improvidence. It is St Matthew 25 all over again. I think of the farmhouse icing up and the pets emigrating. But before one can say ice the special little tanker employed for cart-tracks crunches to my door, and the oilman himself stamps across the thick juicy mat of oak mulch. The oilman is blond with a gold ear-ring, unfazed, accustomed to emergency. I listen to a whole year's warmth gurgling through the hose. The oilman does what I have often seen countrymen do, take a wide look. He sums-up me and my garden. Has he got a garden? 'Just a bit', he says thankfully. Balanced on his iron ladder, he stares around at my realm, sees the soaring bank with its naked trees, the muddy fields with their slivers of sky, and draws an unspoken conclusion. I write a cheque. Never was money more thankfully handed over. We gravely wish each other a happy New Year and I return to raking the lawns, sodden jeans and jersey clinging to me, wellingtons glistening, heart high. How efficient I am.

Meriel the churchwarden-cum-organist and her treasurer husband come to tea and we have some of the Christmas cake which Hugh the vet has perilously left on the doorstep, drink Lapsang Suchong tea and admire the best cups. Over the fireplace the cards are beginning to tumble about and cry, ' Take us down!' The holly blackens over the picture-frames.

3

The beams remind us that they were there some time before the first performance of *Twelfth Night*. Split willow logs make tidy piles where once the copper stood. The radiators begin to crackle with new blood.

Later I visit an old friend in hospital. Wards are worlds outside a world and illness itself is a universe which is beyond the reach of the healthy. The friend is dying, is almost 'away'. The long warm corridors are tinselly and festive, but broken up by open doors which offer tableaux of suffering, of drugged sleepers, of old people reading novels, of young faces waiting for company. The foundations of this big Victorian hospital reach down into a Roman cemetery and its slates reach up into the dull January sky. I am in the part where people of all ages leave this life for another and where some of them are already beyond the diseases on their charts. Should I wake in the small hours, which is not often, I pray for the sick. I hold those I know in mind, using their names like mantras. There is plenty to do for immortality but the time comes when little can be done for mortality other than say goodbye to it. Christmas pot-plants flame on bedside tables. The wife's, the husband's, the children's photographs topple against the Lucosade, the youthful nurses are immeasurably kind. How long does the visitor stay? What is the etiquette? We shall not see each other again. How insubstantial he is already, feather-weight, snow-white. We talk about the Christmas congregations.

Two Thousand A.D.

As something of a minimalist when it come to millennialism, I note all the fuss with good humour but little attachment. Scripture loves 'a thousand' or 'ten thousand' or 'five thousand'. It is its favourite way of numbering. Isaac Watts drew his intensely moving 'A thousand ages in thy sight/Are like an evening gone' from Psalm 90, that threnody on human lifetime, and the figure appears again and again as one which is intended to impress. But it goes nowhere in our calculations of cosmic distance or how many stars create the Milky Way. The old Hebrews were ordered to be jubilant every fifty years, when they were to write-off outstanding debts, take huge holidays and do a number of other sensible things.

My only millennial resolve is to – drift. Drift is good for you. Should in January one still have a fire, then watch the pictures in it. Walk in winter woodland and by winter seas. Or in unfamiliar streets. Hike the entire length of the Thames Path and listen to the river lapping at one's heels and to happy screams from the London Wheel, and think of seasons but not of clocks. Read the Proverbs of Solomon and the Sayings of Jesus. Solomon maintained that 'the length of days is in Wisdom's right hand, and in her left hand riches and honour. Her ways are ways of pleasantness, and all her paths are peace'.

On the first Sunday of Two Thousand A.D. I took Matins at Little Horkesley and Evensong at Wormingford. Their ringing-chambers had ceased vibrating and their naves were scattered with old friends, most of whom 'had seen it all', as they say. So what to show them on such a telling date? A glimpse of the eternal, maybe? This is about as much as any of us can manage. A glimpse of yearlessness. We sang some deadly serious old hymns, shook hands, kissed, then sought our cars. Moles had heaved up the churchyard earth in friable heaps against indecipherable stones, and the chestnut-tree creaked with cold. It might have been 1859 or 1610 all over again. Choose any days you like, poor human creature. Add your birthday to prove that you were here.

Two days later I was talking about Thomas Hardy at the famous Highgate Literary and Scientific Institute, and on the very platform from which Eleanor Marx and Coleridge had held forth. It made my feet shake. When Charles Lamb heard that Coleridge had died, he said, 'It seemed to me he had long been on the confines of the next world, that he had a hunger for eternity.' The old followers of Christ, though ravished by the natural world which he had seen and loved, shared Coleridge's appetite for what lay beyond it. It seemed to them a natural progression, a proper continuing.

The Prospect Before Us

We continue to be puzzled by there being only a kind of tortured acknowledgement in the liturgy to New Year's Day, all due apparently to the Church's unwillingness ages ago to get itself mixed up with the wild fears and festivities with which the Pagans greeted it. Yet it is now the most personally *felt* date in the calendar. On it the hymn writer Timothy Dudley-Smith says we should 'Bring our thanks for all our yesterdays.' On it, too, we must give or accept that peerless blessing in Numbers 6 - 'The Lord bless thee, and keep thee; the Lord make his face to shine upon thee, and be gracious unto thee; the Lord lift up his countenance upon thee, and give thee peace.' Officially, New Year stands for the Naming of Jesus, a feast which has wandered around the months over the centuries.

I take down the Cézanne calendar and hang up the Monet on which January is 'Fishing-boats on the Beach at Étretat 1884.' And freezing it is, with a white choppy sea daring a couple of dabbed-in men to do anything more than stand and stare. A pink sky promises worse. I see Monet huddled against the wind, telling himself, 'I must be mad!' A fragment of talk on the radio about milking cows hurries me back to childhood when my brothers and myself had to be out in all weathers. Goats had to be milked before school. Had to be brought in or staked out. By the time we got them into the cosy old horse-stable our wellingtons would have filled with snow which melted between our toes. The goats, six of them, would gently butt us. The scents and sounds of the milking, our wet cold feet, the watching robins, the gale whistling around our ears, the realisation that we would have to do this until the day we died, goats being goats, would all come together in the simple fact of *being*. 'Happy New Year, boys!' they would say at breakfast. And we, of course, had forgotten to say 'Rabbits!' – so how could it be?

The old year went sadly out with the death of W G Sebald in a car crash. He was the latest loss to the University of East Anglia's wonderful Literature Department. First Malcolm Bradbury, then Lorna Sage, old friends, and now this extraordinary German writer who wrote unclassifiable books in longhand, and who 'connected' us with Europe in a curious fashion so that, reading him, we never quite knew where we were, abroad or at home. His *Austerlitz* – about a boy rescued from Hitler via the Kinder transport and brought up in chapel-going Wales – is one of those tales which alter one's thinking. Max Sebald was 57, a meteor who shot across our parochial vision and then vanished in a wintry accident-darkness, leaving us strangely bereaved and different. I remembered him and the perishable nature of things as, at last, it seemed possible to get the spring garden going, and how tragic it was to die when there were so many pages to fill up.

Richard Mabey's Wetlands Walk

Only in today's ecology would a Twelfth Night guest be sploshed off after a festive lunch to the local marsh. But then I was visiting my lifelong friend Richard Mabey and would not have expected to remain indoors when the wetlands called. All our meetings have been stretched out by giant walks, whatever the weather. This time it is pure wan winter-sun weather with just a nip of Norfolk. Rooks were lodging on the tips of oaks and the Waveney was putting in an occasional appearance. Just down the lane Diss was still dripping with the electric festoons of Christmas. But to the right were the marsh and its sucking sounds as Richard, Polly and myself did what Bunyan's hero would never have done without an urgent plea for divine protection strode happily into the mud. No birdsong, no firm footing - 'Are you all right?' – and no sense, as our forebears would have said. And everywhere an abundance of old deaths and new life, of fallen wood and wild iris shoots, papery reeds and greening mulch. My toes were soon swimming around in a leaky shoe and were still doing so on the train home. But before then it was marshlight, not just that treacherous glimmer ahead which led the country people straight into the slough of despond, but the flat glinting surface of patchy water as it lay in a string of ponds and ruts ahead. This was a Mabey walk to rival his walk with me to Wormingford Mere where, although I don't like to boast, we have a dragon. When the Psalmist slipped, morally not ecologically, the Lord bent down and 'brought me up out of the muddy pit . . . and gave me a firm footing'. Our blessed mud is called, pejoratively,

The Rook

'mire' in the King James Bible. It was something which soiled and held you. We three managed to remain upright.

Emerging, we saw the shadows of Diss and the Xanadu domes of the Bressingham Garden Centre, white in the fire

9

of the sunset. We thought we could smell tea. I had meant to pay my respects to the Diss poet John Skelton before returning to Bottengoms but swift darkness intervened. He had been the wild Rector of the little town in 1502, writing poems like *Philip Sparrow* and *Ware the Hawk* in irregular lines called 'Skeltonics.' Reverend poets are apt to be misunderstood by their parishioners. I can even see today's apprehensive churchwardens, interviewing an applicant for the living, nervously wondering whether they might ask the delicate question, 'Are you a poet?' They made John Skelton Poet Laureate and he was able to sign himself 'Laureate Poet of Disse', an exquisite title. And he could be practical, once catching a man who used the nave of his church to train hawks in. Diss grew up round a great mere and is a true waterland place. Skelton himself is buried faraway in St Margaret's, Westminster, where he was seeking sanctuary from a furious Cardinal Wolsey whom he had lampooned. Richard, Polly and I talked about the Fens, and how they are apt to breed rebels and saints and fancy words. John Skelton, Laureate Parson of Disse, knew a girl who was

> Benign, courteous, and meek,
> With wordes well devised;
> In you, who list to seek,
> Be virtues well comprised.

Her name was Margery Wentworth. I see her catching his eye at Matins.

All Snug Within

Diaries begin. First, self-assessments, then by February a comfortable falling back into old habits. Sensible diarists like Lady Eleanor Butler had no truck with good resolutions and just settled down to a pleasant winter.

'Freezing hard. Windy. Cold, but very comfortable in the dressing room – and an excellent fire. Shutters closed. Curtains let down. Candles lighted – our pens and ink. Spent the evening very pleasantly reading *Tristram Shandy* aloud – adjourned to the library. Worked – laughed.'

Self-lacerating diarists such as Katherine Mansfield tore themselves to pieces. 2nd January 1922: 'I have not done the work I should have done . . . This is very bad. In fact I am disgusted with myself. There must be a change from now on. What I chiefly admire in Jane Austen is that what she promises, she performs . . .'

Ah, if only we all performed what we promised, how satisfying this would be. Nature does. Bulbs tip the surface and will bloom, catkin stubs on the January branch will tassel. The sun just showing above the hill will run up the sky. I observe it, drinking tea by the window through which the old farmers stared, generation after generation. Same sun, same hill, and Shakespeare sixty miles away, writing *A Winter's Tale*.

A letter from Shandy Hall, where my friend Patrick has become curator. He has sent me one of Laurence Sterne's sermons. It is florid stuff delivered by the sound of it from under a full periwig to a well-heeled congregation in St Michael-le-Belfry, York in 1747, to raise funds for a local charity school. The great comic novelist was being dead serious, which wasn't his style at all. He was preaching on 'The Case of Elijah and the Widow of Zerephath' – she of the never emptying cruse of oil, should you have forgotten. And here am I reading it in a room which would have been battered by farming when the glorious charity of *Tristram Shandy* burst on the scene, to do more for humanity than ever did its author when in the pulpit. 'Writing,' wrote Sterne, 'when properly managed (as you may be sure mine is) is but a different name for conversation'. We can only hope that he managed to talk his way into the pockets of his congregation. Georgian charity, how it makes us shudder.

A hundred sheep or more graze in Harold's field along the lane. It is a surprise and a treat to see them there in a now more or less animal free landscape. It is one of those small discrete fields which still belong to the 'old people', i.e. the locals who have been here for ever and ever, who muster in force at the funeral of one of their kind, and who then reveal an unsuspected ownership of much of the village to the incomer, with his quarter of an acre property. The old people's acres would fetch a fortune with planning permission, not much when it is not granted. I like to see their meadows and fields in their modesty and occasional usefulness as they give their owners a ghostly reminder of the old independence. They are sometimes let for trifling sums, either for crops or grazing, and sometimes left to flower, which they do in a far better way than the set-aside. But, like Sterne, 'I pity the man who can travel from Dan to Beersheba, and cry, " 'Tis all barren".'

Winter Wild

The first walk of the year. Over the great field which was once ten fields, or 'several', as they say here. 'Were there many there?' - 'Several.' Fine flints glitter in the set-aside, fine rosettes of thistle, fine puddles in the ridges to catch the clouds, fine gulls on their way to a bit of ploughing. That ultimate smudge down river must be Dedham tower. My little wood whistles and shakes as I come home to it and I am tempted to do some thinning with a bow-saw. But the cold is taking my ears off, so it must be desk work instead. An appalling thought enters my head. Supposing I had come home to one of those television house and garden makeovers, to tons of decking and a blue pagoda and that wild woman with the Rapunzel hair! But all is well. The postman's van is the only vehicle in sight.

My brother telephones from Australia. He is homesick for winter. 'It is 28 degrees here, if this means anything to you. Are you breaking the ice in the water-butt?' A few thin ice needles hang from the eaves. Do I remember skating on the North meadows? Do I! One needs some chilly memories to cheer one up when the stonework round the swimming pool burns one's bare feet. Ian then rings from Edinburgh, from his eyrie-like flat high up opposite the Scott Memorial in Princes Street. A torrent of bagpipers are wailing below and the cold, well he can't describe it. Oh to be in sultry Suffolk in January.

I write a bit then wrap up, go out once more and make a place for the oil tanker to park. Come in, type a page or two, read a chapter, listen to a story on the radio, water hyacinths, answer letters and call it a day. For such is the literary life. All go. The cards and holly are toppling but cannot be removed until Twelfth Night, one of those 'fire' dates when the symbolism of the old religion and Christianity ignite. There were bonfires in the January wheatfields right up until

Kilvert's time. Epiphany light begins to steal into ours. In *Twelfth Night* Shakespeare is wishing us the ambiguity of the season. At the end of the play 'the whirligig of time' brings illuminations.

Keith the farmworker appears, plus his dogs and two little grandsons with Christmas lingering in their eyes. I think of Feste singing for the very first time, 'What's to come is still unsure'.

And the Waters Covered the Earth

Late cards continue to limp in. Mourners go about the churchyard removing dead flowers. Sacks of 'Christmas' await the dustman. The lanes are all under water, the skies awash, the river rising – were it not for the elder and willow line, who could tell where the river was? London commuters splash their way to the station, bravely making amphibious jokes. With dawn also come mallard and swans, and white water as far as the eye can see. It shines harshly. It has come to rule us. 'Flood-time!' it says. So we make what we can of it, helpless as we are in its wake. Our modest streams, Stour, Box, Brett, Linnet, Colne, are in an over-reaching mood and are filling their valleys instead of just their beds. Travellers come home with watery tales. But the ancient and wily men who built most of our riverside farms and cottages for the most part built them just out of reach of these annually flooding streams. But even where they did get in, they were soon brushed out again and could hardly make the ground floors damper than they usually were, and all the year round.

I splosh in the direction of Garnons to survey this now just occasional New Year flooding. Garnons is a manor perched on a man-made Saxon mound and has always kept its footings dry. Narrow knife-slits of sunlight cut into the rain clouds. It is the Epiphany. White or gold? says the lectionary. Take your choice. We hear the voices of John and Jeremiah, enlighteners and poets both. We address God as 'the bright splendour whom the nations seek'. We forget all the wet, the impassable roads, the roaring ditches, for are we not at 'the source of every blessing?' and although it is such a dark day, the old church is luminous beyond candles, beyond all the lights we have switched on. Needles from the vanished tree wither among the armorials of the sanctuary tombs and the vestry sports the undertaker's new calendar. 'Sing unto the Lord a new song', we are told, but we sing Monsell and Heber and Prudentius, of course. It is the best we can do. Their rich language boosts the interior glow.

Back home, I search for one book and dislodge another which whispers, 'Read me instead'. It tumbles invitingly onto the carpet, a harlot of a volume. It is Rose Macaulay's *Last Letters to a Friend 1952-1958*, which I never knew I possessed. Gone the dark day now. High Anglicans surround me, Simon Phipps, and the genuflecting incumbents of Dame Rose's beloved London churches in which she spread her worship, driving to one or another daily in her little car, believed by her friends to be under divine protection as she was the worst driver in town, and richly rising from these pages the learned Christianity of half a century ago. Then I came to her account of the Epiphany floods of 1953 when half of Holland drowned and the North Sea swept into East Anglia for miles and inundated it from the Thames to the Wash, all its seaside towns and villages, drowning hundreds of people in a few hours.

Less tragic inundations invited her wit. 'We are having

floods here; perhaps just a few men will be spared. I should like a voyage in an ark. I wish when in Turkey I had climbed Ararat and found splinters of the ancient ark, as travellers were used to do.' What she found in Turkey, of course, was the stuff, the theology if you like, of her masterly Christian novel *The Towers of Trebizond*. I can see it on a shelf out of the corner of my eye, but it won't do, I must get back to some galleys and be their slave. But I catch one of her frequent asides about the Epiphany. '*Stella ista sicut flamma coruscat* – That star sparkles like a flame. Why is it that Christ as light means more to me than any other aspect?'

On the Eve of the Epiphany

Taking writer friends on recess for their next book requires inspiration. Having swum round Britain for his *Waterlog*, Roger Deakin tells me he is now into Wood. Not into a wood but the grainy subject of wood itself. I rack my local brains for wood as material. Has Roger see Arger Fen? No he has not. Has he seen Tiger Hill? 'Tiger Hill?' He now recognises my genius as wood locationist. 'Tiger Hill,' I explain, where we went for blackberries and bluebells and nightingales, though, except for the fire, never for wood. Where we jumped off our bikes and plunged into what as a matter of fact was a fragment of the wildwood. Where we went to disturb Dr Grace, taking an hour or two off from her surgery to watch birds and listen to the poplars talking.

Glassy rides and rabbit tracks take Roger and myself

through these frigid trees, slipping and sliding. I have lent him an ash-plant walking stick made by John Masefield and it allows him to proceed in a lordly manner, being tall and steady on his feet. The cold is severe enough to make our lugs fall off, as we said long ago. Arger Fen and Tiger Hill are true *Woodlanders'* territory. A hidden community worked it for generations, first as a warren, then as a brickyard, and always as a wood. Its ancient field banks sprout colossal oaks, planted maybe after Nelson's ships had decimated their numbers everywhere. Crack willows go off like rifles in the wan light. A robin tucks his head under his wing, poor thing. The little stream hurries along, as cold as Christmas. Roger the erstwhile merman and now the prospective woodman takes stock of it all. Light snowfall adds definition to the landscape and we ourselves are now burning. Roger looks far beyond this scene. Had I ever heard of the mighty walnut-tree woods of Turkistan? He is going to see them. Arger Fen, Tiger Hill . . . Turkistan. We tramp home to old Christmas cake and warm cats.

The churches, all three of them, have that mysterious 'journeying' feeling which Epiphany brings. The toy tableau of the stable is put back in its box. Gone for a year the doll shepherds, the Magi, the thatch, the Child and his straw. For everyone connected with the birth is now on the road. It was hardly wise, one thinks, for how obviously illuminated they must have been, this handful of people who were present at the birth of God.

My brother telephones from Sydney where the temperature is 35 and the bushfires rage. They have reached the lovely Hawkesbury River down which we sailed one morning. He speaks of blackened skies and charred gardens, of burnt to death sheep and wild creatures, of filling the guttering round his house with water, but also of being safe. We are not to worry. We remember that in Suffolk the gorse and ling used to be fired at Snape, and how, as in Australia, it soon regenerated. I tell him that we have just come back from Arger Fen and Tiger Hill. 'Is it still there?' Still there! What a question. I tell him that it is still only a bike-ride away.

Pictures

Epiphany is for photography. I am on my way to Norwich to declare open Fay Godwin's retrospective at the Sainsbury Centre, that gossamer gallery, so light that it might blow away like thistledown. The train, a favourite, rips along and church towers jump in the bare fields to give it a wave, then vanish. How can they on this level landscape? Four youths on the opposite seat have been to the January sales. Shyly, they peer into their Next bags to take a second look at what they have bought, but it is all too intimate to display and jeans, shirts and jerseys are shoved back into darkness. They laugh nervously and bring out their phones. Norfolk voices. We all take a long look at Diss.

Too early for photography, I too am seduced by bargains. Sale, sale, in every Norwich shop. Already they appear rifled, as though the Vikings had paid a visit. There stands brave Edith Cavell on her plinth. She stares directly into the pub named after her, her steady gaze on its slot machines. Pansies flower darkly at her feet. And here is Elm Hill, Tombland, the Bridewell for wicked women and Sir Thomas Erpingham's superb exercise in flint, St Andrew's Hall. 'Good old knight', as King Henry calls him on the eve of

Agincourt. The afternoon fades in its acre of glass and stone. Sir Thomas's flints are each perfectly squared and not a bit like ours at Wormingford, which were carried straight from the fields to the church walls to be fixed in a kind of builder's porridge.

But now Fay Godwin's thirty years of work lies before us and perfectly tone-matched to a mild winter's evening. I read my speech and so am able to muse a little on what Erpingham would have thought of the Sainsbury Centre and its airy dismissal of flint. Now that it is dark, it is impossible to tell where the inside ends and the outside begins. The photographs are wonderful. They are one woman's meditation on Britain. For decades she has piled her cameras in her small car and set out to discover it, this land which is not that of the News, but the one to which we so individually belong. We note that she does not avoid our litter. There it lies, disgraceful, funny sometimes, ephemeral, tossed around in lovely or homely places, daring us to give a piece of our mind to the local rag. She calls the mess we make on beaches and roadsides, 'stranded material'. She is a poet with a lens, I tell the people. I also tell them about my Norfolk photographer-hero Peter Emerson, whose 19th century pictures of the Broadsmen upset the middle classes by their candour. When these reed-cutters and their wives and children peeped into Emerson's view-finder and glimpsed the vivid butterfly-wing brilliance which his camera saw, they believed they were seeing their toil place turned into the promised paradise to come. Dr Emerson on the other hand wrote strong letters about the poverty he witnessed as a photographer to the press. He and the Norfolk novelist Mary Mann saw eye to eye and were disturbing. Fay too is disturbing, questioning. A master of black and white. A visionary.

Dirty Weather

Rise at six to find last night's rural pea-souper dripping its way off the willows and a gradual clarity in the landscape. Feed wet and ravenous cats, then blackbirds with stale Christmas cake and rotten apples. Eat big breakfast. Listen to Bach. Comfort cats. Wipe fog dirt from the study window and gaze out onto the sodden scene. Observe a dog-fox, damp but debonaire, strolling past as casual as you like. Cats nod to him. Write to an ancient man to thank him for a modest account of himself in the nineteen-thirties. Find some poetry for the Retreat at Hengrave Hall. The subject is, 'In solitude he sought him' – St John of the Cross.

They say that more of us live alone these days than at any other time in history. Christ was for ever seeking an escape from those seething mobs we see on the screen. Writers are taking to garden sheds to avoid their families. I once stood in George Bernard Shaw's garden hut at Ayot St Lawrence, breathing its creosote, smelling his straw palliasse and thinking of Mrs Warren and Major Barbara. Shaw is the patron saint of shed writers.

I am writing out of season about St Luke's little summer and thinking what an age ago it was, the yellowing trees, the generous return of heat, the way in which the garden flowers turned on their last bright colours. I think of the Apostle and wonder as I always do who Theophilus was. Luke sends off both his masterpieces, his Gospel and his Acts, to the excellent Theophilus. His agent? Midday and Robert arrives from Suffolk BBC. He drives his gaudy car which has BBC painted all over it past where the sign says Cars Turn Here into the farm mud. When I reach him the wheels are spinning like tops. We shove bits of duckboard, wire netting, old sacks under them, but still they whirl. No grip. The car settles thankfully into my mud. What will the BBC say? Robert is philosophical. He is twenty-three. We return to the house, remove our shoes, telephone for the tractor, do the recording on 'A Writer's Landscape', have elevenses, talk about Robert's future and his country, which is Cumbria and doesn't sound muddy, and then of Ipswich and the glories of Bury St Edmunds. The tractor arrives and pulls Robert out and I write MUD on a signboard. But other young drivers will roar past it, they always do, it is their custom then their fate.

I de-freeze some Victoria plums and return to Luke, that physician of the soul. Then letters. Father Gabriel has written to me from St Anselm's Abbey in Washington on the blessed subject of Barbara Pym who is the connecting-pin of our friendship. It is now blackest night. I walk up the track to collect the milk and to leave the February services in an envelope for Pip to put on her computer, careful not to fall.

Fine Tuning

Certain tasks on a certain day can set one back centuries. For example, there is nothing like coppicing hazel to turn one into one of those marginalized peasants who toil away in the borders of the Luttrell Psalter. Also, I have been tricked by flowers, mostly primroses, into thinking that spring has come. Not so, says the dark sky in which the moon is rocking about on furious clouds. Not so, warn the birds, angry with my late afternoon felling. Duncan passes with a gun. 'A rabbit for the dog's dinner', he explains. There is an executioner's single shot. I stack up the hazel rods but leave a circle of fragile shoots for coppicing in A.D.2025. Wild winds, wild sounds everywhere by now. The brook runs coldly into the horse-pond whose frigid surface is pierced by the tips of marsh marigolds. Helmeted riders gallop past, which they are not supposed to do because of the track. 'Lovely day!' A helicopter arrives like a hornet. Max stares up from a crumbling wall, starving, waving a black tail. He is appealing to the gods. 'Look at me, a tomcat outside in January!' He looks yearningly towards the farmhouse with moonlit eyes. 'Think of Duncan's poor rabbit,' I tell him. Max licks his chops.

There are bells to talk about at Tendring, re-tuned, re-dedicated and now re-rung bells, all six of them put into St Edmund's in 1907 for under £400, which would now scarcely pay for their ropes. All the bellringers from miles around are there to sing, 'As with gladness, men of old' and Tennyson's 'Ring out, wild bells!' Afterwards, while yet further peals are attempted, I read the memorials and look at the famous and vast hammer-beam. Outside there is one of those wooden porches which fail to weather or collapse although made in 1350. There are a number of them all round here and far from tottering. They were for marriages and will-makings, airy business shelters, with blackbirds' nests in their rafters. The North Sea is near, sensed but invisible, which is why Tendring may have come from 'tinder' – for lighting a beacon on the church tower.

Thursday, a reading from my book *Talking about John Clare* at King's College, London. Tim Chilcott reads from his

John Clare: the Living Year, 1841. The manner in which this great rural poet has gradually emerged to change our thinking about the English village is phenomenal in itself. Having been so slowly discovered, he has rapidly proved to be inexhaustible. A sad irony governed Clare's life. First he had to hide from his neighbours in order to write, then they hid him in Northampton Asylum. There he made lists of everything which meant something to him, his own *mappa mundi* of Helpston. Like its songbirds, being caged never stopped his voice. It was by lying low in the home fields and becoming eye to eye with everything which crawled, ran or flew, with petals and grasses, that he became a pure naturalist.

Priests and Gentlemen

A stunning January day, mild and wild, for a visit to Hengrave Hall, where the wind is shaking dead wood from the park trees and spinning the birds around. And here is the differently stunning house which Sir Thomas Kytson, merchant adventurer, built for himself in 1538. It still does what he intended it to do, takes one's breath away. Iris stylosa and aconites are pressing against its walls. And out comes Canon Armson to greet me, for astonishing as it would have been to a merchant adventurer, it is now a Retreat House, and a Quiet Day has been announced. No fanfares. Instead forty or so subdued folk listening to a meditation based upon a line by St John of the Cross, 'In solitude he sought Him'.

Whispers, chairs being settled, the fire crackling. Guiding a path through the Spanish poet the thought strikes me that this Tudor palace was going up at the same moment when St Edmund's shrine just along the lane was coming down. Sir Thomas was one of the New Men, a tradesman extraordinary. Just one of his warehouses contained cloth of gold, satins, tapestry, velvets, furs, fustians, bags of pepper, cloves and madder. Although his Will mentioned debts were 'good, doubtful and desperate', there was a pile of money to settle them. But my little Carmelite John of the Cross leaves a wealth of words which put a mercer in the shade. And it was the South African poet Roy Campbell who saved what St John had left us from destruction during the Spanish Civil War. Poets stretch their hands across time to preserve each other. St John is among the most passionate of Christians and he saw himself relentlessly pursued by Christ the Bridegroom. Whether in the dark prison or running happy and free in the Toledo landscape, there was one who entered, one who ran faster.

At Hengrave we walk through the garden to the church of St John Lateran to say our prayers before lunch. These are subdued so as not to disturb the great people who lie with clasped hands on their grand tombs. We sing some Taizé petitions. Staring around as writers do, I see the Sir Thomas Gage who gave his name to a – plum. The story is that circa 1724 Sir Thomas's brother John, who was a Parisian priest, sent a Reine-Claude plum to Hengrave but the label fell off, so the gardener named it after his master 'Green Gage'. I went to look at this tree and pat its trunk as I thought of our greengages and their unforgettable deliciousness as they burst in our mouths when we were children. We would shake the wasps out of the part-eaten ones and devour those too. The first greengage tree and St John Lateran with round windows in its Norman tower like portholes for cannon and demi-angels fluttering in the pointed arches. And the grass humpy with spring growth.

Before tea Canon Armson lends me a 1928 Prayer Book so that I can say Evensong. Nobody else has one but memory helps out. Sir Thomas the mercer died in 1540, so he would have just missed the first Book of Common Prayer. Would have missed William Shakespeare too. And the Authorised Version - 'Make not my Father's house an house of merchandise'. But perhaps Kytson was good in a New Man's way. We are, after all, still enjoying his hospitality and looking up to his best window, an extravagant bay over the porch and smothered with welcoming cherubs. On the way home we pass a sugar factory which would have dwarfed mighty St Edmundsbury Abbey. Plumes of sweet smoke belch from its chimneys.

Human Incense

Unutterably moved, appalled, chilled, I sit up late to watch Holocaust Day television. Many an official in the death camps must have been prodded by that question which stopped St Paul in his tracks - 'Why are you doing this?' These officials were after all Lutherans and Roman Catholics, and would have known the famous story. But we know their despicable reply. As for ourselves, have we not lived through a century so riddled with genocide as to make it possible to have a cup of tea whilst watching *Schindler's List*? The truth is that these happenings have been so repetitive and so dreadful as to kill our natural feelings towards suffering. Which is why the Holocaust was so successful – why it was possible, eventually, to feel nothing as one put in a good day's work at Belsen. Or in Cambodia. If we put the kettle on as the now familiar footage passes our numbed gaze, it is to confront those sights with a blessed ordinariness.

John, a boyhood friend, arrives from South Africa. He has just retired from teaching music at Pietermaritsburg although he remains the cathedral organist. We of course never allow organists to retire – whatever next! Do we still have Merbecke? he enquires. Poor Merbecke, the barbarians of his day would have burnt him as a heretic – but then who would have played the organ at Windsor? Music saved him from martyrdom. John says that he has become a martyr to some jingles which have found their way into the Pietermaritsburg hymnal. I see us as teenagers in the country pub, he with a bulging leather music-case, fresh from a lesson with Mr Vinnecombe at St Peter's opposite, myself with a pile of books, and both of us happily stranded between market-day farmers. It was Mr Vinnecombe, whose forebears made the very first church organ in South Africa, who taught the small Suffolk town what church music was. George Herbert adored it and called it 'Sweetest of sweets'. I tell John that St Andrew's, Great Cornard, where he sang in the choir, had for a time shared its chancel with the Roman Catholics. He looked pretty amazed. It is the distant spire in Gainsborough's *Cornard Wood* in which the artist's parents were married. As a boy I imagined him tramping past it, laden with an easel and brushes, looking for a good view.

Unsearchable Riches

The Epiphany sunsets are furious, vast blazing caves of lurid light. Each evening they burn the field across which a dog fox trots, taking his time, trailing his brush through the inch-high corn. I cremated the Christmas holly according to custom. Dry as dust from twelve days in warm rooms, it hurries to become ashes. At night the stars are extra-shining, making the Stanstead planes dim in comparison. Hard frosts having made the footpath walkable, I crackle my way to St Andrew's for a 10.30 Communion and for some of those 'solemn things of mystic meaning', as Prudentious called them. Old tombs stand in white grass; pheasants examine berry-less wreaths, wind comes round the tower like a scythe. The Epistle has St Paul making up his mind to release the starlight of Bethlehem into the world at large and to talk about the 'unsearchable riches of Christ' to anyone who would listen. The altar candles waver and make shrouds, the chancel heating hums expensively.

Back home, it being too good to be in, I cut down some dead cotoneaster, whose name means 'like a quince-tree', and 'staff-like' because its stems make good walking-sticks. I saw-up its slender logs for the stove. Then back to the study to write an Afterword for the Launcelot Fleming Lectures at Norwich.

Now and then I manage to find my way about an area, not with a street-plan, but with what I know of some celebrated resident's life. Thus I am walking with Coleridge in Highgate. It is new ground to me, and poorly lit at that. A self-imposed law says that I must not ask the way. I wander on and it is only when I read 'Millfield Lane' on a wall that I know where I am. For it is where in April 1819, on a Sunday afternoon, 'A loose, slack, not well-dressed youth met Mr Green and myself . . . It was John Keats.' 'Myself' was of course Mr Coleridge. So here they stood. Mr Green, who had tutored Keats at Guy's Hospital, introduced the two poets and they all walked on in a torrent of talk. I pass the buildings they passed. London, five miles away, does not look as it looked to them. Now it is the biggest pile of tinsel ever, glittering, clear. Then it was a fuming sulphurous pit afar off, fed as it was by a million sea coal fires. The smoke, as they called it. Nearby, doubly dark, is the fabulous cemetery where Engels stood by Karl Marx's grave, praising him to the skies. But now I come to the corner shop where an obliging chemist sold Coleridge all the laudanum, and finally to a glass notice-board containing my name, and to Livia Gollancz gallantly welcoming me to the celebrated Highgate Literary and Scientific Institute. Both I and the pleasant Victorian room should be pent-up with revolution but all such passion has been long spent, and I talk bookishly to bookish people, and fancy I hear a great wind roaring by outside.

Sylvia Dies

These Epiphany days alternate between hard frosts and mild rains. It is either crumping to the top of the lane to fetch the milk, or sploshing to the shop. We are poorly, flu-ridden and sorry for ourselves. There is talk of our sickness being brought from Sydney by the English Cricket Team. On the way to the Post Office I pass what was first the pesthouse and then the workhouse, and what was once pitch-black and which is now snow-white. It was built in 1603, the year when plague struck London, and when the Queen died. She had actually been to Wormingford – twice – to stay with the Waldegraves by the river. Michael the vicar is able to see their moated house from his vicarage. It is the best view in the village. In January it is a pencil drawing, in June it would require a palette running over with green and blue. Today it is too cold to look out on without a shiver. Too cold for the gliders, so rooks and duck have taken over the sky. Flints and – if you are lucky – artefacts glint in the thin corn. The roadside verges have been shorn to reveal, shamefully, a catch-crop of lager cans chucked from cars and awful evidence of fast food. Ditches are flooding to the Stour.

Sylvia has died and we cannot believe it, so accustomed have we been to seeing her in an invalid state. It was the flu which finally hurried her off. It has swept her away. I read the Beatitudes at her funeral, each one of which suits her – in fact recalls her. But it is very strange nevertheless to have her gone. She and Douglas lived in the Swedish houses put up just after the war. They came in sections like Meccano, light, airy structures which have served the village well, and which from the back offered wide views for a poet. I read too Sylvia's *Going Fishing* which she wrote for her brother-in-law Phil who can only be found either by the river or the North Sea. Phil asks for little in life, just tackle and a big umbrella, plenty of bait and uninterrupted solitude. At Sylvia's funeral Douglas and the boys are listening in the kind of vacuum which occurs when the reality of what is happening becomes too great to take in. Everybody is present – but everybody from near and far. All the 'old people', of course – those to whom the village belongs by ancient birthright, as we come-latelies know. It is sad beyond telling.

Douglas had been to see me just a few days before all this.

We talked about flour-milling and about the Clovers and the Bakers and the Hitchcocks, the millers who had worked the Stour for miles and miles, and for generations, and whose flour Douglas had driven to London. All this milling had ended in his lifetime. The mills themselves now made tall floury houses and hotels from which the dust would never be eradicated. Not wholly, not entirely. Benjamin Britten told me that when he lived at Snape Mill his piano was white every morning. The millers themselves were white-water men and white-haired men at twenty. Douglas Miller, a school friend who had nothing to do with milling, was of course 'Dusty' to us. The Douglas who drove our flour far and wide shakes his head at our idle river. All that water power doing nothing except flowing over Phil's waders.

Translator's Day

In his thankyou for being given the Whitbread Prize Seamus Heaney at once stood back in order to give centre place to 'the anonymous master' who wrote *Beowulf*, just as Clifton Wolters stands back from that unknown genius who wrote *Revelations of Divine Love*. Where both faith and literature are concerned we are likely to find ourselves in the hands of translators. There are translators who are scholars and not poets, and translators who are scholar-poets, and translators who are simply poets with a dictionary and a nerve. We the common reader and common worshipper are in the debt of all three. It used to be the sign of a formal education to be able to translate a bit of Latin and Greek, though not of Anglo-Saxon, a language which we out-grew and left behind us. It has taken a scholar-poet with a dictionary to release into the sunlight once more those glorious tales which brightened life ages ago, and which are as much an inheritance as architecture.

Swans and alders 1982

Christianity is mightily in debt to translators. We should have a Translators' Day in the Lectionary. We should give thanks to King Alfred for his translation of St Augustine's *Soliloquies*, William Caxton for those translations which made English the language of the printed book, William Tyndale for translating most of the finest passages of the King James Bible, Thomas Cranmer, whose translation of the Latin liturgy into English is a religious work of art without parallel, to J F Goodridge for his fascinating translation of *Piers Plowman*, for John Mason Neale for his restoration of the hymnal and filling the choirs with the words so long forgotten, for Clifton Wolters for his bringing into our light *The Cloud of Unknowing*, for Arthur Golding whose translation of Ovid was such a gift to Shakespeare when he wrote *The Tempest*, for Dorothy L Sayers for her translation of Dante and, especially where I am concerned, for Roy Campbell's translation of the poems of St John of the Cross. And to think that the only record we have of Jesus writing was when he wrote with his finger in the dust. It was his spoken language which was translated to fit the page of scripture.

Please May I Leave the Room?

To awake to heavy frost and hard paths, what bliss. And tonight they promise a red moon because of the eclipse. I am suddenly reminded of a boy in my class who, when asked to recite a poem, always recited the same one. I can hear his husky voice - 'A moment when the moon was blood, then surely I was born . . .' Children have to do the best they can with a huge language. The thirty or so boys and girls at the opening of the new classrooms at the old village school are all seated on the ground. They whisper like leaves and look up at the bishop, the vicar, the visiting mayor, the governors, the M.P. and Mags their teacher. I can smell chocolate éclairs. There has been a welding of 1870 Education Act

Gothic and 1940s bomb shelters to make this new building. Bishop John hands a pair of scissors to a child who is beginning his education this very morning. The ribbon is cut, the prayer said, the door opened, the computers are seen. We all clap Mr Weatherall, the school taxi-driver, who has walked from Lincoln Cathedral to Wormingford to raise funds for the extension. A thousand pounds. He is large and unexhausted. There is a holding-off of the rain and a faint uplift of the sky, then a polite scramble to be photographed in the mayor's chain. It falls goldenly from child to child. We are the smallest school in the diocese, they say. Are we to survive?

I ring Rosa to give her an Epiphany Evensong. She had stamped her feet to keep warm in this school eighty-five years ago, and she spoke ruefully of the tortoise stove with its tall guard, and of the two classrooms packed to the walls with farm labourers' children. A boy puts his hand up. 'Please may I leave the room?' That same brief walk across the tarmac will now take him to the computers.

Rural communities such as ours would be in a bad way if they did not get most of the expert advice needed to run them – for nothing. But far more could be done in this respect. Why should a parish church have to pay the diocesan architect a large fee before it can site a collection-box in a wall? We scan each new retiree for his or her expertise. Craftsmen, money-men, anyone with a trained hand or mind is asked to go on doing what they used to do for free. But retired priests get a fee. My farmer-neighbour is on the edge of retirement. He and I know that there is no precedent for what is now happening to British farming. After the plough-up every yard policy of the Sixties it is bewildering to be told to let some of your fields go back to the old waste.

The Bell Cage

The world is iced like a cake. Frosted meadows look good enough to eat. Puffed-up birds weigh down the berried shrubs. Cats swing along, their tails whisking the thin snow. Although the sun shines for all it is worth, winter prevails. Christopher Hogwood is playing William Byrd on the new radio. Christmas cards totter above the fireplace, begging to be taken down. My study is sultry with hyacinths. Books gape, four or five on the go at the same time. When I take a long walk the cold cuts me up with its knives, letting out the torpor. A white land gives the colourless sky one of its hard looks. I should be thinking about the Euro, maybe, or chapter seven of the new book, or an old neighbour's quick death. But instead I listen downstream, fancifully imagining that I might catch the faraway music of grounded bells. Ringing, they say, travels well by water. But all I hear is wild duck, and the alders groaning with the cold.

A little while ago the grounded bells of East Bergholt turned nasty on a ringer, injuring him badly. Thus their silence. It will cost us a fortune to get them to speak again. They live in an airy oak frame called the Bell Cage, all five of them taking up residence there when the church tower suddenly stopped building in the sixteenth century. Ringers are imprisoned in the Bell Cage twice a week, or were until the accident. No ropes, just delicate hands to heave and push and make a peal. A Quasimodo sight for the curious, which included the youthful me. John Constable drew it and Dorothy L Sayers made notes on it for *The Nine Tailors*.

Constable's family, friends and neighbours sleep around it, the peals shaking their graves. Today I re-read their frozen names, Willy Lott, Johnny Dunthorne, Golding, the dancers at the balls, the peasants in the paintings. Mary Constable, John's sister, wrote of Willy Lott's distress at not getting some education. 'Witness our neighbour Mr W Lott who will sometimes shed tears in his old age that he was left untaught by those who had charge of him in his youth'. Sad it may have been, but who now has not heard of him? I see him taking his place in the Bell Cage on a Saturday night practise for Sunday morning, and outside the miller's son at his easel.

Crumping back to Bottengoms Farm, I endeavour to be serious, for something has to be said about the Epiphany. I play Janáček's *The Diary of One Who has Disappeared* on the miraculous new radio/CD. The sound is quite amazing. Late walkers passing in the darkening snow give little waves. Something from Psalm seventy-two for Epiphany maybe? This psalm is exotic and all about the royalty of Christ. There is a fervent double Amen to end with. 'Prayer shall be made ever unto him, and daily shall he be praised.'

The Fellows' Gate

It is Sunday morning in Cambridge, only ages ago. My friend Denis Garrett is lending me his privileged 'Sunday key' to the Botanic Gardens, just down Hills Road, and soon I am freezing in those familiar forty acres of plants. And the sensuous delight of taking a single step from all this to the tropical heat of the glasshouses and their scented assault of rain forest or desert, from 'fenny humours', as George Herbert called the Cambridge climate, to damp paradise, from catkins to orchids. It is the Conversion of St Paul. The Reverend John Henslow, the re-creator of the Cambridge Botanic Garden was unwittingly guilty of re-creating or diverting Christian certainty. He was a scientist who became the vicar of Hitcham, then a run-down Suffolk village where, to the rage of the farmers, he built a school, thereby robbing them of child labour. Hardly less upsetting was Henslow's turning the entire population of his parish into botanists and, in 1854, as soon as the line to Cambridge was laid, carrying it off to Cambridge to see his amazing Garden. The Hitcham folk, all 287 of them, arrived at Cambridge station, then just four years old, and wound their way to the Hills Road gate, the one which I unlocked with the Sunday key, and went to see 'where the greenhouses and stoves are being directed to contain plants from hot countries'.

I would praise John Henslow in and out of the cold. And then I would mill over his unintentional role in the upset of Victorian faith. Professor Henslow and an undergraduate named Charles Darwin had gone on nature walks. Darwin was blissfully happy, having got away from the revolting study of medicine in order to take Holy Orders. He collected beetles, went to Evensong at King's, went shooting, and went on holiday with this extraordinary man who seemed to know all there was to know about natural history. They searched for rocks in Wales and wild flowers in the Cam meadows, and for birds and fish everywhere, and young Darwin became known as 'the man who walks with Henslow'. Then came the Pauline change of direction. Henslow had heard that a ship named *The Beagle* wanted an unpaid naturalist to join it on a voyage to survey South America. 'I think you are the very man they are in search of', the Professor told his pupil. So Charles Darwin sailed away and kept a diary called

The Voyage of the Beagle which in places contradicted *Genesis*. He was twenty-two. Worse would follow.

After the Botanic Garden, and in all weathers, a later Cambridge botanist, though no great gardener, let it be said, would search for wild flowers along the very railway line, now Beechinged, by which John Henslow had brought all his Hitcham parishioners to see what he was doing at Cambridge. My friend Professor Denis Garrett was perhaps the most single-minded person I have ever met. His face, his entire interest, was perpetually turned to plants. He was not a hothouse man. Chilly streams, the blowy Suffolk shore for which he had a special love, windy heaths and especially the Fens, these his habitats. He looked down to see what was looking up, often a minimal sight to me but to him something great. When his wife and I would carry him off to see architecture he only saw what was growing in its walls. There should be a book called *The Botany of Buildings*.

Snowfall

I know that it has arrived before I draw the curtains. Snow. Its silent voice fills the landscape. Snow is weather with a finger to its lips. A faint cold wind will be blowing towards the house in powdering drifts. John Nash, whose studio window this was, would have stood here to put the snow down, miraculously to me, on his snowy watercolour paper. There it would be, a favourite sight, snow-white on paper-white, and marked with a pheasant's starry footsteps. He is gone, the scene remains with its snow-laden willows toppling about a bit, and the flooded valley vaguely present through millions of flakes. They dance in the London commuters' headlights and settle on the cats, who for some purpose known only to them have left the warm kitchen to plunge about in the soaking whiteness like deceived girls making for the workhouse. The downfall is exhilarating the horses. They canter across the hillside, one of them sporting her winter blanket. 'Hast thou entered into the treasures of the snow?' enquires God of Job. 'No', say we all, men and beasts alike, though it is not for want of trying.

Later this snow morning we drive across a purified East Anglia on ebony motorways to Cambridge to hear a friend read her new poems. All is changed. Modest heights such as Tudy Camps and the Gogs are pretending to be the Himalayas. The windscreen wipers click like Chinese fans, throwing the snow off as fast as it comes. 'The clouds are full of it', we tell each other, this being something which is always said at such a time. Ours is a perilous enterprise for poetry's sake. Will the lane from Rodbridge to Cavendish be adrift when we return? It is the kind of lane down which Mr Woodhouse unwisely ventured to dinner when snow threatened.

It seems not quite right to celebrate Richard Rolle in January, though there he is in the Lectionary. He was the Yorkshire hermit whose love of Christ was too hot to handle by the medieval Church. Or perhaps it felt that it had to stand back from his fire. Rolle is our St John of the Cross, a saint of the interior song. The nuns at Hampole adored him, this passionate young man who did not care much for church services and sang on his doorstep.

> I ask you, Lord Jesus,
> to develop in me, your lover,
> an immeasurable urge towards you,
> an affection that is unbounded,

a longing that is unrestrained,
a fervour that throws discretion to the winds!

The Hampole nuns would have had him canonised – but no. So they beatified his memory. Some claim Richard Rolle to be the 'true father of English literature'. He was a wild boy who left Oxford without a degree, who lived as a hermit without being licensed to do so, and who wrote dazzlingly in English at a time when God expected Latin. Listening to poems in Girton College where I'm told there are now more men than women, fragments of Richard Rolle's enchanting book *The Fire of Love* become entangled with what I am hearing, which is quite a compliment to the poet reading her work. I think of Rolle's concept of the way we should love Christ: 'Reason cannot hold it in check, fear does not make it tremble, wise judgment does not temper it'. He was born in 1300 at Thornton-le-Dale, maybe during an Epiphany snowfall.

You who are the most lovely,
lovable and beautiful,
remember that it is through you
that I am no longer afraid of any passing power . . .

Rolle's life and work are lessons on how not to get on in the Church.

Galanthus

I must go out to look at the snowdrops before the snow covers them. How coming snowstorms thrilled us as children. We would hear the grown-ups say, 'The sky is full of it,' and we would rush to the hilltop to meet it halfway. 'Let it snow, let it snow!' we would holler. And the hill would be so quiet as it waited for the special snow silence. My snowdrops wait for it now, faintly trembling with pleasure, faces to the earth. Any minute it will fall on them, ravish them. Their name *Galanthus* means milk flower and it's milk which describes their particular whiteness, not snow. The whiteness of snow outdoes their milkiness. The few I gather open in minutes in the warm room. Isolated from the garden drifts their variant exposures are breathtakingly beautiful. I hold them up to look at what I would not be able to see outside and remember some of their specie names, *Elwesi*, *Nivalis*, *Nivalis Viridi-spice* . . . Their green-tipped bells have sprung, revealing all. There are snowdrop experts like my artist friend John Morley who are intimately acquainted with *Galanthus* society but I am on affectionate nodding terms with just a few of these first flowers. They drift in my wood, in the orchard, under the roses, along the lane, where the old farm buildings fell down, around the horse pond, where the postman turns his van, countless thousands of them. Snowdrops like to wander about a bit but still keep company.

They drift where I bury Mary's ashes in Little Horkesley churchyard and where generations of her family, the Bullocks, lie. Bullocks' corner it is known as. A stone has been removed to have her name added to it and she will not have to endure one of those stingy set in the grass tablets for the cremated. I have never understood why the latter should have doll's house memorials. Better to have one's name added to a marble book which suggests the divine roll-call than to rest under a tile. I have to cut a snowdrop slab in order to put Mary underground. Her ashes are grey as they slide from a plastic bag. I read John Donne's 'Bring us, O Lord, at our last awakening into the house and gate of heaven' over them to lend the practical business a bit of style. It is true winter and the bare trees clack. 'It is enough to cut you in half,' say the relations.

After which we take Helen to the Crown to celebrate her hundredth birthday. Just the handful of us who have known her for ever. Then back to her bungalow where a card from the Queen totters in pride of place on the mantelpiece. Bouquets cover her jigsaw table. Later, I walk home in the promised snowfall. The wind howls in my ears. The white cat, lengthways on the radiator, says something like, 'Thou fool' but when I set a match to the log fire she changes her tune and mouths, 'Thou angel'. A farmer and his family would have sat around this hearth when Shakespeare was writing *The Winter's Tale*, which is a play set in Bohemia. Flowers are mentioned but not snowdrops. The village people used to believe them to be unlucky and wouldn't have them in the house. White cats too were unlucky. Mine lies on her back and opens to the heat.

Taking Notes

Mid-Epiphany, though the minimum of natural light. Beyond the bright room all is muddy, dull and static. Or, less gloomily, nebulous and still. A jogger pounds by, his white vest intermittently vivid as he runs between the black hedgerows. I am reading about a Puritan sin known as sermon-gadding. Not only did the pilgrim fathers from East Anglia sermon-gad when they should have been at work, but they took notes. It is bad enough to see people taking notes when one is lecturing, but when one is in the pulpit! I did once sit next to a famous novelist and see him covering a ream of crackly paper as he listened to an old clergyman. The learned, or entertaining, or sacred tradition of the sermon has now been pared down to its limit by those whose attention span can just about deal with Thought for the Day. How often I listen to the voices on the Incumbents' Board, stumbling, saintly, disillusioned, eloquent, local, Christ-filled, each of them over the centuries coming from where I am standing, and of course none of them preaching for less than the hour.

Helen is now a hundred. Gordon and I have coffee with her in the bungalow which was the post office which she and her sister Win ran for ages, where they bred spaniels, and which they left at ten-thirty on Sunday mornings to sing in the choir. They would weigh the manuscripts which I, as a publisher's reader, had to return with a report, would look with horror at their scales and say apologetically, 'I'm afraid it will be *three and six*!' They were nineteen-twenties' girls who danced, drove a brake-van rather wildly and starred in the village plays. Guy Hickson - Miss Marples' brother - who ran the market garden next-door, directed them. 'That Guy!' they would say. He was tall and exacting, they could be larky. But now Win is with God and Helen is a hundred, 'eating no more than a sparrow', as the saying goes. However, she remains upright and intelligent, possesses a faithful Aga, dotes on jigsaw puzzles and quizzes, and orders us to bring her Holy Communion. Every now and then she takes to her bed, and the village says, 'Oh dear . . .' Then, driving past, they see her weeding. The Queen has sent her a fine card. A nice coal fire lights it up.

February

Retreats - Mark in February - One Evening in Cambridge -
An Architectural Buzz - Minding the Belly - Desertions -
Mortality Among the Flowers - Walberswick Whisperers and
Sounding Hymns - Interventions - A Doleful Lent - Olney
Hymns - 'Lord, This is a Huge Rain' - More Flooding

Retreats

The Retreat at Hengrave Hall is snowed off and not even a four-wheel drive could get down my farm track. I recall last time when the drifts lasted a week. Every few years it arrives, the world-stopping snow. How we adored its lastingness in the Gull when we were boys, its reluctance to go away, the snowman himself standing firm during the first thaw, his face in tears. We would think of ways of getting him through to the spring, patting his icy sides encouragingly, beating the water from his bowler. Writing from New England on February 11th 1964 Thomas Merton noted, 'Today, brilliant snow, never so blinding. Pale bright blue sky, such as I have sometimes seen in England on rare days in East Anglia.' Our rare days will soon run into meltdown, then into frozen sprinklings which the hares will kick up as they race across the hill. And dwindling drifts will hang about to trouble the postman. The sun is surprisingly hot on the doorstep when I sit to pull on wellingtons before taking a bow-saw to the pile of apple logs.

A wren has found its way into my bedroom four mornings running. I have to open the double glazing to free it, feeling virtuous as the icy blasts rush at me. But, as William Blake rightly said, 'He who shall hurt the little wren/shall never be beloved of men'. And quite right too. One morning I caught the wren in my palms and carried it out into winter. It pulsated tenderly between my hands and was as warm as toast. And when I parted them in the garden, the tiny ex-prisoner hardly dared to take its freedom. And me in my pyjamas. What will the coroner record when I am discovered flat on the cold, cold earth? For the winter's day cuts like a knife, so that even a wild bird hesitates to face it.

I am to write a new introduction to George Herbert's *A Priest to the Temple or The Country Parson*. He was a country parson for less than three years before tuberculosis killed him on March 1st 1633. They carried him to his tiny church a few steps across the lane and buried him no one knows exactly where. Just G.H. on the wall. The poetry then began its astonishing journey into the Anglican consciousness, two editions that very year. But *A Priest to the Temple*, his rule for village parsons, did not come out until 1652 when many a parish was in revolution. Herbert hoped that in future clergymen would build on to what he laid down as a suitable way of life for them in the typical English village, although reminding them that the way of how they should behave had been magisterially laid down by St Paul in his letter to the Colossians. To put it simply, adds the apostle, a priest should do what Christ did, think as Christ thought – as much as he was able. A parson should know about farming. He should know a bit about doctoring, about growing herbs, about music and literature, about old customs and human behaviour generally, about quacks – about everything. Herbert himself was ill all the while he was at Bemerton. He could feel the consumption 'like a mole' working away inside him. He would have his horse fetched from the meadow and ride up to Old Sarum to fill his poor lungs with the best Wiltshire air as it blew across that sacred site. Herbert made the point that a sick priest would be a special help to a sick parishioner, knowing what it was like to be weak and ill. He had not forgotten his dandy Cambridge days. There had to be no judging a man by what he wore, no Sunday best when he went visiting or in church. But the priest himself should be simply dressed in a clean cassock wherever he went. He might find the villagers 'wallowing in the midst of their affairs' but he should bring something higher into their lives but without condemnation of their rough activities. 'He holds the Rule, that Nothing is little in God's service . . . Wherefore neither disdaineth he to enter the poorest Cottage, though he even creep into it, and though it smell never so loathsomely. For both God is there also, and those for whom God died.'

Mark in February

I am reading Kilvert by the sunny window. Snow is sliding along the sill. Kilvert calls his communicants 'guests' - 'twenty guests this morning'. Parson Woodforde calls them 'rails' - 'two rails this morning'. Unrecognisable birds flutter in the bare hazels. The walk I took from Hay to Clyro during the literature festival reconstructs itself in my head. It was where Francis Kilvert walked so often, passing the same trees in many cases and with the Black Mountains in front or behind, shutting off Wales. He had observed ash trees being felled on Ash Wednesday – purely a coincidence, nothing more. His walks along the Clyro-Hay road, and elsewhere, were filled with chance encounters but I did not meet a soul for miles. Festival-goers waved from hurtling cars, just a white hand in a flash of glass. 'We saw you walking', they say. One cat walks miles to watch hares. I see her now at the crest of the hill, her winter fur stirred by the wind, as she walks to where they play. The other cat likes to have a window-pane between her and the wild outside.

It is taking me three whole days to fill up my Wild Flower Society register before sending it to my tutor to check. This time it has to be the wild flowers of Wormingford only. No rich pickings from between the lines of some rural railway station, where plants are plentiful, and none from the Scottish holiday, where they are simply glorious. But so many from Bottengoms Farm itself as to raise suspicion in the minds of those who have never seen this bosky spot. 'It always was weedy', a neighbour tells me.

Candlemas matins and evensong in two different churches, plus three Eucharists for Michael the vicar, and thus our wintry worship drifts on towards Lent. The garden is a million snowdrops and little else. They double and treble themselves every season, jumping fallen trees and the stream to colonise new territory. *Galanthus* from *gala* = milk and *anthos* = flower, the milk-white flowers of February which once seen into the ground should be allowed to journey on by themselves. Which they will do for more than a human lifetime. The Church knew them as Candlemas Bells and recognised them as the flower of purification but the pagans believed they were unlucky. At this moment their porcelain heads are gleaming where the nettles will soon be hiding what remains of the old barn.

St Mark for February – that thrilling, urgent young voice. And that enviable economy of style. And that 'Keep Awake!' parable which only he remembers hearing. How near to us Mark is when Paul tells Timothy, 'Pick up Mark and bring him with you, for I find him a useful assistant', adding, 'and when you come, bring the cloak I left with Carpus, and the books . . . above all my notebooks.'

One Evening in Cambridge

Where one knows a train route backwards one must concentrate on its minutiae. So here are the Newmarket paddocks and rails, and the horses grazing delicately in the damp afternoon light. And here are no end of allotments, more of them than ever, already dug over. And on them the calamitous sheds, all bits and pieces, the patchier the better. As we glide past I imagine their interiors, the girlie calendars and seed catalogues fighting for space on the walls, the broken-bottomed armchairs, the bed for the dog, the beloved odds and ends, the tools, the throw-outs from home which have found a place where they can be appreciated. The allotment shed, and the allotment itself, is eremitical country. Men of all ages continue to flee the lounge for its peace. There dog and master, and mate from the adjoining strip of vegetables, can be as nature would have them, uncountably comfortable den-men. Simply hundreds of allotments are passing and their collective bliss seems to caress the Cambridge train as it says, 'Why go on? All happiness is here.'

I intend to walk from Cherry Hinton road to Pembroke College. 'Walk!' My host is appalled. I shall be mugged, tired, lost, all kinds of things. But like many countrymen I enjoy walking in cities, and here I am on nodding terms with the jaunty soldier on the war memorial, with his victor's wreath nonchalantly dangling from his rifle, and the enormous church of Our Lady of the English Martyrs, and Lady Hilton's surprisingly bare Youth outside the Scott Polar Research Institute, with thick Victorian shrubberies and the faint scent of the Fens. Joggers of both sexes thump past. The

Fitzwilliam looks absolutely beautiful in the street light. At Pembroke I mill around with other lost delegates to APU's preliminary meeting for a new Arts Centre, which is to be held in the Thomas Gray Room. The latter is worth the journey alone. How is it that they never wear out, these old rooms with their portraits and panelling, their squeaky floorboards and handsome ceilings?

John Ruskin was the founding father of APU, the huge university which now runs side by side with Cambridge itself as well as spreading all over East Anglia. The fund-raiser points to vast sums on the screen, to charitable bequests and government subsidies. Everything is possible, although it is not possible for me to comprehend figures which are as numerous as the Milky Way. So I meditate on Thomas Gray, whose father was a 'money scrivener'. An accountant? How did such a father breed such a son? A common question where poets are concerned. I thought of Gray, a timid man, sitting in this room with the shutters closed against the uproar of a Georgian town, fearful of fire, of mockery, of love. They took him back to Stoke Poges when he died to bury him among the best-known anonymous folk of rural England. Like many solitaries, Gray wrote marvellous letters. Highly nervous himself, he sympathised with those who suffered from 'the bad affright'. He would have been scared stiff by the money we intend to raise and alarmed to have it discussed in his room. But, having been on the Grand Tour, he could hardly protest at our reason for doing so.

> Visions of glory, spare my aching sight,
> Ye unborn ages, crowd not on my soul!

An Architectural Buzz

A week of modest snowing. Not too deep, not too flimsy as to be blown from the bough. The mud-flats at Manningtree are white-black and static. No apparent coming in and going out of the tide, but everything thinly frozen and lightly coated. Belated ploughing ripples under powdery drifts. But there is snow-silence, such as we 'heard' in our bedroom as children. 'It has been snowing!' we yelled, even before we drew the curtains, its soundlessness speaking so loudly. Oh, if it would only last for ever. We rolled our snowball along the lane until it was high as ourselves and as heavy as lead, and surely must roll on into April. We saw it turning into a trickling sorbet, then into nothing. At Bottengoms every living thing has felt its mark, rabbits, Mr Death's dog, foxes, badgers, assorted birds, the fastidious cats and Man Friday himself, for someone has taken off his shoes and socks to feel what it is like to have snow between his toes. This takes me back a bit. In the seventeenth century it was 'everybody outside to get warm'. And no wonder, for the houses in Dutch paintings have no glass in their windows. So best skate or dance and drink.

To Sudbury to visit Tony Venison who has alarming winter visitors – mason bees. A previous owner had stripped the plaster from the kitchen walls to show nice red bricks. The bricks are soft and warm looking, with indentations which must have been made by fingers handling the pug. But there are too little holes, very smooth, small pittings and deep dents. 'Mason bees', explains Tony, his anxiety not unmixed with pride. For not everyone's house is a bee's dinner. Mason bees – *abeille maconnée* – build their nests with sand. Tony's bees are taking down his kitchen walls to make themselves a nice hive and, it being cold outside, are working indoors. It is not everyone who has mason bees. All I can boast at Bottegoms are hornets. Builders are summoned by Tony to show the mason bees the door. This can only be done by replacing lime mortar with cement. I advise Tony's bees to fly off to Crowland Abbey in the Fens, where they can join a mason bees' fraternity. Crowland was built by a Mercian prince to honour St Guthlac, a pre-St Francis Franciscan who was so loved by birds that they took his advice as to where best to build their nests. The poet Edward Storey had taken me to Crowland to show me the bees living in – and on – its ruinous arches. I gave Tony Venison his words:

> Each year for my ritual
> I stand near these crevices
>
> to share in the dark buzz of prayer
> droning from stones scarred
>
> by fire and sword and greed
> shattered love's sanctuary.

But Tony reads the builders' estimate.

Minding the Belly

The spring birds sing with all their might. Grass is growing a foot a week. Rabbits have leaped the wire and devoured the sour cabbage stumps. Dinah shins up a poplar, hoping for the fire brigade. Her piteous mewing ceases when she sees no rescuer in sight and she bumps her way down again. It is how a child behaves, passionate weeping then a sensible silence. It is Peter-Paul's birthday and we take him off to Harwich to be gluttonous. We can watch a choppy sea flinging the little boats about from our table, and the ferries coming and going like dream palaces. Harwich is one of those towns with knock-you-down associations. Its nondescript streets are name-dropping with a vengeance. As Peter-Paul tells us about concerts in Copenhagen, his particular dream spot, the Mayflower hoves into view from where I am sitting. They built it just below us. I imagine it heaving in the harbour and Captain Smith asking himself, 'What have I let myself in for!' It is black outside and the North Sea slops over the harbour wall. Best not to look down. Birthday food is carried to our white and silver table. I thought of Captain Smith's table as it lurched, then righted itself, and the heartfelt prayers, and the lowing of the scared cows, and the keeping the victuals dry. Only a month or two on the Atlantic to reach the promised land. Who could jib at that?

One of literature's odd couples now arrive. Dr Johnson and Mr Boswell. The Doctor is fifty-four, his new friend twenty-four. Johnson takes Boswell into Harwich parish church to pray for the future. Boswell is off to Holland to study law. They emerge very emotional and embrace on the beach. Boswell wrote, 'As the vessel put out to sea, I kept my eyes upon him for a considerable time, while he remained rolling his majestic frame in his usual manner; and at last I perceived him walk back into the town, and he disappeared.' It was 1763 and they had known one another for about six weeks but were, as they seemed to know, locked in life together for the rest of their days, and in history.

Much of the talk in the London-Harwich coach had been about food. At Colchester Johnson said, 'Some people have a foolish way of minding, or pretending not to mind, what they eat. For my part, I mind my belly studiously . . . for I look upon it, that he who does not mind his belly will hardly mind anything else.' The menus arrive. Johnson would fast now and then, though not it appears during Lent. On Good Friday he went without milk in his tea. He once told Boswell

Mrs Brown and black 1972

that an ancient Father of the Church discovered that fasting caused him to become 'peevish' towards his friends, so he gave it up. Boswell was for ever giving up something or other, though not for long. But they could never give each other up. Peter-Paul is telling us about his new symphony in his swift, brilliant way, the sentences tumbling over themselves. Harwich is more a place for setting out at a venture than a coming home.

Desertions

When does a virtue become a vice? When saving becomes stinginess. This profound discovery assails me as I cast expense to the winds and insert a new typewriter ribbon. I once had a friend, an historical novelist and book-jacket designer all in one, who sent me letters which were typed edge to edge on the poorest paper with a ribbon so worn out that they made my eyes ache. Although these were nothing to the economies she practised in her cottage. And here was I, a man who picks up his change without counting it and who rarely mends his clothes. When I gave her some good paper and new ribbons, for she was poor, her carefulness was so advanced that I never received a letter on them. I expect she saved them up for 'best', as did an aunt with any gift which came her mildly embarrassed way. There is a quite sensuous delight in doing without and in denial.

I am typing out some poems by John Clare for one of those elegant Greville Press Pamphlets. They are 'tasters' which are intended to lure the reader to some writer he needs to sample for his own good. I was thinking that should my handful of John Clare poems lure a reader to the complete opus of this poet he will be in for a bit of a shock. Clare was all poetry, plus all energy, from boyhood till death. The sad asylum years provided so much isolation that he had to fill it with words or go truly mad. I often conjecture as to what he would have written had he stayed at home – not that he had any choice in the matter. Crazy ploughmen who write books must be locked up. Hidden away at Northampton, he made an inventory of his loss. It turned into a manifesto of the English countryside. How would he have written had he been left to stay at home at Northborough, running a smallholding and bringing up seven children? The reader who goes to the complete John Clare searching for a similar social history of the nineteenth century madhouse, as he called it, to that of an ordinary village in his day will draw a blank. A single poem was made to say it all - 'I Am'. This poem is one of English literature's masterpiece statements on identity. It has a place beside Job and the psalm *De profundis*.

The full Clare reader will also discover what poetry can say on the subject of what Clare called 'thwarted' love. But he took, as well as tragedy, the landscape he shared with his lover into captivity with him. Why are we so moved – overwhelmed – when we read Clare? It is because he was what most of us would have been in his day, the toilers in his fields, the victims of his parish.

Farming news is bad. As bad, they say, as it has been since the war. Not that it shows up to any extent in East Anglia. But I only have to walk through the winter fields which once belonged to Bottengoms to tell that something is wrong. There is, returning, the dreaded inertia, the sense of nothing doing. The spring flowers are early and in abundance.

Mortality among the Flowers

It is difficult to describe the atmosphere of rural life at this moment. Last week a poster was slapped onto the telegraph pole forbidding walkers and dogs to come down the track. There is a primitive fearfulness such as must have existed when coins were placed in vinegar instead of another person's hand and the word Plague was whispered. The world is arrested, still, holding its breath and wondering if it will happen here and not in some far off country of which we had never heard, such as Cumbria. Is then that I hear the spring birds singing and see the primrose profusion in the ditch, and recall how spring arrived at the Western Front, to the surprise and heartbreak of rural soldiers from many lands.

Natural death has darkened our small community. Laura's at six and a half, Albert's at ninety and a half. The latter in his Sunday suit, not a white hair in his head, clanged the bells for me at Mount Bures at nine twenty-five a.m. precisely every Sunday morning. And as a line of Alberts had done since the Wars of the Roses. Using every tactic I knew, I eventually persuaded him not to mow the harebells by the vestry by telling him that they were the origin of the Bluebells of Scotland. After which he skirted round them. But old men like to keep 'the rubbish' down, knowing how incorrigible it is and how given a chance, it will grow up and bury you. Once giving a talk at the village school during Book Week, I found myself listening to the Albert of long ago in this self same classroom telling me how he slid down the mount of Mount Bures on his mother's old tea tray, flattening a path through the bluebells, the slimy stems of which speeded up his descent. It is strange not to count ten after Albert has stopping ringing before entering the chancel to begin the service, giving him time to loop the bell ropes and get back to his pew. And sad beyond measure not find him growing runner beans in his little Eden between the gravestones and the Norman fort. Thinking of Albert's grave, the neighbours are saying, 'Well, he won't have to go far!' But then he never did.

Isolated as I am by the foot-and-mouth restrictions, I miss my walkers whose dogs rush up for a pat, my unrecognisable riders in their helmets, my ramblers with their maps, my occasional mountain biker. This is what it must have been like in the Pest House, with everybody keeping their distance. But at least it could be the ill wind which might blow away some of the nonsense of the Countryside March. Townspeople and country folk alike are drawn into a common plight when the 'plumes' of disease are able to make vapour trails across every boundary invented by history, just as they did during the plagues of long ago, and will do for ever. At Lenten Compline our breath spirals in the cold church, joining that of our ancestors as they muttered in the sacred quietness about the trouble *they* had with sheep.

Walberswick Whisperers and Sounding Hymns

No sooner am I not snowed in than I am toiling in the wood in warmish spring weather. Last week was a Brueghel in which we all clumped about in the bitterness, and in all the knitting we could muster. This week is a Botticelli with floods of snowdrops, primroses and hellebores. Catkins rain down. Thus out to the wood to pick up the debris, to listen to the commotion, to forget all else. The trees crack but it can't be with cold. Birds house-hunt in the hollies. The springs which feed the stream are dreggy with melted ice and need raking. Nobs of butterbur blooms push out of the soil and nettle tips lay out their territory. By mid-afternoon I am so far gone in my clearing that there really doesn't seem much point in doing anything else. The rhythm of gardening has been set.

Voices carry due to geography. The ramblers descending the hill have no idea that they are in a sound box and that I am receiving their talk. In Suffolk they talk of being a Walberswick whisperer who can be heard in Southwold. What I cannot hear is the telephone, the portable one I have been given at Christmas being still in its packing. The chatter of the walking crocodile arrives loud and clear. Perhaps I should have a conversation with the cat for them to enjoy. Instead, I dwell on holy things. Should we dispense with hymns at Mount Bures this Sunday if the organist doesn't turn up? This question leads me to Timothy Dudley-Smith who has given me his marvellous collected hymns, *A House of Praise*. Its magnitude amazes me. Also its revelations, such as 'Tell out, my soul' having been originally conceived as a poem with no thought of it being sung. Then Walter Greatorex set it to a tune called 'Woodlands' - after Woodlands House at Holt School. Then, bringing down a dead bough, I fret yet once more about 'Songs of Praise' on TV never giving the authorship of hymns, and how illiterate and demeaning it can be not to flash Herbert or Wesley or Dudley-Smith on the screen, and how one longs sometimes to know where these words come from. In his poem *A True Hymne* George Herbert wrote,

> The finenesse which a hymne or psalme affords,
> Is, when the soul unto the lines accords.

It is at this moment that the day closes in, the sun goes out, the hour grows nippy. A straggler, a young man appears suddenly - 'Have you seen the others?' 'Only heard them', I reply. He makes off, whistling loudly.

Interventions

Part of my Lenten fast has been silence all the morning, radio silence that is, and so pleasurable has this been that it may prove to be unbreakable later on. In any case, writers exist in their own special silence, work-wise, and all I have done in Lent is to extend it a fraction. However, the extra noiselessness feeds every minute. I listen to the kettle boiling, the rose tapping on the glass, the cat purring, a bird scuffling in the guttering. I look out of the small windows in turn and see the old farm fields lined-up by glazing-bars. Soon a girl will walk with quick light steps along the horizon, as she does every day, to fetch her horse. Soon she will reach the very spot where a walker lost his precious bronze axe-head round about fifteen hundred BC. Shiny new it was when Duncan picked it up and laid it on the dining table. The girl returns leading her horse, each of them balanced on the edge of the view. They will bob along the ridge until my perspective can no longer carry them. Soon too she will trot down the bridle-path, dismount in the unseen stable and go home to her husband or parents, then journey to her work or to the Sixth Form College, for there is never enough of her on view to give exact information. It is simply that at seven a.m. she crops up in the landscape, soundless and thus just right for it, a light-stepping horse and rider who all unknowingly animate at breakfast time a quiet old hill. This every day. What I will never see again is a farmworker's daily stride to his toil. This is a first for local history.

After breakfast I take my Lent quietness out into the garden. The woodpecker rattles away in a dying willow, the pheasants screech and a nippy wind is giving a bay tree a good thrashing. Girl-less horses on the meadow suddenly rodeo around in thunderous happiness, the young postman drives down the track at a fair lick, grinning and cheerful, being newly-wed, and birdsong takes a breather. Ian and Joachim follow him and my silence is filled with tales of the sea, well Southwold, and we are all three far from silent about the books we are working on, Joachim's on Jewish cemeteries, Ian's on Suffolk artists and mine on early days.

I hear all about Mel Gibson's *The Passion of the Christ* and decide not to watch it as gift for cinema sadism. But I am pleased that he has restored Passion to the religious language. This word vanished from the Roman Catholic calendar in 1969 and its observance was compressed into Holy Week. Anglicans can thank the 1928 Prayer Book for its survival. *Passio* - suffering. The Lord's suffering only. What word could be substituted for Bach's St John and St Matthew Passions? For me Passiontide suggests Christ's appalling suffering from knowing what lay ahead. Would he not have seen crucifixions? They were a common sight just outside a Roman city, and a squalid one. Mel Gibson wants us to see 'everything,' yet I distrust celluloid blood. The Gospels are enough for me. John Newman famously described crucifixion to a packed congregation at Oxford, producing a terrible silence when he added, 'And these things were done to the Son of God.' Execution often comes twice nightly on TV, and we do not have to look at the pre-Crucifixion windows in King's College, Cambridge to see what the tormenters of prisoners look like. They look pretty ordinary.

A Doleful Lent

Ash Wednesday, and ashes indeed, with the countryside closed down and pestilence free-ranging. It hitches a lift on the motorway and travels first class on the plane. Our feet carry it along. So does the wind. Indeed, as one farmer said, trying to stop it is like punching the wind. There is a difference between what is happening at the moment and what occurred in 1967. Although such a short time ago, the farms were smaller and more private then, less on the road, less cut down and open. Who now gave a thought to the fact that the chops in our supermarket trolley had already travelled the length of England? Rustling through my book of petitionary prayers, I cannot discover any which touch on the medieval reality of our disaster, and which will do for both our human and animal helplessness. Maligned grey squirrels swing innocently in the trees and among 'the first unfolding leaves' as John Clare called them. So all is well and all is ill. And what can we do? Little, it seems. Sickness must take its course. I recall an ancient petition - 'Have pity upon us, who are now visited with great sickness and mortality'. Although in those days it would not have been the illness of animals.

And so the fast begins. Michael the vicar presses ash from a small silver box on each of our brows as we kneel at the rail and I speak Joel's passionate language. His words echo through the arches. The tower clock crunches into action and claims another hour of our existence. Forty days and forty nights lie ahead. But who is counting! Are we not where the measurable and the immeasurable part company? Our penitence 'for all that is past' is signed on our foreheads. The altar candles gutter due to an untraceable wind which lives in the sanctuary. The coloured windows are blacked out by night and are best seen from the churchyard. Those who have given up whisky for Lent are already battling with their souls, it being a raw evening. Does anyone give up soaps for Lent? How hard that must be for the addicted. Preaching on George Herbert, I talk about his sensible latitude where fasting is concerned.

> It's true, we cannot reach Christ's fortieth day;
> Yet to go part of that religious way,
> Is better than to rest.

Lent was Herbert's season. He was born in Lent, married in Lent and died in Lent. For him fasting was a method of 'starving sin'. But then he was an early dietician and nutritionist where both earthly and heavenly food were concerned. His feast day precedes Ash Wednesday and brings a kind of balance to what is expected of us in the days ahead.

Olney Hymns

A wild week. We battle through the hurtling darkness to say Compline at Mount Bures where gales hoot around the spire and have done some breaking and entering, blowing-in the vestry window. Will trees come down? Will slates fly off? Will there be a power cut? Keep us as the apple of your eye. On a further desperate evening we drive in the opposite direction to Little Horkesley to sing the Olney Hymns and as there are almost a hundred of us we are able to out-voice nature with their piety. First sung in 1779 in the tiny Buckinghamshire town where John Newton was curate and

William Cowper was genius, the Church at large flinched from them. Such intimacy, such a touching of hands with the Saviour, such a keeping in step with him, it could not be decent. Also such an incongruity in the friendship which inspired them, that of an ex-slaver and a depressed poet. What did they have in common? The Olney Hymns give a full explanation, and when we sing them their pathology is so unclouded by the old religious language that it causes us to miss a heart-beat.

John Newton remained astounded that Christ would have anything to do with him, let alone be his close friend. He had gone to sea aged eleven and had both received and given every kind of abuse and degradation. He had done, and had done to him, unspeakable things – and yet at Olney Christ walked with him, a distinguished writer sought him as a confessor and the world respected him. He was clearly redeemed. Heaven assured him so. He was a strange man, very dominant. He had taught himself several languages, theology, morals, Euclid, often using the African sand as his exercise-book as he waited for the dockers of Sierra Leone to load his ship with the eighteenth century's most valuable cargo, black people. But he had been God-fearing and respectable, and would not allow his crew to swear. He said the offices on Matins and Evensong on deck every Sunday. It was a well conducted ship, all Anglican above, all hell below. But in 1764 he was sent to minister to the gentle lace-makers of Olney, the unlikeliest curate ever, and to become the companion of a famous but suicidal poet who likened himself to the most hunted of creatures, hares and deer.

Newton was certain, Cowper uncertain. Newton was Bunyan's Evangelist, 'pointing with his finger over a very wide field' and saying, 'Do you see yonder Wicket-gate?' Cowper was the man who said, 'No'. Then said the other, 'Do you see yonder shining light?' to which Cowper would have replied, 'I *think* I do . . .' Between them, with certainty and uncertainty, they wrote and published the Olney Hymns, all 348 of them, as curious a partnership as will be found in English literature. 'O for a closer walk with God' we sing to the accompaniment of plaintive weather.

'Lord, This is a Huge Rain'

Many fields have pooled and many ditches have slopped over. We drive extra miles rather than dare Little Horkesley pond, now a lake. February fill-dyke is one thing, water pouring from headlands in wide, flashing scallops quite another. Nothing is running away. Lanes are navigable for the four-wheel drivers and for wellingtons, but not for most cars. One almost expects fish to swim across the tarmac. Drains are blocked and rains fall on rains. Winter wheat looks like a paddyfield in China. Keith manages to drag the oil tanker from a slough of despond below Bottengoms. He and the oilman splosh about enjoyably. The gutters round the farmhouse brim over – everything everywhere has more water than it can deal with. And so it stays. It is what deluge means.

My text is taken from a cartoon in the *New Yorker,* now pinned up in the study. It shows a secretary opening the mail and talking to her boss on the telephone - 'Nothing important, nothing on fax, nothing on voicemail, nothing on internet. Just, you know, handwritten stuff'. I tell the damp congregation about the Apostles' secretaries, Epaphroditus, Tertius and Onesimus. They are not always used. Paul's letter to the 'foolish Galatians' comes direct. 'You see how large a letter I have written to you *with mine own hand!*' Outside, the rain will be drowning the dead, washing away the Christ, as holly wreaths and making the first snowdrops think that they have put to sea. Which is what Peter did in the first lesson, put out for a catch which could have sunk him. Nature does not know when to stop giving. Or sometimes when to start.

But I can smell spring. The Stour knows no bounds yet it has to admit a flooding greenness all about it. The footpaths squelch as much with plants as with water. They wait for dry winds to wring them out. I am reminded of the path from Treneague to Burlorne in Cornwall. It is past breakfast and my kind but ruthless (with guests) friends have shooed me

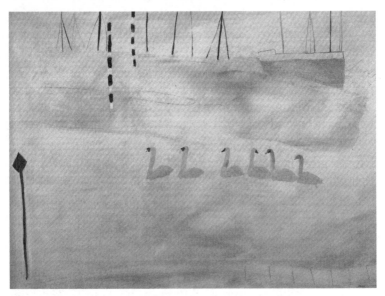

Stationary swans float slowly backwards as the tide comes in

from under their feet. 'Have a nice long walk' – i.e. don't come back until lunch. They have novels to write and other animals to feed. February in North Cornwall is what April will be in Suffolk. Rills trickle down the steep hedges – those slate walls which are now turning into hanging gardens – and the roaring black farm dog rushes out to eat me and turns to jelly when I pat his head. And the scent of St Breock Downs, plus the smell of sties and sheep-pens and rotting hay, and of bluebell and pines, makes a softness of territory which tells me that I am far from East Anglia. Three hours must I walk. I was reminded of my very first visit to Cornwall when I was nineteen and the drill at the Newlyn guest house was all out after breakfast and all back for high tea. In-between, I seem to recall, there were soaking drizzles, foghorns and melancholy, and always the sound of running water.

More Flooding

The day drifts from swamping rains to sunshine, and then back again, every few hours. The fields should steam but instead they confront the changing sky with saturated furrows as evidence of what occurred last week, the near-drowning of the parish. The old church looks as if it had been through the car-wash, every flint of it scrubbed and rinsed. Diana and I note the tottering headstones and hope that our memorials will eventually fall about like this. That our names may become guesswork, due to lichen and February scrubbings. Indecipherable tombs are so eloquent. Let them never be uprooted by the tidy brigade. I see it as part of my mission in life to teach others to let things be. Harold up the road is our master of letting things be. His excuse is that they might come in useful. An old friend, clearing an aunt's house after her death, found a shoebox labelled 'Little bits of string too short for use'. As a boy I heard an aunt say, 'A woman should never marry a man who undid string'. What to keep, what to throw away, these are life's recurring questions. Word-less gravestone reeling by the porch, who do you name? A husband and wife from a muddy farm? A rector no less? A boy who fell from a stack into the path of the trace-horse?

The Gospel for Sexagesima is the parable of the sower, placed there because of February being sowing time. But who at this minute could place as much as a foot on the drenched land? Seed-beds are river-beds and one would not be all that surprised to see carp and dace swimming out of the gate.

I am 'reading' for a new book. There have been writers who 'read' for a book they intend to write until they die, and what a happy thing to do. 'What are you working on at this minute?' 'Oh, I am reading for my biography of John Stuart Mill'. The reply indicates professionalism, not leisure. But I am at the final reading page and at the beginning of the first chapter page and am thinking of the pen which dared to write, 'In the beginning was the Word . . .' The nerve of it. The assurance of it. There would have been no reading into it, that's for certain. I have been reading myself back to a young writer by the Suffolk sea. I can hear again that crashing of the waves between the lines, that ceaseless clinking of the shingle ridge below the window and screaming of gulls. There was an old man outside who sold a handful of herrings for a bob.

March

Modelling - At Bemerton - March Dates - How to Write
Books - Nineveh, that Great City - Lent is Work - Founders'
Day - Lent is Idleness - Lost on the Home Ground - Getting
About - King of the Castle - The Scourge of Tithes - The
Parched Soul during a Downpour - Soldier Poets - Though I
am Sometimes Afraid - The Best Thing Ever - At St
Edmundsbury - Before the Slaughter - *Passio* - Country
Manners - A Power in the Parish - The Waiting Room

Modelling

A wild goose is tacking against the wind, flying sideways in wide swerves. But the garden is calm, so it is books and lunch outside with a woodpecker hammering away overhead. Thousands of primroses and violets line the ditches and there is the distracting scent of buckthorn. I have just returned from Nayland where a roadman dressed for a part in one of those ecological disaster films rides a sprayer through the pretty streets and squirts weedkiller at the little plants which thrive in ancient walls. In the church John Constable's Maunday Thursday Jesus is blessing the Bread and Wine, his hands palm upwards, his face tilted towards his Father. The young local artist painted the altarpiece for his aunt Mrs Smith. I have seen it all my life and it is as familiar to me as the photos on the chimney-piece. 'Why', said his Uncle David, seeing it for the first time, 'that's Golding!' John's brother Golding had indeed sat for the Lord.

Finishing *The Cornfield* in London, Constable had to write home for a list of the wild flowers which were blooming at Flatford in July, when he had begun the picture. Henry Phillips the local botanist obliged. In July, 'all the tall grasses are in flower, bogrush, bulrush, teasel. The white bindweed now hangs its flowers over the branches of the hedge; the wild carrot and hemlock flower in banks of hedges, cow parsley, water plantain and . . . the rose-coloured pesicaria in wet ditches is now very pretty; the catchfly graces the hedgerow, and also the ragged robin; bramble is now in flower, poppy, mallow, thistle, nop . . .' And so Mr Phillips continues. Let Nayland pin his list on its notice-board as a reproach to its spring spraying.

The mad tidiness of the current village, the fear of seasonal growth. However, we are much improved in other ways, heaven knows. When Constable needed a woodpecker to put in a picture, Captain Torin had to shoot him one and send it by stage coach to Percy Street. In Nayland I cross the road to the inn where Gainsborough's brother and Constable's father sat on the catchment board to run the River Stour.

The horrible war leaks into Lent, its sands which bred three world faiths accusing us all. The beautiful Iraqi faces on the screen are descended from the Middle Eastern people in Victorian stained glass. They are accompanied by our incomprehension of Iraq, of Islam. So I read the *Koran* just before reading Compline, then *The Sayings of Muhammad* - 'If you knew what I know, you would laugh a little and weep much'. And so Compline at Wormingford, the drenched tombs of Georgian farmers, the moon making a faint showing, the sticky buds bursting. It is almost All Fools.

To Colchester to model for an art class. This takes me back a bit. Am I sitting comfortably? Then they will begin. May I read – Calvino's novel *If on a Winter's Night a Traveller* – no, because then you will wear your glasses and hang your head. Did not Constable's brother have to roll his eyes towards heaven and allow his big workaday hands to lie heavy on the Lord's table? But his career as a model might have been more testing, for the original subject had been The Agony in the Garden until their mother had objected. 'Adoration was more becoming our Saviour than humiliation', she said. About twenty artists are drawing and painting me. I am not to look. I fall into a reverie. I must be careful in case this falls into slumber. The art teacher tells me, 'You may talk to us'. This is difficult as they know a lot about me and I nothing at all about them. I think what I will have for dinner, and about weed poisoners, and about an Islamic text which says, 'Angels will not enter a house in which there are dogs and pictures'.

At Bemerton

Diaries out. How busy we are to be in Lent. Hardly an hour in which to starve ourselves. I tug marestail from the orchard where it threatens the primroses. Cold winds run along the track. My green woodpecker flashes across the set-aside with an alarming shriek. The P.C.C. rattles along in Jenkin's Farm. What have we here? The diocesan chancellor's threat to visit us if we do not move the plastic flowers from the churchyard. What surprises me is to see florist's packaging left on bunches and sprays, whether they are for graves or soloists, or for Princess Diana, the lovely blooms peering through plastic. Churchyards are now places which reveal an absence of the old religious language. Those who put up memorials either do not know it or do not feel confident to use it. Hence the frequent banality. The memorials tell one more about churchyard rules than about the dead. A hundred or· so twentieth century stones rise from the dust of many thousands of Wormingford burials of those who went into earth coffin-less and above whom the weeds waved until a Victorian clergyman tidied them up, planted handsome trees and laid out the gravel walks.

I once sat in Bemerton churchyard, which is no more than a wedge of land acting as a breakwater to the flood of Salisbury traffic. Here, I thought, a young parson sat in rural peace, playing the lute. Knowing him, I see him playing it at a funeral. His own memorial inside the little church could not be more discreet, just a tile with a cross and G.H. 1632. He died not at all certain that the bundle of poems he sent to Little Gidding would come to anything. While I wrote in this churchyard, the man mending the fence came over to see what I was up to. Did he know where he was? Not really. He had come from the New Forest, and so wouldn't.

'A poet named George Herbert was rector of this church.'

'Lately?'

'Long ago.'

Some explanation.

'George Herbert, did you say. I don't read a lot.'

I told him that the ploughmen would tie-up their horses when they heard him ring the bell for service and come in just as they were. He told them how 'to keep God's watch'.

'Imagine that!' said the New Forest man.

March Dates

Everything begins. For a start, the Wild Flower Society Register. My tutor says that this year I should confine my discoveries to the village and to Bottengoms Farm. No bog plants from Perthshire, no treasures from Glen Lyon, one of my most favourite places on earth where, it is said, Pontius

Pilate was a child. So I walk around listing the common
loveliness of the home ground, primrose, violet, catkin, etc.
Then to the Aldeburgh Literature Festival where I read from
a novel which I wrote ages ago, so distant is it that it might
have been from another author. I can hear the North Sea
slapping behind my back as I typed it, rather than my own
words. After the reading we go to the White Lion for an
Organic Dinner and where, instead of the hum of 'Down with
GM crops!' I am once again listening to Imogen Holst in this
very same room as she tells us about her father or Mozart at
the Sunday Gramophone Club. I can see her clearly, a figure
of infectious joy, her body dancing in its urgency to make us
feel, if only for an afternoon, what she has felt all her life,
that human existence is a burst of song. Catch on! she
seemed to be telling us, before it stops! Well, dear Imo, I
have done my best.

The following day I preach on St Francis and the
Benedicite. Just a couple of miles away, down by the river,
they painted him preaching to the birds on the north wall of
Wissington church – blackbirds, all listening to him from a
tree. They say that this picture was put on the wall less than
twenty years after the saint's death at Assisi. 'You are all our
riches', St Francis tells God. We sing the Benedicite and
command the wells to bless him. Hearing 'wells', I am a boy
again and letting down a galvanized pail to a ledge from
which will gush icy water when my brothers and I heave the
bar round, for it is really a horse-pump and it tires all our
strength to get it going. The Benedicite is the song sung in a
furnace, and no wonder it praises every kind of coolness and
greenness. I go to check the springs at Bottengoms. There
they are, never ceasing, never ending their gentle disturbance
of the soil, always trickling, always pouring, always rushing,
for ever on the way to the Stour, but with a courteous call at
my water-tank en-route. 'Praised be my Lord for our sister
water, who is very serviceable to us, and humble and

precious and clean'. Not, it has to be said, that St Francis took much advantage of water's cleaning power, but then few did in c.1200 AD.

On Mothering Sunday we sing 'Once in Royal David's City', this to my mind being the best hymn about the childhood of Christ. The Sunday ramblers chattering through the churchyard will be perplexed. Little bunches of spring flowers wait on the altar before being distributed to each woman present. A choirboy once expostulated, 'But she isn't a mother!' But she had a mother. 'And you have a mother'. He receives a posy with consternation. That's what you get for speaking out of turn – daffodils. So many mothers below the first cut of the year, all tidied under the lawns, all above the deep blue sky, each with her God. We sing too Tim Dudley-Smith's 'Tell out, my soul, the greatness of the Lord' and feel that we have had a small holiday from Lent.

How to Write Books

One of my favourite biblical scenes is of Baruch reading the book which Jeremiah dictated to him to the king. Dictation, it seems, was no unusual method of writing a book. 'How didst thou write all these words at his (Jeremiah's) mouth?' they asked Baruch. 'I wrote them with ink in the book', he explained. How else? They said that the book should be read to the king. But the king was young and did not want to know what Jeremiah had dictated to Baruch. However, there was no escaping it, and then we have this wonderful vignette. It is winter-time and the king sits listening by a brazier, and as each unwelcome chapter is read to him, he chops it off with his penknife and throws it into the fire. And so, when it comes to 'finish', there is no book. Nor were they any more keen on Jeremiah's book outside the palace. 'Why', they said, 'You are no more than a singer of fine songs with a lovely voice!' This is what happens when a writer possesses a delightful literary style. One is sometimes more apt to be read for it, than for what it advocates.

I thought of Jeremiah as both stylist and dictationist when I was editing Henry James's novel *The Awkward Age*. Because of arthritis, he was recommended by his brother William to employ a stenographer, i.e. typist, when he began writing this book. And so, after decades of longhand, the pen-to-paper days were over for the great novelist. For the first time in his life he would have to compose with another person in the room and to listen to the clatter of keys and not the scratch of a nib. And talking the story down instead of writing it down had an extraordinary effect on Henry James's famous style.

Some editors have suggested (almost demanded) that I use a computer. Poor creatures, little do they realise that the sound of a manual typewriter will be all that is heard in my work-room until God calls 'finis'. I take comfort from other Luddites. Alan Ross, poet and cricketer to perfection, could not even type and edited the *London Magazine* by fountain pen. But now I have to give a talk to a class of middle-aged folk suffering from all kinds of handicaps, including blindness, who intend to become writers on the internet. And I have to go to the village school and watch nine year-olds engrossed with mice and screens. And presenting me with some good poems which have never seen a ballpoint. So I comfort myself with thoughts of Ivy Compton-Burnett and Iris Murdoch writing their marvellous tales on ruled paper with HB pencils, and with a recollection of Martin Amis saying that the bell of his manual typewriter was a sound which, like the Muse herself, said, 'Go on!' But like every writer, I find the mechanics of the trade ever interesting. It is the harnessing of them to the imagination which is the hard part. The trouble with Jeremiah was that he was often too great a poet for the politics of his day. 'Why', they retorted, 'You are no more than a singer of fine songs with a lovely voice!'

Nineveh, that Great City

I was piling up the dead wood when spring came. It was shortly after lunch. The birds changed their tune and the flowers could wait no longer and made a collective opening about two-thirty in the afternoon. There was a smell which was not decay and a disturbance of the ground cover as those who were sleeping beneath it raised their heads. Were I nearer to the neighbours I might have heard the first mower. But Bottengoms Farm knows only its own sounds, on the whole, though with memories of its once roar. Plough horses, pigs, children, poultry, machinery, dogs, shouting wives, arguing men – it could have been a boon to go to the Crown for a pint and a civilized conversation.

All the talk now is of war. I re-adjust the petitionary prayers so that they can make sense for God. A farmer could have knelt in this self-same room asking to be saved from the Spanish Armada and the Pope. How strange it is that at this very moment planes from East Anglian airfields might soon

be on the way to Iraq. 'Go to Nineveh, that great city . . .'
When Jonah went to Nineveh he told its inhabitants that it
would be overthrown in forty days if they did not mend their
ways. Forty is a measure of time much favoured by the Bible.
People knew where they were with it. If Jonah had told the
Nineveh-ese that they would be conquered in thirty-eight
days they would have continued being wicked. But forty
days! From the king down, the population covered
themselves in sackcloth and ashes, and God spared them. I
look up Nineveh that great city in the *New Oxford Atlas*, also
Babylon, and the fabulous rivers of the Tigris and Euphrates
which skirt Baghdad, all marked. Though not Eden, which
has fallen off the map. 'Asthur built Nineveh' – Genesis,
chapter ten. If all goes well, those who want the war will get
it in Lent. And in those very same deserts which provided the
conditions for Christian and Islamic fasts, and dusty answers
for such questioners of religion as myself. But needing some
kind of answer, I search for it in T.S. Eliot's *Ash Wednesday*
(1930) and hear Ezekiel's dry bones confessing.

> 'We are glad to be scattered, we did little good to each other,
> Under a tree in the cool of the day, with the blessing of sand,
> Forgetting themselves and each other, united
> In the quiet of the desert. This is the land which ye
> Shall divide by lot.'

Those youngish sincere faces of Blair and Bush on the
screen, what do they mean? 'Go to Nineveh, that great city
. . .' The troops scratch their heads. The children sick from
our sanctions weep.

Lent is Work

Procrastination hangs around. I look through the window, I re-read the letters, I turn up an obscure composer on the Third, I walk to the stream and finally and fatally I open a book. Except today I have the added memory of what happened yesterday to mull over and prevent my getting down to it, that of a visit to London. How was it, other than a miracle, that my watch-strap should snap just as I was passing the watch-strap repair shop in High Holborn? 'It will cost you,' warned the man. He meant ten pounds for a leather band and three minutes of his valuable time. I tell him about the coincidence of its breaking outside his premises and he says, 'Where better?' This rain drives me into an ex-gin palace off Covent Garden. It is an acre of dun carpet and a pile of mahogany and engraved mirrors waiting for the first customers. The Beatles are in the woodwork bawling out a dull old song. This apart, the atmosphere is tranquil and given to recollection. I recollect the reading going on around me in the Liverpool Street train. Edmund Burke's *Reflections on the Revolution in France* (pretty girl opposite); airport novel the size of the Bible (dressy woman across the aisle); *Nikkei News* (Newspaper crackling in the little hands of a Japanese lady); and then on an obituary page of the *Independent* (bearded commuter), looking out at me, the face of someone I knew. Only it would have been an old face when he died. Not the face of a friend exactly, but that of someone from my world. So we stared at each other all the way from Ingatestone and until the fellow traveller turned the page. Writers possess memories like litmus paper. Everything sticks.

Richard the church treasurer is crossing the river, a move

of all three miles which will take him into another diocese. 'And I, even Artaxerxes the king, do make a decree to all the treasurers which are beyond the river, that whatsoever Ezra the priest . . . shall require of you, it be done speedily.' So I inscribe his leaving present, Richard Mabey's *Flora Britannica*. Then I write a description of the cover of my new book, which is George Herbert's *A Priest to the Temple, or The Country Parson* (1652), plus some of his poems, although why it should be called 'my' new book I can't imagine, having only put it together. But I did choose the cover picture. It is a painting by William Dyce and it shows Herbert in the rectory garden at Bemerton, the River Nadder flowing by and Salisbury spire in the distance. Fishing tackle propped against a willow is a reminder that Izaak Walton was the poet's first biographer. Herbert's lute rests against a seat. Dyce painted it in 1861, Herbert slim in his cassock, a finger keeping place in his prayer-book. His position is not unlike that of someone told to stand in a certain place by a photographer and who will return to what he was doing before this request was made. The mid-nineteenth century photographers and artists alike were beginning to find a not entirely welcome common ground in portraiture. It has often seemed to me that Dyce and Herbert might have returned to the rectory for tea. 'Same time tomorrow, Mr Herbert?'

I heard someone say that Lent is 'hollowness', thinking about deserts and such like, I imagine. But for me Lent is work. The desert was where early Christians went to work with all their prayerful might. It need not be sand. Norwich provided excellent, or dreadful, desert conditions during the Middle Ages. No need to go to Palestine, really. Norwich was where many seekers laboured hard to come close to the heart of what they professed. Lent can blow sand into our eyes. It rubs its ashes onto our heads. There is nothingness and there is everything.

Founders' Day

To Dartford School to give the annual Founders' Day Address in the parish church. The founders sleep under my feet. Or maybe they are wide awake and listening to, among hundreds of other young people, including Sikh lads in turbans singing 'He who would valiant be'. The church is filled to overflowing. Mary the School Captain reads that there is a time to cast away stones and a time to gather stones together, and the congregation, knowing that Mick Jagger is an Old Boy, will be updating the text. The choir sings Palestrina's *Sicut Cervus*. The Kentish light creeps through the windows. In my sermon I read Shakespeare's account of Jack Cade's tirade against grammar schools. Cade is haranguing poor Lord Say and giving no quarter, telling him, 'Thou hast most traitorously corrupted the youth of this realm in erecting a grammar school and whereas, before, our fore-fathers had no other books but the score and the tally, thou hast caused printing to be used, and contrary to the King, his crown and dignity, thou hast built a paper-mill!'

A few steps from me is the memorial to Sir John Spilman who did indeed build a paper-mill, and just up the road. And which most likely provided Shakespeare and most of the Elizabethan writers with what they required above all things – paper. The 'grammar' of the Tudor grammar schools was Latin, not English. Hence Jack Cade's wrath. Feudalism was passing but it would never disappear if the educated classes used Latin and the rest of the population used English. I urge great bedside shelf-fulls of books on those listening to me. Novels, poems and lives which will challenge the resident hi-technology. Later I talk to Mick Jagger's father, an old schoolteacher. He said that when he was a boy in Yorkshire he and his friends would roll stones over the moor to make cairns. Mick cavorts in blown-up photographs on the walls, and has a House named after him.

Tony Smith, the Headteacher and an old friend, drives me towards Dover. He has a surprise. The pear blossom is out. There are oast houses and clapboard cottages and blue distances and coastal cars. We come to a halt at Tudeley, and

Willow 1980

still no explanation for this Founders' Day outing. Tony opens Tudeley church door and tells me, 'Be amazed.' And I am. All the windows are by Chagall, the colours and shapes those of a drowning and a rescuing, or rather a spiritual saving of a girl, Sarah d'Avigdor-Goldsmid, who lost her life in a 1963 sailing accident. She clasps a small boat as the sea casts her up to the Cross. The Marc Chagall animals are all round us, of course. It is unexpected and wonderful.

Lent is Idleness

I have some difficulty with Lent. It makes me feel on top of the world, which is not what it is supposed to do. Maybe it is the way in which the breakfast sun spins up from the back of the hill like a new coin, blinding the rooks, and the clouds begin to parade their spring gold, and the way in which the orchard fritillaries begin to show. And this Lenten difficulty is made worse (or better) by my being naturally austere (I suppose) so that I have never possessed some of the things which my friends are now doing without. As for Lenten silence, I have it here at Bottengoms all the year. It is the constant background to the old farm's unstoppable sounds of birdsong, stream and wind. But then we say Compline in church every Wednesday, which is a Lenten treat, so no doing without in this respect. Compline from *completorium*, the completion of our daily prayer. We squash into the chancel for this and are measured and quiet. Real worship unwinds from its formality. The church says, 'Take your time. There is nothing to add, no train to catch. The day is far spent. Abide with me until the morning watch'.

A fine dog fox trots by as I clear the kitchen garden of the sticks which a gale has brought down from the aspen. Nettles are coming on nicely. Were I not so far away I would hear the first lawnmower. 'Put in your earlies (potatoes) now' says John. And I do, of course. Some garden advice must be taken, some ignored. When I tell neighbours that the Magnolia Stellata is in bloom they say, quick as lightning, 'The frost will get it!' But it never does. Listening to the just leafing trees might be a good discipline in Lent but it will be too soon for aspen music, my favourite sound.

England is crowded with societies wanting talks from writers. 'But you've heard it all before!' I protest. How modest he is, they reply. Come and tell us about your having been young here. About how you and your brother used to climb the church towers. One of these climbed towers, Stoke-by-Nayland, is framed between ash trees in the classic Constable manner as I walk down my track. It is a hundred and twenty feet high and five miles off, and is constructed from a mixture of tile and rubble, flint and septaria – anything which they could heap into it – and its colour changes from hour to hour like Monet's *Rouen Cathedral* series. 'You can see Harwich Water from the top', they used to tell us. But I cannot remember if we did. 'You could turn a wagon and horses on its roof', they'd say - 'That's if you can get 'em up there!' A big joke. The church still has its lovely original doors, all silver-grey now from Suffolk weather. They swing open mightily, just as they did when we were children, to reveal the vast interior. The tower arch – what a sight!

Lost on the Home Ground

Needing a new water purifier according to the water inspector, I found myself quite lost where once everything had been most found and familiar. And having to ask the way. For what had been the secret fields of boyhood was now the Chilton Industrial Estate. Gone the deserted lime-pits, the marshy meadows, the weathering timber – 'the Logs' – the dark ponds into which we squelched, the remote neighbours on their World War One chicken farms, the green lanes, and come scores of hi-tech buildings, in one of which lurked the water-purifier. But which one, for none advertised their contents, just the firm's symbol. I must find the water-purifier because the inspector is less despairing of me than he usually is and I do not want him to find me slipping back into bad habits. I am now walking on sacred ground, for just under the concrete lies the agricultural ruin of our play-land, the peggles and white violets, the dens and old reapers, the hides and private territories of the old country child. I found my way to the right hi-tech shop by using the church as a compass. For although everything else had been flattened out, there it rose, perpendicular and eternal. My sister Constance had been baptised in it one September Sunday long ago before the corn had been cut, so that her long robe trailed over the wild flowers. It was a hot afternoon and father beat a path along the headland for the christening party. In the churchyard there was a large tomb with railings round it and an inscription which petered-out in ivy. It read, 'George the third . . .' and I informed my friends that it was, of course, the King. Inside the church were the tombs of the Crane family, and equally royal where I was concerned, for had they not built Chilton 'Castle', with its moat and crenulated roof? A most royal house. Later on it would remind me of the enchanted chateau in Alain-Fournier's haunting novel *Le Grand Meaulnes*, and indeed it still does, even if the hi-tech estate is only fields away. But now I was with the water-purifier man. He wanted real money, not some new-fangled card. When I carried it back to the car I felt more like a water-diviner with his ash-stick than a modern customer. 'You will know where to come next time', said the salesman. I thought of Sir Robert Crane and his wives, probably drinking from the moat, and of their fine tomb in the church. A sculptor named Gerard Christmas had carved all three of them for fifty pounds.

Getting About

Giving. David brings me a cutting of *Rosa Lutea*, a thornless rose planted by the wall of Beacon End farmhouse in 1886. He says it will grow to over thirty feet. Gerard mentions it in his 1633 herbal and says that it has an excellent sweet smell. But later rose-growers disagreed and re-named it *R. foetide*. I shall introduce it to the Rambling Rector on the dead apple tree and trust that they will make a go of it. David sits in the kitchen with his beloved dog at his feet. It tries to hide its longing to go on and its hatred of 'sit'. I think that David is off to the village, but he is actually on his way, to Cyprus 'to search for plants which grow in the cracks of ancient temples and such like'. I am off to Selwyn College, Cambridge to the annual Readers' Day Conference. The Backs will have their sweet March smell. In Cambridge they are using the tallest crane imaginable to insert a new building between some old buildings. It is like one of those silver pick-ups in an amusement arcade. Will it grab King's College, then drop it into the sugared almonds? Cambridge observes its antics with consternation. It is building students' accommodation where other builders cannot reach, piling them high in the cold sunshine. I have looked up Selwyn College in Pevsner - 'Not bad'. Well, that's a relief. Soon the lilacs and laburnums will be flowering in Grange Road, soon it will be May.

Back in Wormingford Michael the vicar will be running round the village to prepare himself for the London Marathon. His energy astounds us. He says it will be his last Marathon, but tell this to the Archdeacon. I am notorious for walking everywhere. The spring ramblers pass Bottengoms in starling gaggles, chattering away. They wave their sticks at me and call out pleasant half-heard things. Sometimes they pass through the churchyard at service time and I want to rush out and lead them in. Sometimes I have to walk with them to give a kind of peripatetic lecture on local history, when I remember Lancelot Andrewes teaching the Westminster schoolboys during muddy strolls along the Thames path. Although group walking is not for me. I think of leading about fifty walkers through the Piers Plowman country, and then through the Elizabeth Barrett country, and then into the John Masefield country, all in six miles. This bookish ramble as part of the Ledbury Poetry Festival. The walkers wore great boots and carried life-saving flasks. I had shaken my head. We were off to the Herefordshire Beacon, not Everest. But they were joyous, like birds.

King of the Castle

The third temptation of that 'Exceeding high mountain' from which could be seen 'all the kingdoms of the world, and the glory of them', suggest that now is the moment to climb the new millennial wooden steps which have been built alongside the mount of Mount Bures. So off we set between the Lenten services. The wind is icy but the sun fierce and the motte of a castle which was never built is shiny with new bluebell leaves. The mount is a monster version of a sandcastle at the seaside and, although far from being an exceeding high mountain, it is pretty dizzy by our standards. Up the ladder we go. When we reach the summit we find ourselves assuming the correct sentinel postures as we look this way and that. Below us, stunted oaks stick out from the mount like holly from a Christmas pudding. We can lord it over all the territory between the Colne and the Stour. And there lies the churchyard, rather cheered up from this altitude and turned into a Stanley Spencer painting, the graves rocking about in the grass as if about to give up their dead. We train the binoculars on the vicarage to see if Michael is gardening, and then to another height where Edmund was crowned King of the East Angles, and then on to the church clock at Bures itself, which says twenty to four. Our mount is thirty-five feet high and two hundred feet round. The church below would have stood in its bailey. But all is dizzy conjecture, what with the climb and the wind and the vagaries of history.

Conjecture reigns too in a field in the east where a hopeful young man swings his metal detector. Mr Chaplin, ninety in the autumn, stares at him scathingly. That old iron he is filling his pockets with comes from a wartime work-shed. Our thoughts are more elevated. We are above trove and within nodding terms of the spire. Who piled up this motte? Every poor labouring man from miles around. And then did their lord say, 'Not here, but Hedingham?' And so they deserted the best bluebell raised bed for miles. Poor work force, deep down now but not so buried in time to be rewarded with a Stanley Spencer resurrection. At least it can boast of having marked the earth for all time. Those diggers knew what they were doing, but we do not. We descend to Mr Chaplin, truculent among the broccoli. Ancient, wise, mocking. Fancy spending all that money to make steps up the mount! Fancy waving a metal detector over the site of a Hitler war shed!

The Scourge of Tithes

It has to be explained that the milk is left one mile away, and the papers further still, but that the post is left a mere two hundred yards from the house. The daily journeys to these various locations are taken up with nature-study, idle dreams, haphazard meetings with dog-walking neighbours and to returning waves to faceless figures in cars. About once a week I do the village round and encounter various mishaps and gossipers.

Harold rushes from Festilla to tell me that he is drying out my *Revelations of Divine Love* 'and some other old book' in his Rayburn. Accompanying him to his kitchen, there they are, Mother Julian, faintly baked, and my nice blue Compline, rather wavering from first being left out all night in the rain, and then put in the oven. I had dropped them and it served me right if the school bus had run over them. Later that day Harold discovers another page, which I read as best

I can. It has the quality of one of those letters from Prince Owen Glendower to the King of France which someone of the radio is mentioning, but it is the Contents page of the Recluse atte Norwiche, and smelling faintly of roast chicken.

These Lenten Complines, said in all three churches, plus some reading and little addresses, have steadied us. I think that this is the right word. I consider this Wednesday worship as I turn over the dark earth in the kitchen garden. I plant as I go, earlies. The main potato rows will be set later. Then to Wortham on the Suffolk-Norfolk border to give a talk. It is one of those villages which have been severely marked by authorship. Richard Cobbold wrote *Margaret Catchpole* there, his fictionalised account of a real live woman horse thief which became Suffolk's most popular folk novel. He was the Rector and I see him wandering around Wortham's wide greens with ample time for watercolours and storytelling. And Doreen Wallace wrote dozens of novels there, some of which still deserve a read – *The Time of Wild Roses, A Handful of Silver, Billy Potter*. In-between she was the scourge of the Church of England, a Boudicca come to sweep away its tithe system. It was indeed called the Tithe War. Supporting the clergy by the tenth of the agriculture of each parish may have been a good idea in 786 A.D., when the Synod voted for it, but a very bad idea in 1930, with farming on its uppers and the Church in the eyes of most country people compromised by its often enthusiastic support for the Great War, when thousands of young labourers were hustled into the trenches by their parson. Doreen held rallies, wrote protests and was in the van of those who were to put Church of England finances on a very different level. She gave her recreations in *Who's Who* as gardening and politics. The latter became extreme, as was apparent when young men in black shirts helped to get her corn in.

The Parched Soul during a Downpour

There is a flurrying theatre of snow and the cats take up the best window-seats to enjoy it. Lower Bottoms opposite is already covered and white, except for where a lone horse is chomping his way through it, leaving a vivid green line. But soon the snow turns to a brittle rain which hits the panes, making the cats withdraw to cushions. They haven't paid good money to watch this kind of thing. Journalists declare that the spring has come too soon or will come too late. A cock pheasant paddles majestically in the cold stream, gorgeous, with hungry eyes. 'Delicate stepper, Cathyan bird, you fire the landscape' wrote Sidney Keyes. This poet came to mind when a couple of old Desert Rats arrive for tea, Gordon and Peter, talking of Sidi Barrani and Tobruk. Alarming reminiscences fill their heads. 'We washed our shorts in petrol!' Could this be possible? Sidney Keyes would have been thinking of his own obliteration in the Western Desert on an April day in 1943 when he wrote,

> 'They said, It will be like snow falling –
> To-night a hollow wind beating the laurels,
> And in the morning quiet, the laurels quiet,
> The soft sky resting on the treetops and
> The earth not crying any more,'

At night a Duke of Wellington climber rattles my sleep. It knocks away to the guttering and scratches at the tiles. 'You want to take that down a few feet', advises everybody, but I don't suppose I will. They shake their wise heads. 'He won't do what he's told – did you notice? – he don't do what we tell him.'

At Compline I stand on the chancel step and talk about aridity, an odd subject when the village is practically afloat. The fields are ponding, the lanes waterlogged and parted like the Red Sea when a car comes along. Whoosh. But, as I point out, none of this can affect that drying up of the spirit which happens to each of us at some time or other. How thirsty we are for that sacred refreshment which alone can lay the dust in our hearts. 'For the Lord your God is bringing you into a good land, a land with streams and springs and fountains.' When? That is the question. 'Today!' answers Christ, for whom it is never tomorrow. Compline broaches a spring and there comes that bubbling-up of the clear refreshment of the spirit.

Soldier Poets

The best or most interesting anthologies are wayward. Who is allowed in and who is left out should be the anthologist's personal choice. I have anthologised both prose and poetry in this mighty fashion. The dividing of the sheep from the goats played no part in it. I had a writer friend who went nearly mad with rage when he opened Philip Larkin's *Oxford Book of Twentieth Century English Verse*, as of course did the first readers of Palgrave's *Golden Treasury* or any other selection of poems. I was thinking of this when I went to see R.N. Currey, another literary friend, who, long ago had edited *Poems from India,* a little collection of work by men from all three services who had been stationed in the sub-continent during the last war and who used poetry to describe the enormous effect which the Raj had on them. Currey had gathered it up and put it together in a way which created the full impact of their experience. It remains a startling book.

But here we are in the familiar house where we have talked literary shop for decades. Over the garden wall the residential roads lead to where Wavell was born. A plaque points it out. This house is a larger version of the one we are in, tall and spiky, and in 'grounds'. It would have been new

Magpie flying up from a wet road

when Wavell was being wheeled through them by his nanny that May in 1883. Wavell made a great anthology called *Other Men's Flowers* during World War Two. Everybody bought it. His choice was what most people would have chosen. And Wavell's son John had assisted Currey with his anthology, *Poems from India*.

Colchester, home of both these anthologists, is one of those towns which pile it on where history is concerned. The foundations of their houses went deep into a Roman cemetery and it was quite usual to dig up tesserae with the potatoes. All in all, they were surrounded by some two hundred acres of Roman graves. Below their hardcourts and shrubberies lay soldiers from all over Europe, their wives and children and slaves. They would have been the kind of folk the Lord met and St Paul knew. One of them was 'Longinus, son of Sdapezematycus, Duplicarius of the first Wing of Thracians from the province of Sardis (who died) in his fortieth year . . .' and who was buried by Currey's garden wall. His tombstone in the local museum has enthralled me since boyhood. It shows a cavalry officer riding in triumph over a barbarian, poor man. Longinus had lost a hand. And then, 'what do you think?' said Currey. 'Last week they found it!' They were building a new house between his and Wavell's and there in the soil it appeared, the victorious hand of Longinus, waiting to be joined to his arm by expert archaeological surgery. Currey's ninety years fled like an evening gone, as they say, in the light of his discovery. It was a Longinus who pierced the dead Christ, and a Longinus who was an excellent critic in Athens, and a Longinus who was governor of Judaea. After I left the anthologist I walked to the museum to see my Longinus and his victim. Would they stick his hand back on tomorrow? Oh no, archaeological surgery can take years. You see, there is no blood in stone, no nerves, no warmth unless the sun catches it.

Though I am Sometime Afraid

St Cuthbert in March, so I talk about him. He was a Lauderdale shepherd, a tall young man, they said, with a gentle face, and no go-getter. He liked wandering about the Lauderdale hills, talking to those he met, and was in flight and hiding from those who wanted to set him to 'proper' work, i.e. that of a bishop. He clung to Celtic ideas and the Romanised part of the Church was often rude to him. He took to living on Farne where he could only see the sky. He could have been sensitive about his appearance because the plague had left its mark on his gentle face. Solitude would have suited him. He fits grimly into a Lent which is being marked with the culling of the Lauderdale sheep by sharp-shooters, for they too have the plague. A huge sadness fills the countryside as foot-and-mouth infects it. What to do? The government says one thing, the farmers another. Visiting a sick neighbour I have to tread through disinfected straw. 'Come and cheer me up', he says, as I enter the close room. Outside the ditches are full of primroses, and a helicopter cranks its way overhead like an injured dragonfly. We have tea in the old house, once the grange, or home farm to a medieval monastery up the road, and we shake our heads. What to do? This is what everybody is asking. Coming home, I note a faint greening of the trees. When they carried Cuthbert's body to Dunholme above the crashing Weir, they made a temporary shelter for it with green branches and it turned into Durham Cathedral. St Cuthbert's Day psalm is 56 - 'Nevertheless, though I am sometime afraid, yet put I my trust in thee.'

Back to my old school to tell the children about books. Forty angels of both sexes listen to me. They are all about nine. Over their heads, through the window, All Saints Church glitters in the sun. Samuel Crossman ('My Song is Love unknown') was rector here. Why is not this great hymn, based on a George Herbert poem, not in *The English Hymnal*? But back to my class, now bursting to tell me what it reads. Hands wave in the air. Little do they know how totally ignorant I am of their authors. A boy nails me. 'How many pages are there in your longest book?' I hazard 'Three hundred . . .' He holds up Harry Potter. 'There are six hundred and thirty-six pages in my book!' Well, one can only do one's best. Then we have our photo taken by the local paper, all seated on the floor and looking up like St Cuthbert.

Night now and I am splashing along watery roads. Soaked sheep over the hedge, Paul's probably, and plague free, thank providence. Their lambs cry out.

The Best Thing Ever

I have moved my desk by as much as two feet to have the light fall better on the page. Why did I not do this before today? Before ten years ago, to be accurate? Furniture has a way of taking up a stance of its own, a moral or aesthetic position which says, 'Don't dare to shift me. I know where I belong.' I have friends whose rooms are tips but move a chair to the window, and they are dreadfully put out. Writers can have an affair with their desks – the poet Robert Bloomfield addressed his oak table quite passionately. Some do not have desks at all. Angus Wilson liked to write on the window-sill and D.H. Lawrence on rocks above the sea, under trees, in railway carriages, any old where. Penelope Mortimer wrote on her kitchen table, as did the Orkney poet George Mackay Brown, although he with his back to the window for fear of distraction. Ivy Compton-Burnett wrote in pencil whilst lying on her sofa, and Virginia Woolf wrote in ink whilst seated in a baggy armchair, the bottle strapped to a piece of board. But I write on a respectable Victorian writing-table, such as one would have found in a decent hotel at the time. Only work in progress is permitted on its top. Everything else is strewn around. And now it faces a different view, and so must I. And now, with the harsh March day full on the typewriter, I must prime the pump.

The primer this morning is Calvino's *If on a Winter's Night a Traveller* . . . with, in the first chapter, perhaps the most alluring advice to a fellow writer ever given. It is about how to buy a new book, how to bring it home, and how to sit or lie as its pages take you prisoner. 'Yes', writes Calvino, 'you are in your room, calm; you open the book to page one, no, the last page, first you want to see how long it is. It's not too long, fortunately. Long novels written today are perhaps a contradiction: the dimension of time has been shattered, we cannot love or think except in fragments of time each of which goes off along its own trajectory and immediately disappears.'

But no sooner am I settled in the Calvino position for reading his amazing novel, and rejoicing in my added light, than a thought hurries into my head. Which is that it is Book Week at the village school and I have to be there to help celebrate it. The school is two miles away and the children, like the shepherds, will all be seated on the ground, or the library floor to be exact. No transport. The church clock says nine as I run past it. Alas, it is slow. Drawing breath – the local author must be dignified – I stroll in. The children are on the floor and hoping that maybe I had come the field way and fallen over a cow or into the mere. I have to talk about Characters – the kind found in stories. There are characters in the Bible stories called 'types'. Types of angels shoot up their hands to ask questions, some leaving them wearily up in the air until Mags the Headteacher draws my attention to them. Alice, Mr Toad and William Brown fight for places next to Harry Potter, about whom I know nothing. I am a Potter virgin. A little girl tells me that she has an aunt who writes books with characters in them. She puts them onto the page with her pen and then onto the computer. Another William, just off to the Royal Grammar School, says that he is reading *Moby Dick*. The trouble with the bookwormship of children is that it makes grown-ups feel unsafe. I tell them that Beatrix Potter used to stay with *her* aunt just up the road from here. Well, at Long Melford. The other William takes me on an educational tour of the classrooms. They are miniscule Tates, artwork of every kind covering up the painted Victorian bricks. There are greedy paintings of pizzas and pancakes, the latter no doubt inspired by Michael the Vicar's cookery on Shrove Tuesday. And here are everyone's names in the Viking language. Kirk in runic script – it alters him somehow. 'Here', says William severely, for I am not paying attention, 'is our wormery.' The poor things do what worms do but between glass plates. Outside in the playground I observe the return of the Hula-hoop. Nothing quite goes away in school.

At St Edmundsbury

Notions of heaven play around in our heads as half a mile of choir and clergy come in singing, 'We love the place, O God, wherein thine honour dwells'. What an afternoon, and everybody able to tell their grandchildren how they found a parking place in Bury on a Sunday. Geoffrey, Deidre and I are to be installed as canons in the ancient pilgrim church of St James, now the cathedral. Here come our Bishops, Ipswich and St Edmundsbury, Thetford and Dunwich, here comes the tall Dean, here come all the Suffolk priests, all practising 'the triumph song of heaven'.

On the way, coming through the village where I was born, I see the site of the old thatched house, burnt down these fifty years, with bungalows marking the spot. Also a squadron of trumpeting daffodils. And the avenues to vicarage and church dark with summer heat to come and not at this moment at all spring-like, and the little low-roofed school, and the ancient huddle of thatched cottages known as the Spong. No glimpse of our pigsty or pond. Running away on either side are the lanes where I biked, some pre-Pevsner guide in my saddle-bag, to Bury St Edmunds to wander among the jagged flint piles which are all that is left of the king-martyr's shrine.

But here we are again, seemly and rehearsed. Having given us our Deeds of Collation, Bishop Richard takes his throne and we all praise the unity which is pouring down on us like the dews of Hermon. We swear in turn to observe the Statutes, Ordinances and Laudable Customs of the Cathedral. And then, one at a time, the Dean, holding our left hand high, leads us to our stall, pressing us into it, making sure that we possess it. Geoffrey is pressed down into the stall of St Ethelbert, King of the East Angles, Deirdre into the stall of Anselm, Abbot of St Edmund's Abbey, and myself into the stall for Writers, a new seat, the cushion for which is not yet quite embroidered, though it will be by the time of my next visit. The Cathedral is so big that all the East Anglians in the nave have become a pale, singing mist, featureless yet intensely present as individuals. The liturgy is severe, for it is Lent Three. We feel guilty when we listen to the choir children sadly beseeching God to 'Wash me thoroughly from my wickedness' and brave when they refuse to 'flee as a bird unto the hill' in order to escape the arrows of their critics. For all will be well as 'The Lord is in his holy temple'. The latter is certainly true at the canonical moment. What a business it all is, life with its 'bane and blessing, pain and pleasure', with its foolish politicians and its obedient armies, its deaths in the desert, its unending ritual of war.

Then afternoon tea among the ruins. Or rather among the materials for the new tower. A friend has brought me an Albertine rose to commemorate this lovely day and I prop it up carefully against a Norman wall. Lydia brings me a cup of tea and Helen some saffron cake which a stranger devours in error. The late afternoon light brings shadows. They stretch over the ruins to where the barons stood, swearing on Edmund's altar to force Magna Carta on John.

Before the Slaughter

A Raphael card has arrived and I am staring into it, needing to see it all, the sleeping knight, the women in his dream, the little city beyond, the minute horsemen wheeling where the road bends. The knight is dreaming that Flora is bringing him spring flowers, and that his Muse is bringing him a poem about his heroic deeds. But these deeds have not as yet been accomplished and he stretches out on a sandy bank, his armour undented and his body unscratched. The radio speaks of some American soldiers lying on the ground in Kuwait as they play Monopoly on a board made from an old carton. Nearby, and probably unknown to them, is the site of the Garden of Eden.

Soldiers waiting for the fighting to begin have often seized the imagination of artists and poets. Men have rarely seemed more innocent than before they kill each other. F.T. Prince brought painting and poetry together in his *Soldiers Bathing*, which might well be the finest poem from World War Two. In this poem he says that he too has been staring into a Renaissance picture and has been recognising that the artist 'knew war's sorrow and disgrace'. But the sleeping soldier in my Raphael does not know this. All he knows is bravery and heroism. We sing about a sleeping Christ and about his nightmare dreams of earthly conquest. He too is a young man on his own, stones his pillow, earth his bed. Raphael was thirty-seven when he died – on Good Friday, which was his birthday. I prop the Raphael on a bookcase and then re-read F.T. Prince's *Soldiers Bathing* and re-see the faces of those who made the Iraq war and wonder how it is that nations throughout history find, or lose, themselves with such leaders? Prince saw 'war's horrible extreme' as 'the obverse of the scene' 'Where Christ hangs murdered, stripped, upon the Cross/I mean, that is the explanation of its rage'.

The March sun is warm enough for lunch on the doorstep. Garden birds are energetic, loud in song and swift in flight. The young man making the reservoir in the valley below roars away. I pack up working and rake weed out of the horsepond, hauling frightful stuff from its depths. The rills which feed it make tiny sounds like a xylophone. From these droplets escaping from the mud, the rills are a positive Zambesi by the time they reach the pond, splashing away in fine force. But the leafless trees retain their winter silence. I think of all the rustling to come. Raphael painted his sleeping warrior on poplar wood. Wormingford is rich in poplars. They run along the main road like a thin curtain, tremulous in summer, shaking and whispering, talking back to the traffic. And not far off are the rare black poplars which our neighbour Edgar Milne-Redhead, whose name will for ever be associated with them, put back on the tree map, so to speak. One would not think that a living tree species could get lost, but this one did. It had become invisible to the unseeing eye.

Seeing Lent anew year after year tests one's vision. Particularly when it has to be done from the pulpit. The poignant tale of the young Christ testing his resolution in the desert hardly needs analysis. What I always see is the appalling aloneness after the warmth of a Jewish home, and the companionship of his friends. Also the equally appalling realisation that there was no alternative way. Our plaintive worship filters into the cold churchyard but is briefly warmed by Benedicite, the nature hymn.

Passio

At twenty past eight precisely a watercolour sun comes into the farmhouse, picking out the gold picture-frames and promising the earth. The cats hazard a paw or two into the icy garden, then retreat to a radiator. Birds de-moss the lawns and daffodils totter about in the new grass. It is England's famous spring, and not to be missed. The air is strong and sweet. Foot-and-mouth keep-out notices are in tatters on the telegraph poles. Ditch water pours away. The old men with their leaping dogs go by. I divorce La Reine Victoria from a blackberry bush. Easter is coming. 'Therefore let us keep the feast' we will soon be singing. Keeping feasts and Sabbaths, fasts and such likes, if only with words, keeps Time itself in tune. Admirers of W.H. Auden were puzzled when he did so. Robert Craft found it surprising that he could refer quite readily to his religious conviction and practices, informing his New School audience that he will not be lecturing on Holy Saturday: 'When they told Auden Saturday wasn't a holiday, I told them it might not be for them, but it certainly was for me'. Passiontide reminded me of Auden's, bizarre to some, Christianity.

Passio=suffering. The road to Resurrection had to be trod with gravitas all the way. A few have trodden it for the many, which has been unfair but blessed. Faith's serious business has always been attended to by the saints. We have to make sure that faith's serious business is not reduced to pleasant customs. Christ's suffering and what we sometimes suffer because of it intensifies in the week before Holy Week. Julian of Norwich could not separate his suffering from our own. 'For the fundamental thing about the passion is to consider who he *is* who has suffered. I began to think about the majesty and the greatness of his glorious Godhead, now united with his tender body; I also remembered how we creatures loathe to suffer pain . . .' And thus Passiontide, that sweeping into the calendar of all that we understand all too well, and from which God as man had no way of escape. For Julian the Passion was 'the greatest gesture our Lord God could make to the soul of man'.

A letter has arrived to ask if I would mind looking at one of the handsome eighteenth century tombs in the churchyard to see if it is the writer's ancestor, who lived at the Grove. I get a chair from the vestry and try to make out its weathered lines. The letters are crammed with lichen. Moss makes fat fullstops. Here is the figure five, here a curlicue, here nothing at all. A gentleman lies below, but who is he? Sticky-buds wave over him. A honeysuckle feeds on him. His quarterings are smudged.

Country Matters

A crisp white world. Field edges have been trimmed-off by frost. The oaks are creaking. I am up early to write a new Introduction to George Herbert's *A Priest to the Temple or the Country Parson*, first published in 1652. He would have had the Bemerton windows wide in order to breathe – in order to live, indeed. I re-read his famous little book. What a nerve to write a rule for the rural clergy when one has only just joined them. And how did Mr Herbert come to such an understanding of his parish in such a few months? And, considering what a dandy he was at Cambridge, what a lot of ordinary common sense he has at his finger tips. By mid-morning the March sun is hot on the window and the ice is slipping. 'Immortal heat, O let thy greater flame attract the lesser to it'.

Commotion below – the hunt is in the garden. A river of hounds is flowing through it, one of them having the impertinence to gollop up the cats' leavings en-route. Three huntsmen appear behind the hedge, though hoping that it hides them. One does a little bugling but the dogs stream on, soft muzzle to whipping tail. Then they have gone, all of them, men and animals. The cats! I tear down to save them. One is sitting many feet up in an old willow doing her famous Lewis Carroll act, the other . . . Where is the other cat? I rush around calling, beseeching, composing in my head a letter to the Master of Foxhounds which will scare him stiff as I see pretty Kitty swallowed whole. The night comes and Bottengoms is in deep mourning for her. Look where she once laid, her favourite place, the imprint is there still. I put out, as usual, Whiskas for two and her sister eats the lot. Blinded with rage and grief, I fail to notice the sleeper in the piano. She stretches and makes a dissonance along the wires, a spangling of notes to accompanying a greedy purr. Would Herbert, saint though he was, have put up with it?

Herbert told his country folk to 'think well – or better – of yourselves. But not without good cause'. The more tumbledown the circumstances, the better to make Christ's mark on them. What a privilege to be installed in neglect. And what a nuisance to have less than three years to reverse it. I climb the hill to have a word with the horses. Their nostrils steam and it makes them dragonish. No, they were not in the hunt, they tell me, just grazing. One of them rolls around on his back. Is it because he is happy or itchy? Gulls fly overhead, too high up to see anything to eat.

A Power in the Parish

The churchwarden as a literary character is a fairly rare bird. Which is odd when one remembers their prolixity. He emerged from the late medieval church. There was one for the priest and one for the people, and now there must be thousands of them, still quite extraordinary men and women who, as well as holding the old reins, now have the main say in choosing the incumbent. Yet it has become an avoided if possible office and one firmly refused. Most PCC members say, 'No, not me'. To our relief there are churchwardens who go on for ever and ever. Surely these have been called as much as elected and who are we to say your time is up? 'Three years shalt though reign' says the Rules. Forget it, we say.

There are three churches and thus six wardens, whose price is above rubies. But John has gone to God. A good musician, he brought the choir up to a Royal School of Church Music standard and we will for a long time continue to hear his teaching when we sing. As for Gordon, he has only to be away a week and we go to pot, or we think we do, which is as terrifying. However, writers don't have much to say about churchwardens, not even Barbara Pym. Trollope's first Barsetshire novel was called *The Warden* but it is not about a churchwarden. The poet George Crabbe chooses a parish clerk as a victim of his exposure - Jaquin, 'the gravest man on the ground'. Poor Jaquin, 'when christening fees were small, the weddings few, the parties paupers all' to helping himself, and his end was grim, as it would have been in Aldeburgh. Literature's classiest churchwarden was T.S. Eliot. Long-serving like our friends, he was warden of St Stephen's near Grenville Place for a quarter of a century. It was said that in church he looked like a businessman and in business he looked like a cleric. He saw the 'piaculative pence' drop from the choirboys' little hot hands.

My own history of churchwardenship was not all that businesslike, I must confess. Thrice was I called to this high office, or rather told to do it, once by the patron, an earl, then by what was clearly a misinformed common consent that I was the right man for the task. I was first churchwarden of All Saints, Great Glemham, then of St Peter's, Charsfield, then of All Saints, Debach, all in Suffolk. At Glemham I was youthful and writing my first novel, and greatly fascinated that I was helping to look after a church of which George Crabbe had been the rector. It was a beautiful church with an airy interior and there were few Sundays when I did not hear the Suffolky voice of the poet-botanist-doctor-priest. The parish had got four professionals for the price of one. They said that on a winter's afternoon Crabbe would carry his book nearer and nearer to the window and when he could no longer read, would slam it shut and cry, 'All go home!' But in summer he would take the whole congregation round the village after service and instruct it in botany. The Hall gardens were flooded with his snowdrops still. At Charsfield there was a medieval bell which said in Latin, 'Box of sweet honey, I am Michael's bell.' At Debach, 1853 and soon to be turned into a house, I saw the ghosts of Edward FitzGerald and Omar Khyyam. When I looked up churchwarden in the dictionary it said that it was a clay pipe.

The Waiting Room

To the rather fearsomely named Oncology Department at the hospital. To wait for a friend. Below us the Roman dead, centuries of them, the last ones lying East to West. I imagine them singing Ambrose's hymns such as 'The day draws on with golden light.' The waiting-room is warm and homely. Nitwit afternoon television flickers in a corner. About twenty patients, some in wheelchairs, and including a nun, two white-faced women in wigs and a boy in jeans. Each is identified by a birth-date. There is no indication where the cancer is. The staff is as unlike that of a TV hospital as it could possibly be, calm, kind, sensible, just quietly at work.

I find a vast old armchair from the Thirties and read. Not Colm Tóibín but the Joseph Conrad paperback which I found in a charity shop en-route. It is *Lord Jim*. This works every time, not the plot but the novel as the provider of the trouble-free zone. How this barrier irritated the grown-ups when I was a child. Faintly even now behind the wall of words I can hear the complaint, 'I am talking to you!' But bookworms soon learn other sounds. The patients gossip, the nurses gently call out names and 'Your birth date?,' the car park operates softly over the Roman tombs, a keen wind shifts the corporation daffodils, and Lord Jim son of a dicey Essex Rural Dean, holds my full attention.

Like most Conrad heroes, Jim is far from home. He emerges hesitantly from the dense prose and is not to be viewed all at once. His is the world of infinitely slow travel on untrustworthy ships skippered by untrustworthy men, the world of close quarters, a world which Conrad understood, from the Congo to the East Anglian shore. The latter would bring his unlikely lessons on English in the form of the *East Anglian Daily Times* and *Eastern Daily Press*, sent to the crew by their wives. I glance at the current issues, bursting with house agents and petty misdemeanours, football and fine editorials, ambitious letters and death notices. Hugh Walpole once outraged Conrad by bringing him the English dictionary as a useful present. He who had graduated D.Litt from the *East Anglian Daily Times*!

Lord Jim is carefully hesitant when it comes to words. Young men such as he, crushed together on old ships, unwittingly touching, are masters of self control. But when something does slip out in a Conrad story it leaves the reader in shock. 'Date of birth?' asks the nurse. 'Fourteen-six-eighty-four' answers the boy in jeans.

April

Serious Calls - At West Mersea - Blowing the Gaff - Waiting for Salvation - As it was - As it is - Good Friday Music - A Meditation on Puddles - Light from the Black Mountain - 'Little Lamb, who made thee?' - The Hares on the High Ground - Anselm at Norwich - The Emmaus Walk - Noises Off - Low Sunday - Mark at Tiger Hill - Proofing George Herbert - The Seekers

Serious Calls

Motionless April days but warm enough to have elevenses on the doorstep. The garden is noisy with birdsong. Cats lie back in the primroses to watch the gliders, turning now and then to give each other a lick. The world is all death and resurrection, half-mast flags and blackthorn. Riders and walkers pass, full of praise for the day. Church-wise it is Exodus and Corinthians, Corinthians and Exodus. News-wise it is terror in Manger Square. I tap out Finis to a new book, lay out the Contents, then pack it all up for the publisher. It is like having a new child and sending it straight to the orphanage. The study has suddenly become one big space, my head another. Which is why I sit on the doorstep to pass time with cats and strangers.

We are to remind ourselves of William Law, it says. He wrote the next best guide to life to *The Pilgrim's Progress*. Like Jeremy Taylor's *Holy Living* and *Holy Dying*, Law's masterpiece is now in the realm of style rather than piety. It is entitled *A Serious Call to a Devout and Holy Life*. Law himself led a charming life in what is now the John Clare country round about Stamford. He freed birds from cages, confused the orthodox, educated the boys and girls, and took the milk from his four cows to his poor neighbours. He ate raisins for tea and he walked a long way and wrote long works. Dr Johnson, the Wesley brothers, the Quakers, the Anglicans, all eyed him uncertainly. And no wonder when he was packing up for the publishers books with titles like *The Soul Rising out of the Vanity of Time*.

Spring weeding. Now here is true contemplation if you like. Muddy knees, earth-filled nails, and all the usual guilt over the sheep from the goats business. Should such a fine ranunculus give way to a tottering iris? Buttercup flowers were once warmed in Vaseline to make a potion for skin troubles. I shall give this magnificent buttercup honorary Garden status and let it have a bit more of the vanity of time. Nettles come up in easy skeins. In the churchyard the mighty horse chestnuts are making their sticky candelabrum above the tombs of John Constable's uncles and aunts, their branches swooping down from on high to dip in graceful sconces for May blooms. Some of the aunts were so young, mere girls lost in childbirth. Young husbands often felt that their lust had sent their young wives to the grave, when it was usually the old midwife's dirty hands. Poor May Constable, poor Anne – poor Abram too. I see them weeding up at the Hall, the April wind catching at their hair, their bantams getting under their feet, until a bell cries, 'dinner!'

It is the Annunciation. Art has translated Mary to suitable surroundings for hearing that she is to be the Mother of God. On the postcard from Italy, she and the angel are in perfect juxtaposition in a Florentine palace, her modest gaze, his rosy wings. The psalm is eighty-five. 'Righteousness and truth have kissed each other'.

At West Mersea

'And here is Ronald Blythe, who needs no introduction!' smiles the chairman of the W.I., the Parent-Teachers' Association, the bellringers annual do, even the Professor at the local university. And here they are in front of me, the dear familiar faces, all of them curiously unaged within the bounds of the get-together. To not need an introduction was not always a lazy compliment when it came to being a villager. Much suffering was caused by everyone knowing everything about you. The news of the world which runs across the screen every night is often spoken of as the destroyer of the provincialism which gave stay-at-home life its rich flavour, but we are apt to forget its benefits. Among these is an hitherto unknown tolerance of what is going on next door. Or just an indifference to it. When one remembers the killing gossip, the cruel laughter, the persecution even of the recent past. The hopeless longing for not being known. Those who were born not to belong, fled. But many who needed no introduction on account of their already notorious families brassed it out. All this has gone, as has the drama it created, the amusement, the misery. 'I publish the banns of marriage between . . . both of this parish.' Both of Sweetpea Cottage, of course, and for at least the last three years. But they are still only twenty-one and as pure as flowers as they drift down the church and into the disco. But it makes it hard going for the rural novelist. They have knelt probably for the first time in their lives at the rehearsal.

Those who seem to know everything about us these days are the junk-mail folk who reveal a disturbing familiarity with our birthdays, debts, wealth, ailments, diets, dreams even. There is still a strong parochiality in the shape of the PCC or the darts team, but the ancient savagery which made life such a bloody business, though interesting, has been long defunct. Some mourn it. Their eyes light up when they see on the local News some scandal which exceeds anything which is allowed to go on without comment these days, and the next door village at once assumes some of the old ferocity towards what is beyond the pale, and is envied its right to rage. All that we have is a years-old debate about putting up one of these faux-rural signs which have recently become a parish coat-of-arms on a stick, and seen on every green. The debate is tepid, unfiery, and such a far cry from the question of whether to clash saucepans under the window of an immoral couple or whether to report the rector for popery. There are now people who never draw their curtains or who get up at ten in the morning and who do not belong to anyone or anything. 'And how do they manage it?' is all we long to know. And where is the Chief Gossip, the female 'loudspeaker' of our boyhood who was first with the news should it be bad? I can see her now, putting on her coat and hurrying off, ostensibly to fetch the milk but really to give her little world something awful to brighten up its day. Now all we have is genocide with the cornflakes.

April north-easters tear at the magnolia and rock the fruit bushes. It whines through the lattice of Mount Bures vestry and defeats the hot-air heater. Thrushes are appearing at Bottengoms and are welcomed like errant sons come home. I set potatoes to the sound of rattling hedges and screaming gulls. They make me think of all the sailing folk de-hibernating to drag the covers from their boats at Mersea, and to caulk and scrape to the music of ropes slapping against masts, and to iron pennants, and polish and scrub the weekends away. Some of these yachtsmen must be the descendants, it occurs to me, of Sabine Baring-Gould's 'sailors tossing on the deep blue sea', a wild lot in Victorian Mersea, where he was rector, and where he wrote, 'Now the day is over'. East Mersea, it was, a marshland parish where one would have kept one's mouth shut. How one longs to see when it is mentioned. Now, had it been 1880 Wormingford, it would have been all over the village 'His trip to Mersea. They say he walked all over the marshes in the rain and came home fit to die, they reckoned. Writes books. Needs watching.' And here begins a history.

Blowing the Gaff

The spring is like an Olympian runner who paces himself for what to the spectator seems like a risky age, then sprints ahead of the field with a brilliant burst of strength. I thought that I was keeping up with it by way of mowing and planting, but now it is way ahead of me. As indeed is St Mark, whose Gospel famously runs so fast that it takes the reader's breath away. Less rushed, most thorough, Keith paints the front of the house, his ladder rattling against the guttering. The cats sit beneath a handsome stand of Butcher's Broom, just watching.

I am working on George Crabbe, a poet who would have denied T.S. Eliot's plea that 'Human kind/cannot bear very much reality'. Crabbe's neighbours could bear it all too shockingly in Aldeburgh, but not on the printed page. In his time the borough was a pair of tumbling streets being gnawed away by the German Ocean and a huge flinty church with its feet well out of the water. Crabbe had an affinity with Christ's rueful description of what happened to him in Nazareth - 'A prophet is not without honour, save in his own country'. Crabbe was the saltmaster's son and the slave-ship captain's brother, the duke's chaplain, the herbalist, the apothecary, the unflinching eye and pen. Aldeburgh detested him while at the same time being uncomfortingly proud of him. He not only knew the local game, as it were, but gave it away. One day he was the cack-handed young man rolling butter barrels along Slaughden Quay, the next he was doctoring them with cures made from the weeds which they had seen him gathering from sluices in broad daylight.

As a youthful writer I worshipped in his church and wrote its guidebook. I sang in the Festival Choir and observed from the corner of my eye the Jacobean pulpit in which Crabbe had stood and held forth to Aldeburgh, daring to speak 'for the full hour'. I thought I saw the restless congregation, the seething, the muttering. 'That George Crabbe daring to preach to us, and his father no more than a wild beast at home!'

Ports breed sailors and sailors are wanderers. One of them was wandering around London when he saw a familiar figure with his foot placed hesitatingly on the step of Wesley's pulpit in Moorgate and his gaze going this way and that in the empty chapel. George Crabbe! So the new curate at Aldeburgh had Methodist leanings! Thirty years later came that devastating exposé of a small town, Peter Grimes and all. Crabbe's *The Borough* spares no one.

Waiting for Salvation

Birds everywhere. Carefully stepping pheasants among the hellebores, hungry mobs of thrushes, blackbirds and sparrows gorging on the rotten apples which I have thrown out, keepers no longer. The sky is dove grey and soft, with here and there a rash streak of yellow. Sheets of snowdrops on the banks. The horse ponds glitter. I am telling lies on the telephone to keep the week free. 'Thursday? I am so sorry. I can't manage Thursday'. Or Friday. What about next week? 'Next week . . .' On the radio Lional Blue says that the Holocaust produced the most un-answered prayers that were ever made. He does not demand or expect answers and nor should we. It is the actual praying which does one good. I run over some of my private prayer as one would a score before singing, and discover that, on the whole, it is not petitionary. More a few reminders of things which God may have forgotten. I ramble on as I cut the wood. For church I edit other men's prayers to fit what is happening, earthquakes, the arrival of the new Bishop of Colchester, starving multitudes, life. Having glimpsed some farmers and their wives in the congregation, I pray for the crops. These are low on the ground and marvellously green.

My subject is private prayer in public places. Here are two old people in the Temple, Simeon and Anna in their eighties who are praying, praying and waiting, waiting. 'Hurry, hurry, little consolation of Israel, we haven't got all day! Soon we will be lying in unmarked sand!' They were expectant. Yet praying without overdue expectancy of answers can be a healthy way of passing the time. To have the ear of God – what more could one want?

Keith is decorating the study. Shifting the books was Herculean. It reminded me of one of my first literary tasks. Canon Gerald Rendall had died and left half of his classical library to Colchester. It had to be fetched from his house to the museum. The removal men were grumpy, scathing. 'I don't mind what I do', said one of them mournfully, 'but I hate moving a parson. Half a ton of bloody books before you start!' Keith stares at the mountain of my books and asks if I have read them all? He doesn't read, being too busy. But give

Linda his wife a book 'and she's away!' He is painting the study white. His work is beautiful. 'Do you know, Keith, people were sleeping in this room when Shakespeare was alive'. I imagine them, going to bed, looking up at the bumpy ceiling, making love, snoring, dropping their boots on the wide floorboards, dreaming, dying. Shouting at the children. Smelling of toil. Worrying. The deeds say little about them. They just drop a name here and there to comfort posterity.

As it Was – As it Is

Good Friday, but long ago. The early morning Suffolk town was barely awake when they sent us off to collect the hot-cross buns. Other erranding boys and girls boasted how many they would eat for breakfast. Bakers' vans, like Arks of the Covenant, were being trundled through the waking streets, steaming with buns. Good Friday was in half mourning for Christ and half at play. The Boat Club rowed down river to devour hot-cross buns and bitter at Henny 'Swan'. Henny means an island on river land which is frequented by wild birds. The Boat Club boys needed to be wild birds in order to stand the cold. They shook in caps and mufflers and were as pink as blancmange or as white as death. Their oars cut into the icy Stour as fast as they could as their crews lusted for buns. They would not have heard of the young rector of Little Henny, Samuel Crossman, who had written a book called *The Young Man's Meditation*, a little collection of poems which included 'My song is Love Unknown'. He had been reading

George Herbert's 'Love unknown' and Herbert had been reading Psalm fifty-one. For this is what happens to divine love. It streams through the imagination of poets, rhyming up here and there, catching a tune, catching a congregation.

But back to small town Good Fridays. Should they be early, then it would be snowing, if late, the sticky buds were glistening on Miss Baker's vast horse chestnut and the first swallows would be whirling around the green copper spire on St Peter's. But whether early or late, the Three Hours would slowly pass in ice-box conditions. The wan Welsh rector Canon Hughes would fidget in his miserere stall and the well-off old ladies would come and go in fat fur coats, their powdered cheeks turning blue. The truly saintly sat it out. Every little while Mark Fairhead the organist would play a verse from 'O Sacred Head' and we would stand and sing, 'Thy beauty, long desired, Hath vanished from our sight'. Although where I was concerned this was not true. I found his beauty all too terribly present. It was heartbreaking. All around, Suffolk voices were pleading, 'I pray thee, Jesus, own me' and the tower clock would say another hour to go.

Good Friday these days, in the village, that is, amounts to ante-communion for the two or three, and one hour for the many. Stainer. No talking when we leave. Car doors going, clump, clump. Smiles through glass. Cries from the footballers. At teatime I look up the recipe for hot-cross buns in *The Universal Cookery Book*, a very pre-Delia authority acquired by mother about the same time as I was sent to the baker's before breakfast. It said, 'Cassis, 3 tabl. yeast, mace' and a surprising number of other ingredients. The buns had to be brushed over with warm milk and 'baked a nice brown'. But as every child knows, hot-cross buns must come from a shop, not from mother, and on Good Friday morning, not from the deep freeze. They must arrive plentifully, not just one for you and one for me, and they should never be eaten except on this tragic morning, then fillingly.

Good Friday Music

There is a greedy welcoming of the cold April rains by every growing thing. The weathermen apologise for them, the Benedictus says glorify their maker. It is a running time. Hares, rabbits and pheasants are on their legs. The kitchen garden soil falls from the spade as rich as Christmas cake. A watching neighbour says, enviably, 'No stones'. Her garden is like Shingle Street, she grouses.

Back indoors I choose my music for Michael Berkeley's *Private Passions*. How about one of those measured hymns which Britten used to bring gravitas to a Church Parable? Shall it be 'Lord Jesus, think on me' (*Noye's Fludde*) or 'God moves in a mysterious way' from the *St Nicolas Cantata*? Perhaps the latter. The memory of it roars like the North Sea for those coming into harbour, the slow pacing of the lines, the April wintriness of the fifth verse:

> His purposes will ripen fast,
> Unfolding every hour;
> The bud may have a bitter taste,
> But sweet will be the flower.

On and on I choose - 'anything you like', says the producer. My musical education, such as it was, began at Little Easton Rectory with the ample figure of Canon John Barnett at the piano, and the drawing-room walls stacked with seventy-eights. None other than Thomas Ken had been a previous rector of Little Easton. Nearby was Thaxted and Holst. John Barnett rose at midday and went to bed at two a.m. The rest was food and music. Every Maundy Thursday men from the village hauled his Steinway to the church opposite, where he played his meditation on Good Friday. Listeners came and went. There he sat in his rusty caped cassock and chained cloak and in his icy chancel, just himself and Bach, and with his nervous little Dutch barge dog trembling at his feet. Having a poet friend whose religion included cold churches, I took him to listen and he wrote, 'Our music celebrates the High Wood of Golgatha', a poem I sometimes include in the Good Friday worship. One of these years, when the PCC debate is all comfort for us who do the worshipping, I might wickedly suggest that the church central heating might be turned off for Lent. I might raise my Amos voice against the luxury of these times.

A Meditation on Puddles

With no wind to speak of to divert it, rain falls in verticals like the glass bead curtains of the cake-shop through which we pushed our ravenous way as children. The rape fields are drenched. The rain never stops or wavers but drums away on the smart conservatory roofs. It dimples the black surface of the river and looks as though it might stab the pike. The cycling club on its first spring run hisses through it, the tyres leaving wakes. I walk in it and hear rainy birdsong from willow warblers in my willows and from larks who believe that they can rise above it. How nature wallows in a downpour! A sopping wet hare bounds along. A rainbow comes, one end in Polstead, the other in Layer Marney. Puddles are everywhere to reflect it.

There are two great Christian meditations on puddles. First, John Bunyan's. Bunyan had convinced himself during a bout of religious madness that he was guilty of a sin which was outside God's forgiveness. He was very fond of bell-ringing, tipcat, his wild friend Harry, dancing and many other shortcomings which are apt to take over tall young men. Thus he strode between Bedford and Elstow in the rain, the devil on his tail, his head bursting, his tongue crying, 'What shall I do?'

One day as I was betwixt Elstow and Bedford, the temptation was hot upon me to try if I had any faith, by doing some miracle: which miracle at that time was this, I must say to the puddles that were in the horse pads, Be dry; and to the dry places, Be you the puddles.

Much about the same time, a boy in Hereford who had only just outgrown the pleasure of splashing in puddles, stood by one of them rather as Alice had at first stood by the Looking-Glass before entering its reversed world. Thomas Traherne, the poet of joy, could only imagine such an entering. In *Shadows in the Water*, a matchless puddle poem, he wrote:

> Of all the play-mates which I knew
> That here I do the Image view
> In other Selves; what can it mean?
> But that below the purling Stream
>   Some unknown Joys there be
>   Laid up in Store for me;
> To which I shall, when that thin Skin
> Is broke, be admitted in.

Evensong over, John climbs the tower and comes down pregnant with our flag, having stuffed it up his waistcoat the better to manage the ladder. It had been no more than a wet

thing slapping against the mast. The church is aromatic with
spring flowers, smoking candlewick and the smell of new
hymn books. We are as dry as Ezekiel's bones. But not for
long. The puddles are waiting for us, mine deep enough to
drown the lace-holes in my shoes as I splash down the track.

Light from the Black Mountain

To Hereford now. April slides past the carriage window. Its
interior is fretful with mobiles. Inane communications back
the wide scene which slides by. It is yack versus sublimity.
The youth opposite is quiet enough as he works his way
through a novel as fat as the Scriptures. Granny reads a
twelve-page story to two small girls, and also to me, though
she does not know it. Then the Malvern Hills and the dizzy
Beacon where Elgar liked to sit, gazing for miles. Then a
quick, looking stroll through Hereford before my hosts arrive
to carry me off to Discoed. No time to see the Mappa Mundi.
How curious to think that Thomas Traherne would have
looked at it, a local boy tracing that Jerusalem centred atlas
and maybe gathering the longitudes and latitudes of his own
ecstatic earth. His geography took him far:

> This world is not this little cottage of heaven and earth. Though
> it be fair, it is too small a gift. When God made the world, he made
> the Heavens and the Heaven of Heavens . . .

which for Traherne remained Herefordshire in spite of his
vision of some angelic outer space.

It was Richard Birt, a Welsh border priest, who showed me Traherne's country. George Herbert's, Henry Vaughan's and R.S. Thomas's country too. And now the Fenland poet Edward Storey has settled in it, the rough old church which is practically in his garden telling him to make it good for a further thousand years. At breakfast we watch the swallows diving it, the daffodils crowding it, the westerlies caressing its stones. We are within sight of a ferocious battle-ground where Welsh women finished off the fallen soldiers. We walk over it. What a hopeless place for a battle, a steep, rocky hillside for rolling corpses down. Shakespeare could hardly bear to describe what occurred: Lord Westmoreland tells Henry IV;

> there came
> A post from Wales loaden with heavy news;
> Whose worst was that the noble Mortimer,
> Leading the men of Herefordshire to fight
> Against the irregular and wild Glendower,
> Was by the rude hands of that Welshman taken,
> A thousand of his people butchered;
> Upon whose dead corpse there was such misuse,
> Such beastly shameless transformation,
> By those Welshwomen done, as may not be
> Without shame re-told or spoken of,

We stroll over the massacre slope knowing what the women did to the wounded men, but not saying a word. Then drive on to where the Quakers hid, past sheep farms and crying lambs, past walkers with packs and maps, and vans doing a little business. And so it is, history. I see Presteign for the first time. It reminds me of the kind of quietness which towns in Suffolk possessed when we explored them on our bikes long ago. Then to Bryan's Ground, that lovely Border garden on the River Lugg. Lugg = Light. 'They are all gone into the world of light' said Vaughan. 'You are as prone to love as the sun is to shine', declared Traherne. I plant a tree to start a new wood then catch the train home. There is an Easter collect which says that God only can over-rule our unruly wills and affections, can fix our joys and make us love what is best for us.

In our churchyard celandine curls like goldleaf. In our fields Farmer Rix's onions are resting under acres of flint and the limes leading to the church door, having outgrown what we required of them, stand mutilated, their lopped branches thrusting like wounded arms. A sad sight but of course we must not be sentimental. That would never do.

'Little Lamb, who made thee?'

The sacred images of shepherding darken as I listen to what is happening on the sheep farms, autos-da-fé of the folds. Christianity is a divine pastoral in which the Shepherd becomes the Lamb. It was Christ's cousin John who first created this disturbing imagery. And it was that Lancashire shepherdess Beatrix Potter who said that 'Every lamb which is born is born to have its throat cut'. The use of sentient creatures by humans for their religious rites, and food, cannot escape questioning as we watch each evening what is happening on the pastures. History reveals that foot-and-mouth is no new thing but what was once accepted by previous farmers as a fact of life as it made its cyclic rounds, has in our day to be stamped out at all cost. These thoughts distract me as I kneel at the altar to chant Agnus Dei. The Baptist took his words from Isaiah 53, perhaps the most poignant passage ever written on the helplessness of animals, and of Christ.

My Compline address, by way of change, comes from Kilvert, the Easter entry for 1870. The young curate, he is twenty-nine, sees 'droves of white-faced cattle hustling and pattering to the Fair' and, later, their owners reeling home

The cockerel 1983

drunk. But this time the Swan Inn over the road from his rectory is 'marvellously quiet and peaceful' for once, with nobody sprawling in the gutter 'cursing, muttering, maundering and vomiting'. On Good Friday Kilvert takes cross buns to give widows. On Easter Even he rises at five in the morning to write his sermon. At eleven he pays a visit to the school and its distracting girls. Then he goes to church to see what Mrs Morrell has done to the font and finds, 'a round dish full of flowers in water . . . and upon this large dish a pot filled and covered with flowers, all wild, primroses, violets, wood anemones, wood sorrel, periwinkles, oxlips and the first bluebells, rising in a gentle pyramid, ferns and larch sprays drooping over the rim'. Then bands of ivy and moss. But 'at two all my arrangements for the afternoon' are upset by his having been told that old man Pritchard is dying and wants to receive the sacraments. Off Kilvert strides, meeting the schoolmaster and his friend gathering primroses with which to spell out 'Christ is Risen' on the board in the east window. It is one of those burning hot April days and Kilvert 'envied the sheep being washed in the brook below by Price and his excited boys. The peewits were sweeping, rolling and tumbling in the hot blue air about the Tall Trees with a strange mysterious hustling and quavering sound from their great wings'. When he reaches old man Pritchard he finds him far from death's door. His niece had heard him cough and wanted Kilvert to witness his Will in her favour. Kilvert refuses to sign the Will and walks home, rattled. He finds the fierceness of the sun 'tempered'.

All this at St John the Baptist Church, Mount Bures, with healthy lambs on the slope.

The Hares on the High Ground

Climbing the steep fields in front of the house, we find four hares about their amorous business. Its madness is little different to ours when similarly preoccupied. They actually sit up in four corners and are so absorbed in their ungainly courtships that they fail to see three men and a dog in the offing. When they do, it is flight in all directions. 'Lepus!' I want to call after them, 'take no notice of us. This is your land. Take no notice of the legends we have burdened you with, that you can change sex, sleep with your eyes open, dance in time to music, herald our deaths and attend the goddess Freya. Let us be honest with you, like the poet John Clare and, if we must, call you 'tasty'. He saw what we are seeing at this moment':

> The timid hares through daylight's fears away
> On the lanes road to dust and dance and play.

You have been halted in your love and we have been halted in our tracks. Give us pause. We have been baffled by your innocence, your limping towards your fate. Richard Jefferies marvelled how you would 'come as it were to meet people on country roads' and went on, 'Of all sport, if a man desire to widen his chest, and gain some idea of the chase as it was in ancient days, let him take two good greyhounds and 'uncouple at the timorous flying hare', following himself on foot. A race like this over the elastic turf on the downs, inhaling with expanded lungs air which acts on the blood as strong drink on the brain, stimulating the pulse, and strengthening every fibre of the frame, is equal to another year of life.' So spoke a young consumptive.

Someone else is being hunted all this week, passiontide. *Passio* = suffering. Someone else is being terrorised, brought down, raised high. Sad hymns allow no more than a glimpse of this redemptive suffering which is first mental, then physical, then both at once during a climax of pain and desertion. The readings are dark and harrowing, but stabbed through with a unique light. Who is this? None other, says the writer of Hebrews, than 'the effulgence of God's splendour and the stamp of his being'. What, this poor man sweating blood as he comes to the inevitable conclusion to his claims? We are told that Christ 'hid himself' before he arrived where he would be tracked down by the authorities. And what have we learned – taught ourselves – since then? To look at the News, only to find new ways to be cruel.

How cold it is at night. I live in a frost pocket. From the upstairs windows I can see the hares' field shining as white and still as a cake below a slice of moon. I fear for the greengage blossom, so delicate, so vulnerable. Planes steer in to Stanstead. They will be buckling their belts, closing their novels, filling in their landing-cards.

Anselm at Norwich

It is assumed that if one lives in the wilds that one lives out of it – the melée. But the very space which one has, and the silence of the fields, makes accommodation enough for the troubles of the world. At this pre-Easter moment all its troubles are crowded into a single face, that of a smiling boy whose parents have been torn from him by an Allied missile. He should have vanished, like all victims, by now beneath mountains of journalism, this little Ali Ismail, but of course it often takes a single person to prevent the win or lose war statistics from adding up.

Easter is as late as it can be – I think. The Golden Numbers of the full Paschal Moon in the front of my prayer-book are beyond me. All I know is that it is just a step to May-Day and that the happiness of the Resurrection will run full pelt into memories of Cornwall's wild flowers. Those who first showed them to me are long gone but at Easter, when we were so often together, and during May Days at Padstow when we sat on the doorsteps as the procession passed, they return, and I am at Trethias again, or kneeling in their damp church with its frigid floor. Or we are lolling high up on the cliffs with their granite biting into our backs and the Atlantic crashing below, and the wind a bit sharp still. For nothing ever dies.

I revisit my hares. They give me their lasting look before scampering off in all directions. What a frustration it is not being able to convince a creature that one will do it no harm. To the hares we are all tarred with the same brush, presumably, and out for the kill. Or just for the sport. They know all about the kill but nothing about the sport. And they certainly do not recognise all the names we have called them over the years. Jumper, Rascal, Dew Flirt, Grass Biter, Wood Cat, the Wild One, the Lurker, the Sitter still, the Sudden Start, the Home Late.

Holy week in Norwich. I must not go on about Dame Julian in my talks, as folk who live perpetually in the light of a famous local saint tire at hearing her name being dropped by every visiting preacher. The last time I stayed at Norwich Deanery was when I helped judge a children's poetry competition. The Normans built their cathedral in a dell. So many holy places take shelter in the landscape. I see by the programme that I am to witness my first Pedilavium or washing of feet. I will read St Anselm because a prayer of his is contemporary with all these angel-perching arches. 'Come now, little man (the saint is talking to himself) turn aside for a while from your daily employment, escape for a moment from the tumult of your thoughts . . . free yourself awhile for God and rest awhile in him (but) what shall I say? What shall I do? Whither shall I go? Surely you dwell in light inaccessible – where is it? Lord I am so bent I can only look downwards . .' So that is why they created spires.

The Emmaus Walk

Faith is full of walks, long and short. Faithless friends it was who walked home from Calvary. Their frightened retreat from this dashing of their hopes has printed itself on the Christian imagination because of its realism. It is all part of that upheaval which threw the little band in all directions. Who were the walkers? Luke does not say. Apparently these two shared a house because when the pursuing stranger finally caught up with them and took away their terror, they said, 'Abide with us, for night is here.' All the same, though their guest's scholarship had impressed them as they tramped along, they remained wary of him until 'He took bread and blest it' - then no further explanation was needed. They *knew* him. Diana Collins used to tell me about her walk along the Emmaus road with John her husband and George Appleton, Bishop in Jerusalem. She gave me his *Jerusalem Prayers*. There they were, faithful old CND marchers, walking to Emmaus, with today's traffic whizzing by, kicking up the old dust.

The Jerusalem which the unknown walkers had left was a

dangerous place. They had slipped away from it as darkness fell and were in turmoil. They had quite forgotten their Master's assurance that, as their Comforter, they could never escape him. And now a government spy was on their heels. When he caught up with them 'their faces were full of gloom.' There was no recognition and so the third walker passed the time by giving these runaways a history lesson. The seven miles home dwindled, the nerviness too fled to such an extent as to make it safe to invite him in. Bitterly, bitterly disappointed though they were, they did not forget their manners. Also, as faith-sharers with the stranger, they would have known all about entertaining angels unawares.

My Emmaus road is a mile of flinty farm track with a soft rise in the centre which lovingly strokes low-slung cars. A brook rushes by on the right when I come home. The tract is made of stones which women and children picked off the fields for generations, a few pence a tumbrel load. The Easter rains give them a good shine. Larks sing over them. However hard it is, we dread the ending of the road and that 'Abide with me.' We want to go on making history.

Holy week was dominated by a fine stem of Crown Imperial (*Fritillaria imperialis*), the orange one named after Aurora, the goddess who opened the gates which released the dews. But how did this single stem grow where it is? Then I remember. An inconsolable woman, a school teacher who had shared a house with her mother all her life, had given it to me after the funeral. Its five flame-coloured bells hang down like the bells in the tower before they are raised by the ringers. Seeing it, the plight of the giver runs round in my head. Because although mother was very old the daughter had been unable to so much as think that the day would come when she would no longer have her. Their relationship reminded me of Stevie Smith and the Lion Aunt. Such grief. The Crown Imperial was to be a wordless expression of its irrationality. Staring around at my garden the bereaved

teacher apologised for it, saying 'it was coals to Newcastle.'
But it was not, I insisted. The mourner, the unwed sister of a
friend of mine, just smiled, being too bright for platitudes. I
told her truthfully that my Crown Imperials had disappeared,
taken themselves off somewhere, as plants tend to do when
one isn't looking, and now they were back and I would not
let them out of my sight.

I was gazing at my gift when the paper arrived. On the
front page was a photograph which in a previous age might
well have been a painting. A freshly shot Iraqi soldier lies on
the sand surrounded by his appalled friends. His face is at the
moment of purity when the spirit leaves it to go to God. No
sign of pain, just a noble beauty. He is young, still in his
teens. His companions, though uninjured, are in agony. They
reach out to him with their big spread hands and with
anguished expressions, and are aghast. It is not his face
which they stare at, but what should have been his white
flesh when they tug his shirt up to look for the wound. Only
it is what Isaac Watts so unflinchingly gazed at on Calvary.

> His dying crimson like a robe,
> Spread o'er his body on the Tree.

The soldier is indeed robed in his own blood, a sight more
terrible than any cinema blood could ever be. I think of the as
yet unaware family, the swift burial the next day, the shots in
the vacant air, the sun coming up and going down as it always
did, the discredited politics. And for the dead man the wholly
unimaginable business of countless newspaper readers seeing
him like this, naked and in such a mess.

Noises Off

The train stops by a nice wood but the woman on the mobile does not cease talking. She interviews a young man in her clear voice. She repeats everything he tells her, which is courteous of her. We trapped listeners might as well have both sides of her call. 'Your name is Raphael?' She writes it down on her pad. 'You are twenty-three, and you did say that you were a post-graduate?' She scribbles away. We hear that he will have a month's training and then be on his own. For four hours per evening. Soon, we realise, that we will be picking up our telephone and hear, 'My name is Raphael and have you a minute whilst I tell you about our fitted kitchens?' We are told his full address and his number, and so we could ring him up and tell him not to bother us. A strong wind throws rain against the carriage window. The only passenger who doesn't know all about Raphael is a boy plugged into a Walkman. I can hear it faintly sizzling, like a chip-pan. We travel on. Here is Manor Park cemetery, acres and acres of applicants for jobs. Miles of workers who applied 'in the first place' in handwriting on Basildon Bond, but who are now at rest. The phoning woman goes on, filling other vacancies, asking the same particulars, promising the same rewards. I am sitting next to Jenny who is on her way to the Royal Horticultural Society, being a famous gardener. She squints at the hirer and firer woman and says, 'Well, we do see life!'

When I get home I think about what Shakespeare called 'Noises off'. I think about James calling from Cornwall and hearing in the background his gold clock striking, and Peter calling from Orkney and hearing a door banging in a gale, and John ringing from Nottingham and his little daughter butting in. I ring Jane in Cambridge to ask, 'What can you hear, other than my voice?' She answers, 'Be off with you, I am listening to *Madame Bovary.*'

The TV ads for BT tell me that it is good to talk, and then communicative lovers fall into each other's arms. Three times a night they do this. Talk, embrace, or both, one interrupts the programme. Long ago I was told that some means would be invented to capture all the talk that had ever been on a retrieval system. Think of asking in the Talk Shop for 'Adam talking to God'. The voices of the first recorded talkers are enthralling. Tennyson, Yeats, Eliot, Marconi himself. Queen Victoria, who in her eighties sounds bell-like and youthful. I rummage out some seventy-eights from the Thirties of Viennese orchestras. Here is Beethoven's *Gosse Fuge* being played by the Lener String Quartet just before Hitler put a stop to it. The players are/were Lener, Smilovitch, Roth and Hartman and not the kind of musicians one would want to listen to in the Third Reich.

Easter leaves its Noises off, cruel noises, then the quiet mighty sound of Resurrection, and the sound of following footsteps on the Emmaus road.

Low Sunday

This was the day when those who received baptism at Easter put away their white clothes. The altar is heavy with the scent of lilies which are too full of life to be thrown out. Cold churches make flowers last, sometimes for weeks. They thrive in the sparse congregation, reminding it of crowded processions and rites. The tower flag has been lowered and folded. The graves suffer their first shearing and have their Easter tributes re-arranged. The mower is started up, as are the rooks. We ask God to put away from us the leaven of malice and wickedness, the thing which makes our tempers rise.

Duncan sits in the kitchen and foresees farming trouble ahead. Change anyway. More change than our fathers could ever have imagined. Contrary to what is popularly said of them, farmers have an opportunistic plus imaginative streak which comes into play when they are forced to alter their ways, and some of them find excitement in having to head in another direction. Part of their present trouble stems from their lives and work not being of the remotest interest these days to their neighbours – to the rural community at large. To most country people farmers are landscape-minders, not food producers, and they are praised more for their footpaths, etc. than for their crops. Duncan's dogs sit obediently on the doorstep, eyeing the cats. He sits in the chair in which his father sat when he paid me a visit. Many visits, and William approaching his hundredth birthday. His father, when things failed in Ayreshire, took a brave direction. He left his stoney Scottish fields for loamy Berkshire. Old farmhouse kitchens have always been debating chambers. Polite talk went on in the parlour. The fields used to be easier to respect than to love, so hard was the going. But what to do now? I say that, having had double our usual fall of rain, we could not have got on to the land at all, had it been 1890. We could have starved. As it is, Dave arrives to mop up the mud in the track with hoggin, and we go out to look at the corn. Every few yards it becomes waterlogged, peering from the flood like rice, and a moorhen is actually having a little swim in a furrow.

Mark at Tiger Hill

It is St Mark's time and his Ezekiel-like swiftness seems to be carried on the north wind. His Gospel, like Keats's poem, remains unfinished. Mark, they say, was probably the young man who escaped naked when Jesus was arrested, leaving a sheet in the hands of the police and running away. Mark writes at a tremendous pace. 'Stay awake!' is his message. His very first words are about a herald's cry, his last words about 'going out into all the world', and not skulking in safe houses. 'I say unto you, stay awake!'

We go to the annual bluebell party at Tiger Hill. Wandering from the crowd, I find a girl lying full length in the intoxicating blueness, her eyes closed as she listens to the nightingales, a pair of them in sublime communication. Trodden bluebell stalks surround her. Water glints in boggy patches. It is at this moment that I too hear it, the teatime nightingale with its classic wheet-tac-tuc-kerr sequence of divine song. Overhead the evening clouds pile up like draperies, promising but not giving rain. Fragmented conversation drifts through the budding trees. Those who meet here once a year are telling each other who they are. Creatures who live here always lie low. The girl sits up. She too can smell white wine, tea, sandwiches, cake, and we return following the slippery bluebell stems to the party, and now and then catching the sparkle of our cars through the woodland. They are parked on the rare mat-like 'bitter grass' of Tiger Hill which is not the kind of plant to raise excitement in any but the most accepting of botanists.

'We go back a long way', I can hear my old friend Jane telling her neighbour. As we splashed through the little flood which crosses the lane, and in which we paddled as children - 'Try your brakes', says the sign – she was telling me that her parents were married by Percy Dearmer, her uncles Martin and Geoffrey Shaw being colleagues of his. It was our childhood friend Dr Grace Griffith who had saved both the water-splash from being filled in and Tiger Hill from being destroyed, so we always talked about her when we came to the bluebell party. Clear as the chiff-chaff somewhere above our head, Dr Grace's familiar voice re-enters our consciousness, patient, learned, faintly cracked, as she told us how to identify birds and flowers. As a young woman she had known gruelling toil among the victims of the farming depression and had nursed the consumptives at the sanatorium on the hillside, with its arctic wards where the iciness of Suffolk weather prepared them for the iciness of death. We saw them lying on beds in the snow, waving when we waved, thin arms with big hands, brave grins and even sometimes a shout. There they were, Dr Grace's patients, exposed to winter like Eskimo grandmothers on their icefloes. She warmed them with her Christian Socialism, her absolute goodness. They too listened to the nightingales, whole choirs of them singing together in those days. As for bluebells, for some reason we had to pick more than we could carry, could strap to the crossbar, could ever do anything with. Giles our local cartoonist showed a farmer hollering to a mad bluebell gatherer, 'Look, you've missed one!' I pick about a dozen so that I can have them lolling from a vase on the window-sill and their unique scent in the study.

Proofing George Herbert

I am proof-reading 'my' edition of George Herbert's classic rule for the clergy, *A Priest to the Temple or The Country Parson*, first published in 1652, some twenty years after *The Temple* itself, his poetry. His spelling is all over the place, where it has to be left. There is a great deal of getting up and down to consult authorities and much gazing out into the garden. At first there is an unaccountable silence, then I remember that this is the day when the earth-shifters finish the new reservoir and will have rumbled back home. I place a marker in Herbert and wander off to see what they have done. It is breath-taking. Where there was a hilly sugar-beet field there is a sparkling lake, blue as blue. Its edges are frilled by a slight breeze and its surface mirrors passing clouds and birds – a plane even. Watery places like the Stour Valley are coded to receive reflections of all kinds, including philosophical ones. I am seeing a lake on its birthday, on the day when it came into a famous rivery scene. 'No longer call me clay', says Hugh's ancient field, 'I flow'. Mr Death arrives and his dog plunges in, paddling mightily.

But back to the proofs. It is the tradition for writers to howl when proofs arrive. 'Somebody loves you', says the postman, as he hands me the big soft packet of Herbert's latest edition. One cannot be creative with proofs; publishers do not like it and will charge if you do something extravagant, such as adding a chapter or cutting out a character. No, proofs have to be the original text suffering from printer's errors. I always place a ruler beneath each line to prevent 'block' reading, something which most of us unconsciously do. A sermon about St Mark creeps into my head and has to be driven out.

A man should never be more single-minded than when he is correcting proofs. David and *his* dog enter with a present – wild tulip bulbs in a white envelope. 'I mustn't disturb you.' But he has, thank goodness. So we talk on the doorstep, have tea, look out.

An hour later I am on Chapter eight, which is reproachful. 'The Country Parson', says Herbert, 'as soon as he awakes on Sunday morning, presently falls to work, and seems to himself so as a Market-man he is, when the Market day comes, or a shopkeeper, when customers used to come in. His thoughts are full of making the best of the day, and contriving it to his best gains'. The hours drift by, filled with semi-colons, of 'leave a space here' of added es and ls. Cabalistic signs crowd the margins. What a slow business. Every page read twice, and then not read in the normal fashion, but haltingly, nit-pickingly. George Herbert himself did no proof-reading – did not know what it was like. He was in heaven when he went to press, leaving others to see him through it. But, being a realist, he did teach us the high calling of domestic drudgery and how to elevate ordinary things.

May

Angelic Blythburgh - Footing it - The Deaths of King David
and King Redwald - A Birthday - Ben, Sam and Haggai -
Ascension and Nettles - Death of a Roadman - John Constable's
Ascension - The Queensland Pilgrims - Preserving Samuel
Harsnett - Memento Mori - A Problem - May for Proverbs -
May in Colchester - The Whitsun Cantatas - The Morning
Stint - Diana Dies - A Retreat - The Seekers - More Food -
Spring as Usual - Ringers' Banquet - Cathedral Camps -
Woodland Week

Angelic Blythburgh

The old familiar journey to Blythburgh, this time to make a talk on Radio Three with Martin Newall. Martin is to tell me about Black Shuck our Suffolk hell-hound and I have to tell him about architecture. Terrifying dog and comforting glories come together in this building. The producer lines us up against the churchyard wall and says, 'Talk'. Martin is a spiritual Pagan and I am of course an Anglican. We know that Black Shuck has his dreadful whirling eye on us. Legend raises its sensational head as we do our stuff. We each burst with Suffolk pride. Black dogs terrified half of England but none more so than our Shuck. How he slavered! How the brimstone tainted his hungry jaws! One bite from him, my boy, and it was breakfast with Old Nick. Meanwhile, over Martin's shoulder, flashes the reassuring flintwork, the Virgin's monograph, the Trinity, the serried windows, the quatrefoils, all the lovely patched-up thing of a medieval fish-church, so called because it was paid for by herrings. Once the herring fleet sailed up to it, now the A12 roars past it, though half a mile from it, which is not too damaging.

Martin lights a cigarette and smokes it in an unconsecrated direction. I warn him that malefactors are buried 'on the dog', i.e. to the north of the church, where Shuck hangs out. But, poor beast, he has lost his frightfulness. Gorse blazes on the heath and elderly couples are making their way to the White

Hart for lunch. The noonday light intensifies as Martin and I entertain the Radio Three listeners as best we can. It heightens the names on the reeling tombstones, putting, as it were, flesh on bones. I am looking at 'Sarah' carved unusually large, and fancy that the Bloises (baronets) are up in arms once more, seeing-off those who Shuck saw-off long ago.

However, neither old hounds nor new guide books can supply a satisfactory explanation of the angelic nature of Blythburgh. Visitors leave with the enormous roof angels on their minds, usually so stunned by them that they fail to have seen that the entire building is an angel roost and is as smothered in them as a white buddleia is smothered in butterflies in August. They cling inside and out wherever there is angelic purchase. They always make me think of David the poet-king who told his Chief Musician that God had made both of them only 'a little lower than the angels', although what a pity he had not given them wings. 'O that I had wings like a dove! For I would fly away and be at rest.' All David and the Chief Musician could do was look up, the Lord being their 'high tower'. Whoever it was built Blythburgh was for ever looking up. Martin takes me to the north door and looks down. Horror, for here are Black Shuck's paw marks as he scrambled his way back to darkness. Plain as day, they are, so no doubts there. It is a church full of messages for smoking Pagans and saintly Anglicans, though one can hardly mention them on Radio Three.

Footing it

Michael the vicar is a runner. He runs in marathons and each dawn he runs much further than our parish boundary, it being not nearly long enough for his purpose. Years ago he would have been a familiar sight but due to the late rising of the village on the whole, only the commuters, the postmen and the milkman are likely to see him jogging past. Not being up and about by seven would have been called sloth, and a dreadful thing it was, character destroying and shameful. So a running parson would have run the whole gamut of toil, should he set out before breakfast. Farmworkers, craftsmen, labouring children, nearby factory folk, women hanging out the washing, everyone in the world would have watched him with wondering eyes. Parson Hawker at Morwenstow swam and sunbathed, and was believed to be part-merman. But Michael has his seven o'clock parish more or less to himself and is not seen until he collects his *Guardian* from the shop at nine-thirty, or dawn to most of the population.

I am famous in Wormingford for walking. We have neighbours who do not as much as set foot on earth, so to speak, bounding from doorstep to car, and are thus not famous for anything. There was a ministry for running into people, for the casual encounter, and I may exercise a little of this. When I think of young Kilvert and old William Barnes, walking, walking, meeting, meeting, and maybe doing better than they ever did in church. Michael is writing a paper on the philosophy of running and I toy with anthologising the poetry of walking. It would be a fat book.

The rape is out and asthmatics stay in. There is money in rape and a yellow county declares it to be true. Its garish beauty adds a psychedelic dimension to landscape, what one might call the Van Gogh touch. It is fashionable to hate it, to whine about it, to hold one's nose when passing it, but it has to be granted glory of a kind. It flowers in huge blocks of colour which lock-in the other crops, and which make the corn look insipid. It stares brassily at the skies before it rots and stinks and is harvested. Corn is of a subtler gold, ravishing, rustling. I could listen to ripe corn for ever. It too has a scent, but who smells corn? Birds can smell it from afar, but not us.

This notion came into my head as I sat at supper in Bury St Edmunds in an eyrie-like room high above the Abbey ruins. Everything which could be viewed was below us, Anselm's fearsome gate, the grid-pattern streets, the tall house in which Daniel Defoe invented Man Friday, and even the swifts and swallows. We watched them firing themselves into the sunset. I thought that if I could clear away a couple of buildings to the left I might be able to glimpse the racehorses dozing at Newmarket.

Walking in Bury makes me think about these Bible runners, the road-watching father who at last sees a bedraggled son approaching and runs to meet him, arms wide, the verse in Mark which says, 'And when he was gone forth into the way, there came one running, and kneeled to him, and asked him, Good Master, what shall I do that I may inherit eternal life?' The running, the kneeling, the passionate question. Mark says, 'Jesus, beholding him, loved him,' this young man who had everything except what lasted. King David, watching for the return of his son Absalom from battle, saw 'a man running alone' and knew the worst.

The Deaths of King David and King Redwald

May winds roar through the poplars and honk in the chimney. They raise the horses' manes, ruffle the cats' fur and bring down spirals of laburnum. Birds are flung about the sky. It is wind of an inspiring sort. It shakes but does not cut through the hollies, so I can read in their protection. I am reading the last words of David, 'the sweet psalmist of Israel'. A king, he said, had to be 'as the light of the morning, a morning without clouds, and as tender as rain-washed grass'. And I see the translator making his way through a sopping English meadow in May-time, his gown trailing through wet buttercups as he makes his way to the desk.

Paul arrives to have a drink before putting his sheep out, forty here, fifty there, only twenty in a little paddock which has not been munched these ten years. The sheep will eat down the roughage and, if they stay long enough, will leave behind flower-rich meadows. Shearing-time draws near, though shorn of its old wealth. Paul is sad. 'Nobody wants our fleeces anymore. They are rubbish'. The word is shocking in an old room which must have heard 'wool' as another name for money. I tell him about the magnificent chapter in Thomas Hardy's *Far From the Madding Crowd* where the shearing in the great barn is turned into a village equivalent to all the other human achievements, however mighty, and of which the Psalmist sang. Hardy's favourite Bible words were from Kings I. 19. in which Elijah, discovered cringing in a cave by God, is ordered out and to climb a mountain. Reaching the summit, Elijah waited for the Almighty to speak to him in Wagnerian language. But when at last it came the divine message was in a still small voice. These are the words written on the memorial window in Stinsford church, the epicentre of Hardy's imagination.

We are off to see what they are up to at Sutton Hoo. Container traffic from Felixstowe makes canyons for the little car to pass through. Heavy land turns to light land, Suffolk's sandlings with its conifers and seabirds. And how changed Sutton Hoo is. What we last saw was a group of rather battered humps above the Deben and some rabbit fences. Nothing more. You needed your wits to see the wild, grand funerals of East Anglia's royalty, the Wuffingas sailing away to heroic bliss in their treasure-laden boats, the cold gales filling the sail, the screaming, mourning gulls, the down-to-earth thud of burial. I shared this mixture of reality and dream in 1967 when I biked over to watch the British Museum re-dig out the now treasure-emptied ship. It was hot and breezy, and the young archaeologists had become a shirtless crew, and the plastic erected to protect their excavation had billowed into a huge cracking sail. One good blow, and they would be well on their voyage back to Sweden.

The original dig in 1939 was made by the local archaeologists plus two gardeners, Mr Jacobs and Mr Spooner. It was only when the amazing gold and garnets began to show themselves that Mr Kendrick from the British Museum was called in. To prove that so great a man had not been brought on a wild goose-chase, he was met at Woodbridge station by the leader of the local historians with one of the fabulous buckles in a tobacco tin and shown it in the waiting room. And now we come to English Heritage in, one must admit, as sensitive a mood as possible, confronted as it was by little more than humps and rabbit tracks. I carried Seamus Heaney's *Beowulf* with its uncanny account of what occurred here, although the unknown author was in another place altogether:

> Silver and jewels buried in the sandy
> ground, back in the earth again
> And forever hidden and useless to men.

A Birthday

Florence's hundredth to be exact. Evensong pauses to allow her to make her way to the chancel step, sans stick, sans anything which might assist such an age. Slight, smiling, upright, she takes from me a little basket of pink flowers. For her this past week will have been no different to all the past weeks, washing, ironing, shopping, letting in visitors. I make a birthday speech and as an acknowledgement of Florence's early Methodism we sing from *Golden Bells*. As this and other hymn-books poured into the Victorian churches there was frequent alarm from on high. Throughout the nineteenth century there were official protests about hymn singing. Finally in 1890 Archbishop Benson's 'Lincoln Judgment' announced that hymns could be sung as long as they did not interrupt the service! Florence's hundred years have interrupted our service but clearly not her life. Ghostly behind the hymns of her girlhood, with their zippy choruses and strong sentiment, lies the old poverty, the old clinging to faith truly as a lifeline and the close odour of chapels long ago. There are other once-Methodists present as always. Once-Salvationists too, and some once-Presbyterians with nowhere else to go, a still-Roman Catholic, a Baptist or two, and Anglicans of various levels, this being the usual congregation.

Easter lilies continue to trumpet headily from the altar; the Paschal candle wavers, and a now forgotten hymn beloved by my mother, 'My glorious Victor, Prince divine', comes back to me. It was written by Handley Moule whose brother Horace taught the teenage Thomas Hardy classics as the pair of them walked the fields around Dorchester. Handley Moule became Bishop of Durham. Horace Moule longed to be a writer but was forced to be an Inspector of Workhouses. Hardy went to visit him at Cambridge and they parted amicably after walking on the roof of King's Chapel in order to see Ely in the distance. When his guest had departed, Moule committed suicide. Thus Hardy lost his greatest friend. He left writing *Far From The Madding Crowd* to attend the funeral at Fordington. All around were the fields where Moule had taught him classics.

Ancient and not always first class hymns run through our heads carrying unstoppable thoughts known only to ourselves. Once, standing by the door of the dilapidated chapel at Eastwood where D. H. Lawrence was taught his Christianity, I remembered reading how he was unable to get a hymn fragment out of his head – how it lodged there all his life. It was 'Galilee, O Galilee, where Jesus walked in Galilee'.

We are singing 'Blaze, spirit, blaze' for Florence, which is asking rather much for a centenarian dressed in blue and silver. When the hymn is over there is a brief silence in which I hear a night bird calling. Something from Barbara Pym's description of the typical retirement home enters my head: 'The flowers were certainly past their best, though, in the curious lingering way that chrysanthemums have, they were not exactly dead. Most of the leaves have withered, but some of the flowers might still pass, arranged with fresh leaves or massed together in a bowl'. From the pulpit I can see Florence's lips framing, 'And thanks never ceasing, and infinite love'. There is to be a cake later with a single candle. My text is 'Walk while you have the light, less darkness comes upon you'. Squashed between large relations from Canada, she does not have to listen.

May days. Soaking growth, saturated dawns, and the cold not a winter's cold but something which promises to warm up after breakfast. Duncan's towering hawthorn hedge is full out and its sexy scent speaks volumes of earlier goings-on – maybe in the meadows opposite. Our ancestors adored May-time. It made them glad to be alive. I see them in the pre-Reformation aisles spattered with pollen and in good need of being shriven, and the priest shaking his head. And the women keeping blossom well away from the house.

Some dashing about. First to Nottingham Trent University to unveil a sculpture of John Clare. He is in profile, like John Keats in Severn's drawing, young and swift – and 'lost', of course. Poets are often lost and have to be found. They say that Nottingham is a city beloved of the young – that it suits them. John Clare and John Keats shared the same publisher. He commissioned a bust of Clare – these days he would have sent a photographer. I talk about statues and images, and how the Angel of the North flashes by when I am on the train to Scotland and how, on the same journey, John Clare's universe at Helpston becomes a momentary blur through the same carriage window. I say how moved we were by the man-sized Christ wearing his barbed wire crown on his plinth in Trafalgar Square, and how touched to the heart we are by some war memorial of no particular artistic worth, or by a recumbent knight in an old church, his praying hands lopped off.

A trip to Southwark Cathedral for a meeting, but too early, so time for an exploration. Here is St Hugh's, Porlock Street, 'Blessings by arrangement', and here are the hospitals where Keats trained to be an apothecary, and here are the London toilers, young and not so young, some elegant, some blown about, some straight out of bed, some beautiful, some not so, all hurrying along the back streets, taking the same short cuts which Shakespeare and Dickens took. Then a rush back to the Cathedral, for the more time one has, the later one is.

Ben, Sam and Haggai

Peter's geese wing it over the roof to the river every evening regular as clockwork, and sounding rather like it as well. I am training Madame Alfred Carrier and Albertine to climb dead apple trees. Pear blossom curdles above me. Earlier, Ben and Sam, plus various adults, arrive for tea after tidying-up the family graves at Great Horkesley. The boys used to lie on the floor building domino palaces but now they sit still and watch and listen. The ritual of the annual visit, the catching up, the wonder and admiration, the spaced out love. More cake? Another cup? The children's hands darkened by the tomb dirt.

I preach on Haggai, the prophet of divine priorities who always insisted on first things coming first, which as we know is not always the case. Haggai's little book would have echoed in the mind of George Herbert, who repaired his church before he repaired his rectory. What happened in Haggai's day was that, having laid the foundations of the Temple after the original building had been let fall down, the Jews turned from completing the job to put a roof over their own heads. So there they were, complained their prophet, dwelling 'in your ceiled houses – and this house lies wasted!' The planners of post-Great Fire of London might also have read Haggai for Wren's churches were built before the new housing. Haggai wrote about the actual disappointment of secular gain. 'You eat, but you haven't enough, you dress but you aren't warm, you earn money but put it into a bag with holes'. He has a dry way with him.

Ascension and Nettles

The lanes close in and the river vanishes as an army of plants conquer every growing inch of earth. When I walk to the spinney it is like dipping into a green bath and I am wet to the waist. A north wind then lays it on with all its chilling might. Then the sun comes out and I steam and burn. This is mid-May for you. Moorhens sculpt the frigid surface of the horse-pond towards which I have to scythe a nettle highway, otherwise it will vanish for ever, or until the winter when the water will glint through black stalks. Yet I feel it a shame to take the nettles' young lives on my sharp blade. So new and so tall, and morally with as much right to a nettle-y bloom as the roses have their right to flower. Nettles flourish where men have lived. They draw a stinging curtain over our enterprises. Discreetly veiled in nettles, one finds on most farms a cemetery for dead machines in which iron monsters lie entangled with each other in their uselessness, and who must be thankful when winter no longer exposes their rusty parts. Observing the changing lessons of nature, Emily Dickinson wrote, 'God is a noted clergyman whose sermons are never long'.

Queen Elizabeth the First came to Wormingford – twice. She was entertained by Sir William Waldegrave down where Mr Rix now has his acres of onions for Tesco, but then a deer

park. We still ring the church bells which she heard. More
Emily Dickinson:

> This quiet dust was Gentlemen and Ladies
> And Lads and Girls,
> Was laughter and ability and sighing
> And frocks and curls.

It was Dame Julian's time. What a struggle it must have
been for her to sit in that stuffy anchorage during May, with
the nice rivery smell of the Wensum drifting up through the
Norwich stink, and all the spring birds calling from where
the football ground is, and her old colleagues sitting in the
priory garden in Carrow Road. It would have been the time
of the year when she saw us, humanity and its Lord,
gardening side by side, 'Digging and banking, toiling and
sweating, turning and trenching the ground, watering the
plants awhile . . . making sweet streams to flow, fine
abundant fruits to grow . . .'

Death of a Roadman

Hiding from a cloudburst, we talk of Jack the roadman, the
final earth of whose grave is at this very moment being raised
over him. The lanes were not turned into lakes every time
there happened to be a downpour in *his* day we tell each
other. Jack's sharply cut grigs carried the rain to his sharply
cut ditches. Blind and deaf, long retired, he may not have
noticed how the litter is concealed by summer and exposed

in winter. But always our roadman. The flag on his coffin spoke of Empire parade grounds, dry climes and bands.

It is the annual Bluebell Party at Tiger Hill. The faithful are already gathered when Roger Deakin and I arrive. The rain has held off and the sun is surprisingly hot when it has a mind to.

Rogation at Little Horkesley – the asking time. Considering the needs on the screen, it ill becomes any of us to ask for a thing. Last Rogation we asked to be delivered

Young cuckoo 1977

from foot-and-mouth. We process through lanes and farms and gardens and back into the churchyard, singing here, praying there. Some of the earliest rogations took place on volcanoes where God was asked to stop their irruptions, and hellish they must have been. Ours are fairly heavenly although women who have come in un-sensible shoes complain of wet feet. A sinner gazes from the window of the

Beehive pub. No knocking boundary information into numskull boys. A glance here, a petition there, symbols and rites, let them say something relevant to our day, we ask. Don carries the golden cross through the cow-parsley. Robes darken at the hem. I count thrushes in David's drive – a tree full of them.

Then the visitation, the Ofsted to the village school and the Rural Dean to the church. And various callers to me, this being the time when pilgrimages are made to writers. 'Such lovely weather!' As Jack the roadman's territory did not include my track, I fill in the worst potholes and chop out a few grigs for the rain to run away. British Telecom comes down to untangle its wires from my oaks and wild winds rock their ladder. The young man aloft laughs and shouts and waves, knowing that May is the best time of all.

John Constable's 'Ascension'

'It is getting on top of you', remark the friends as they wander through the garden. And this just before my one big spring weed. The beds shimmer with sweet cicely, buttercups and campion, and look not unlike Giverny. Trailing behind them, I think of the in and outness of existence, the weeds and the garden flowers, the wheat and the tares, the sheep and goats. What a lot of it there is in religion – in life. The chosen and the unchosen. The useful and the merely beautiful, the good sons and the bad sons, the listening sister and the bustling sister. My first dandelion clocks, each telling a different time, blow across the land.

On Ascension Day at Dedham Constable's painting of the ascending Christ is lifted up over the north door of the parish church in which he would have run wild, the grammar school being a few yards to the east. He and the other boys climbed the mighty tower to try to glimpse 'Harwich Water'. Soon his relations were all for him painting altar-pieces, a respectable trade and not badly paid. So he had painted *Christ Blessing the Elements* for Nayland, his brother Golding modelling for the Lord, and *Christ Receiving the Children* for Brantham down by the estuary. He had a sensuous-mystical love for the human body, calling it a kind of divine landscape, and drew it in the life-class at the Royal Academy School long after his student days. A favourite model was a discharged soldier from Wellington's army, a Suffolk lad whom Constable had helped get a job as porter at Somerset House, and who may have sat (soared) as the ascending Christ. There are many drawings of him. A distant relative of the artist, a Diss brewer named Edward Alston, had offered Constable £200 to paint the picture, some said to win favour with the Archdeacon of Colchester who licensed ale houses. But here it is, the Lord vanishing from our sight as we crane our necks.

Brother Abram who worked Flatford Mill down the road advised John 'It would be certain *pay*, and now *you could knock it off*.' Trade was in the doldrums and money scarce. So, believed some of the family, was John's talent. Thus, find him what local jobs they could. 'Job' was to become Constable's most detested word. Abram reminded his brother, 'My floodgates at Dedham and Flatford must be repaired, several millwrighting bills coming in so that I cannot keep my money in my pocket'. Later, he never failed to send John his share of the Flatford profits, slender though they sometimes were. Christ, humanly beautiful, rises above their sums.

Staring out of the Window

George Mackay Brown the Orkney poet turned his back to the window at nine in the morning. He pushed back the breakfast things and began to write. And then, every afternoon, he would stoke up a nice coal fire and, he said, 'Interrogate silence'. He meant to dream whilst being especially wide awake. I wake up like a child very early in the morning. One minute I am sound, then I am thinking, wondering, making things up. But I do nothing at all except look out of the window, tea in my hand. The window is that which centuries of farmers would have interrogated for the day's weather. It faces due east and lets in the merciless sun. There is a steep hill in its frame and the tops of trees which are growing in the next valley, dawn fire on the horizon and wheeling birds. The foot of the hill deepens into the boundary ditch which was cut during the Middle Ages to separate Wormingford from Little Horkesly. Soon the silhouettes of girls who feed the horses will appear. The girls wait on horses like devotees on gods. At this time of the year their shovels blink in the hard light. The window's glazing bars line-up the view like a drawing. I wait until the sun rolls towards the catch, nurse a cat or two, ignore the pleadings of the radio to turn it on and marvel at the inspired sentences which effortlessly spill through my brain but do not put them down. Window-watch, kettle business, alert idleness, you could hardly call it prayer.

The postman arrives with a present to be signed for, the

second volume of an interpretation of church architecture which is similar to my own. It is a hand-produced work, idiosyncratic, amateur, the product of pleasurable outings to various buildings half lost in lanes, and is entitled *Seeking the Saxon in Suffolk*. Now here is a hold-up to the morning's toil. The author-artist-motorist is one Lorna Lincoln, late of the Probation Service. So this is how some people splash-out on their retirement! Her advice is sound. Always look first at the north wall of an old church because it will refute what the south wall is saying about the past. Poor north wall folk! How roughly they were treated. And often with the Devil waving his tail over the north door. Our north door will be opened on Sunday, weather permitting, to allow us to take a glass of wine. As I read on, breakfast cooks, and now I am poking about with Lorna Lincoln, discovering long-and-short-work, mean lancets – as contrasted with the best Perp and Dec windows along the south façade – humpy grass where the suicides and stillborn lie, and pre-Conquest things left alone. 'Sign for it', says the postman.

The Queensland Pilgrim

Travellers are apt to delight in what we would not have them see. My sister and her husband are here from Brisbane and are ecstatic about our rape. They were politely pleased when I took them to see the bluebells at Tiger Hill but amazement overcame them when we drove through the rape, fields and fields of it, and apologised for. We have to get out and be photographed in it. Will my neighbour come along in his land-rover and report an outbreak of rape worship at Assington? We must get right in the field, insists my sister, breast the Van Gogh yellowness, let it break against us. *Brassica campestris oleifera*, you are adored. Make the most of it. It will be dandelions next. As if intoxicated itself by our act of love, the rape becomes yellower and yellower as we make for Bury St Edmunds, though mercifully it is too early for oleifera. 'It stinks', I tell my sister. She looks at me reproachfully, then at the latest rape farm we are passing. 'I'll never forget such a sight', she says. Intoxicated by being loved, the rape casts all its colour at us as we wind along the old pilgrim road which threads the fields where our ancestors worked.

But the Australians appear to have unburdened themselves of their history. Standing before the flint stumps which once carried the dizzy roof over St Edmund's altar when the barons met to force Magna Carta on wicked King John, my dissertation is stopped by their polite disinterest, their failing to pick up the threads. They are thinking of rape, of English grass as lush as, well, what? I noticed in the garden how they had sunk their hands into it. Later that week, when they had left, I did the same. Cool, long, faintly damp English spring grass waiting for the first mow.

St Dunstan and Deuteronomy for May. Dunstan who was made Abbot of Glastonbury when he was twenty-one, and who they said had heard of young Edmund's murder from the king's own armour-bearer. Office after office was piled upon Dunstan – Canterbury whilst still in his thirties – yet he found time to paint, for music, for making bells, for getting education going, for being a craftsman. How interesting it would be if the Church made a few twenty-five year-olds bishops.

Preserving Samuel Harsnett

Shopping, I occasionally look up at Archbishop Harsnett in his niche on the town hall. My memory of him will always be permeated by the reek of the British Museum preservative which, as a youthful librarian, I had to rub into the leather covers of his books to prevent their decay. The bookworms would have perished in that oily fumigation and the leather made pliant and breathing once more. Harsnett was intolerant it was said. He left about a thousand volumes to his home town, Colchester, a mighty gift in 1631 and an unlikely one from a baker's son. I read parts of them through the rancid smell of their survival. Predestination, Salvation, Arminianism, Rages against Rome, the occasional lovely travel-book or poem, the intimate signatures of Erasmus and Calvin. One of Harsnett's problems was how to re-install ceremony without popishness. He certainly had a way with words and was a mighty borrower of them, for the names of the spirits in *King Lear* jump about in one of his furious declarations. But I admired his honesty when he wrote of 'the painful trade of teaching', and I was touched that he had turned these same pages. As a local grammar-school boy he would have smelled of bread.

Wormingford is drenched in May-scent, heady and sexy. The honeysuckles planted in the garden by German prisoners of war wind about the lilac. The cat sprawls along the debris of Whiskas and souring milk. The washing snaps in the wind. Insects and birds fly low and my neighbour's little Amy Johnson plane takes a look at me. My farmhouse would have been new when Sam Harsnett was irritably keeping his balance on the Puritan-High Church tightrope, not to mention his head. How glorious the title-pages and capitals of his books are. Their forests and monsters, towers and mythologies tell a different tale to what follows.

Memento Mori

The blossom of a more or less frostless May begins to vanish. For what seems like ages it has hung in creamy swags but now the fruit is setting, and the rhubarb, named they say after the barbarians, begins to bolt. *Gloire de Dijon* roses clamber over the walls, the cow parsley shows that it has had its day. At Mount Bures the grass has not been cut enough to expose the dead and the Reverend Mr Davies, B.D. Oxon is still in hiding. He lies by the vestry door. They have planted a fine new avenue up to your rectory, I tell him as I pass. Mr Chaplin, who pumped the organ for you is ringing the bells for me, although you left this life in 1939. I robe and wait. I read the Register of Fees and remember God. The wind shoves its way through the cracked lattice like knives. Mr Chaplin stops. A minute to let him loop up the bell-rope and to return to his pew, and then the formal entrance. All stand. The organ will not be able to come to an agreeable halt for a few bars yet, so I find the first hymn leisurelily and glance out of the corner of my eye to see Diana, Andrew, Gerry, all the dear ones. And right at the back a little holy family, the boy from Scotland, the girl from

Tonga, the baby asleep. The candles are made impotent by
sunshine. We begin.

They are building five-bedroom houses behind the village
shop. They will be grandstands for our games. All the year
long their new owners can sit upstairs watching gratis our
football and cricket, dog walkers, children on swings, old
men at their gates. All free sights. Starving young bricklayers
rush in and out the village shop for Mars bars, Kitkats, crisps,
pork pies, cokes, their cruel wives and mothers having sent
them to work empty. At the parish meeting we hear some
shocking information. That the new residents not
infrequently hear the footballers and cricketers swear. They
have erected a thirty-feet high net to save their windows
from the balls, but what can save them from bad language? I
suggest Eric Partridge's *Dictionary of Slang*, that
dispassionate interest in the subject. Am I being serious?

To Aldeburgh to open the Suffolk Group Artists'
Exhibition. We have halibut – holy butt or flatfish – for lunch
in the glitter and turmoil of the place. After looking at the
paints and craftwork, I vanish for a few minutes to see once
again a particular house along the Crag Path which held a
fascination for me when I lived in Aldeburgh. It was the
home of the novelist Margery Sharp (*The Foolish
Gentlewoman*) and I regarded, not without amusement, as an
idyll purchased out of fiction. I would glance up at its little
balcony late of an evening, and there she would be, elegant
with her husband Major Castle and a glass of wine beside
her, playing chess to the roar of the North Sea, framed in
lamplight, secure in her publishers. This evening the balcony
was deserted and the folding doors behind it closed. But the
tall thin house itself remained utterly desirable. Just behind
stood the clapboard villa in which Wilkie Collins had written
No Name, a novel about two ladies who had come a cropper
where identity was concerned.

The following Sunday at Wormingford we sang the tragic

psalm thirty-nine, the one about our being but sojourners here, and about one day our being 'no more seen' from the old Burial Service, though put there for the living, not the dead.

A Problem

The countryside is perpetually racked by conflict between the obsessively tidy and the unconsciously untidy. There are grandees who emerge with bin bags and spiked sticks to collect what is always referred to as 'visitors' rubbish', we ourselves of course not guilty of dropping a match. My rural untidiness rises far above this and, mercifully, is beyond our self-appointed roadmen and women, who can only shake their heads when they pass some old barn lurching this way and that, some frank evidence of cows, some tiles on the slide. I hate mown greens but most people seem to love them. As for the burglar lights which black out the stars, ruining the lovely darkness of rural England, to criticise these creates genuine bafflement. Do I want their owners to be murdered? Thinking about the conditions which exist in and around my ancient dwelling, they shake kindly heads and tell me to join the twenty-first century. Why am I not terrified? 'All by yourself down there . . .'

Vestries of course must enter the tidy-untidy stakes. Those must remain nameless which tolerate old field-maps crooked on strings, a vase of half-burnt tapers, unconsulted almanacs from the undertaker, greying hunks of oasis, ten pens which don't work, nests of palm crosses, a surplice fit for dusters, five hundred hymn sheets of 'O Valiant Hearts', and a gallery of incumbents since the invention of photography, plus a gallery of choirs long gone to heaven, but thank God they do. They and their holy smell of sacred detritus. As for the churchyard, nothing is more evident of the moral torpor or spiritual progress of a parish. Here is a Brownie snap of me as a boy, my dark head just above the cow parsley as I lean against a tomb. What a disgrace. How wicked we were then. But at least we did not have plastic flowers and teddy bears left out in the rain. Or real flowers sealed in cellophane to make an opaque cushion for the dead. Some questions and answers. Who makes us untidy? They. What keeps us from the sin of untidiness? The lawnmower. Is there a service of blessing for the lawnmower? Not yet. What can we do about Mr N's disgraceful farm/garden/untidy manners generally? Nothing, it seems. Should we love him as ourself? Theologically, yes, socially, certainly not.

It is Flower Festival, Rogation, Songs of Praise all in one. Folk descend my farm track with esoteric wants, a dozen stems of allium, willow wands (the Vicar's wife), my wind-up gramophone. It is rainy and warm, and blowy and sunny. Phyllida's barn is packed with bargains and antique dealers rush in first to buy first editions for 50p or a Constable for a pound. The churchyard is unholy with Richard's raffle. Mammon stalks the land. 'Quota! Quota!' he cries. But at least we are not selling pardons. To pardon is to forgive freely, and so those old indulgences were a contradiction in terms. Chaucer's *Pardoner's Tale* is strong meat. Armed with a relic – the shoulder-bone of one of Jacob's sheep set in brass – the Pardoner preaches the same sermon up and down the countryside. His text is *Radix malorum est cupidites*, the love of money is the root of evil. Out of the pulpit he brazenly confesses, 'My only purpose is gain. I'm not interested in correcting sin. After they are dead the souls of those who are buying my pardons can go blackberrying for all I care!' But the people are not taken in and just laugh at his spiel, give him a kiss and send him on his way. Even the Church proper must have discovered that some of its teachings could never make headway when confronted with the commonsense of ordinary folk.

Flower festivals apart, the most glorious show at the moment is in Lower Bottom, the pasture surrounding the little stream which runs past Bottengoms where a million buttercups bloom. This dipping acre or two is at this moment a sheet of thin beaten gold. 'Buttercups', wrote Nicholas Culpepper, 'grow so common everywhere that unless you run your Head into a Hedge you cannot but see them as you walk.'

May for Proverbs

I write with the window wide, with a horseman passing, with a bumblebee furious against the pane. Last night, walking in the dark, I was startled by crashing and yelps in a ditch. Two badger snouts rose out of the crushed cow mumble to see what kind of creature was plodding by. They kept utter silence as I passed, then resumed their quarrel. Bluebells overpowered their musk.

In church we are to read proverbs and wise sayings. These Rogation month lessons are a favourite. The Book of Proverbs ends with two feasts, the Feast of Wisdom and the Feast of Folly. A proverb is a form of words which one cannot get out of one's head, and thus it constantly reinforces certain beliefs and actions. I check the lesson-readers' names. Who shall stand at the eagle-winged lectern and give us a feast of wisdom or folly? Oh, the power of the lesson-readers' master! I say unto Gordon, 'Read this', and he readeth it. He reads, 'There be three things which are too wonderful for me, yes, four which I know not. The way of an eagle in the air; the way of a serpent upon a rock; the way of a ship in the midst of the sea; and the way of a man with a maid'.

Later, nodding in the hot garden, made semi-conscious by a monotonous chiff-chaff, I come-to with a start, remembering that 'a little slumber, a little folding of the hands to sleep' is all that Proverbs permits after lunch. I watch the horizon through my lashes. A pretty muntjac deer is trotting along it, taking care not to fall off. I had been reading *The Apocrypha*, my mother's copy, I see, with her name on the flyleaf. 'When I was born, I drew the common air, and fell upon the earth which is of like nature, and the first voice which I uttered was crying, as all others do.'

May in Colchester

The north wind is busking at the street corners, the sixth formers are puffing their cigarettes or holding each other tight, the corporation flag strains at the mast, the flower baskets swing from the lamp-posts, wild music bursts from shops and old women speed along pavements in their electric chairs. Huge people squeeze through the check-out with gigantic groceries. Do I want any cash back? To the Public Library to look up something which Virginia Woolf said about the town in her *Common Reader*. It is a gently mocking account of the Jane and Anne Taylor circle ('Twinkle, twinkle, little star') as it discussed poetry on the town wall in moonlight. The wall is Roman, the girls are gone. I sit on it too, on orange bricks contemporary with the Apostles, and which are warm to the touch and starting to sprout toadflax. Bells ring. Surprise Major? Caters? Royal?

Swan on her nest 1977

Christopher would know. They peal-out with confidence and passion, altering the afternoon. Lovers lie below me on the spring grass, the boy on his back, the girl saying, 'Open your eyes'. Whiffs of fast food and lilacs. I remember a friend once telling me how depressed she is sometimes by the scurrying multitude on the concourse at Liverpool Street Station as the doubt comes to her that God could not love each of these individuals as He loves her, then feeling ashamed and bewildered to be having such thoughts. Looking down from the Roman Wall, I note that some young men have saved God the trouble of numbering the hairs of their heads. Craning forward, I watch archaeologists gently brushing the dust from somebody's bones.

It is the week when we remember the 'English Saints and Martyrs of the Reformation'. There, where the lovers embrace, Colchester burnt men and women and boys and girls. Once, a dozen of them chained together in a single bonfire. Terrible processions would have come this way. Religion delights and worries me. But then so it did the Lord's friends and enemies, for the worst and best things descend or rise from it. It is the seat of light and of darkness, of intelligence and idiocy, of tenderness and cruelty. The lunch-time lovers jump to their feet and brush dust from each other's clothes. She smoothes his hair. I suddenly remember May Days in Padstow, and the morning and evening songs throbbing through the narrow streets, and Cornish boys and girls lost in ancient emotion, the tipping 'Oss and its teaser', and the feeling of strangers such as myself stumbling into 'something' strange and wonderful but which is not our concern, and of the world being divided between observers and participants.

The Whitsun Cantatas

Two winds disturb the imagination, the rushing, mighty one
of Acts and that in the poplars. I lie in the new grass to take
my first hearing of the latter. Poplar-sound is counted
among the perks of summer. Today it leads me to the
incoming breakers at Treyarnon Bay and I think of them
ceaselessly hissing towards where I sat to read, and never a
line making sense because of the Atlantic dominance and
that regular roar. The gale of Acts was – is – empowering,
and so I suppose is the delicious wind which orchestrates
trees and water. At the moment it riffles the pages of the
book I am supposed to be reviewing and telling me that I am
always working. 'Listen', it is saying, 'just listen'. The
British Telecom man then arrives and says, predictably,
'Some of us have a cushy time!' May he chop-off the
branches of the hedgerow growth which are tangling around
the posts? More B.T. men arrive, one with a huge corkscrew
with which to dig a hole for a new post, the present one
having being put there in 1943. They try out the new line
with old jokes, laughing like Edison when their voices come
through. Shortly after they have gone, a tawny owl tests the
new post to see if it will bear him.

To Long Melford with Ian for Bach's Whitsunday
Cantatas. 'No interval, although a short break for tuning'.
And here comes further gusts of that Pentecostal breath
which shakes walls. If only the dizzy elms which grouped
themselves at the foot of Long Melford Green could have
survived to hear it. The Green is the grandest panache of
village imaginable, rural England on the greatest scale. At
the top the parish church offers a glass parade of all the
aristocrats who walked in before the Reformation, knights
and knaves and ladies from playing-cards, hieratic, drenched
in heraldry, emblazoned with mottoes for idlers to make out
during sermon time. When my grandparents, David and

Martha, were wed here somewhere round about the 1880s, they would have looked down on them, as was their right. They would have been puzzled by Bach and the winding Pentecostal voices. And so must the congregation of St Thomas's, Leipzig, when the latest Whitsunday score was spread before it and the old man began to teach it to them.

The Morning Stint

I am fond of being told how writers write. Virginia Woolf in her sagging armchair, bottle of ink - Stephen's ink - taped to a board, Hazlitt anywhere, inns, banksides, his house being so uncomfortable, Ivy Compton-Burnett on her couch, Iris Murdoch in her chaos. I sit in an old room at a leather-topped Victorian table and on a chair bought from a field for thirty-five shillings many books ago. A local dealer used to attend auctions and leave his less valuable finds out in the rain for pitying men like me to take in. This chair has nice wooden arms and a hard seat, and is unsleepable in. 'Another page', it creaks.

Trinity Sunday in all three churches, thus *Holy, Holy, Holy* sung thrice. Its poet author young Richard Heber turned down the bishopric of Calcutta twice but eventually said yes to what proved to be the diocese of all British India. It killed him at forty-three. How he struggled, travelled, taught, weakened, died. His God against the Hindu pantheon, the conviction in all the heat and dirt that 'Only thou art holy, there is none beside thee'. The letters from home smelling of

Yorkshire Dales. On Trinity Sunday afternoon I journey to
Colchester for the launch of R.N. Currey's *Collected Poems*
in a garden close to where Lord Wavell was born, and thus
fitting for a poet of the Second World War. It was Wavell's
son who persuaded Ralph Currey to make a collection of
servicemen's writing about India, that near-mythical pinnacle
of empire which they were now seeing with their own eyes.
Poems from India reveals the impact. Now in his nineties and
blind, Currey listens to our praise whilst the rain flashes
against the conservatory glass, a lifetime friend. His work, as
so often with poets, is youthful, disturbingly so at times. We
toast him and praise him. Back home I change into horse-
pond gear and splash about clearing weed. All around,
everything is as tall as teenagers, nettles, butterbur, Japanese
knotweed, quince suckers. What to lop, what to leave.
Everything seeks light. I am the enlightener – am I not?
Ramblers pass. The rain stops quite suddenly and the
evening sun blazes away in the west like a battle charge.

Diana Dies

It is crack of dawn on Ascension Day and I am typing out
Diana Collins's funeral for the local printer. The scented heat
of the night garden hangs about the house. Spring birds are
noisy, roses biff against the window and the cats are licking
breakfast off each other's chops. The study is fretful, not
being accustomed to being useful at such an early hour. After
her chosen hymns and readings Diana has scrawled, 'No

need for sadness. I have had a life full of interest and excitement, I have lived in beautiful places, who could ask for more?' This is all very well, but what about us? Our first week without Diana. I can hear her little car bumping down the track, stroked all the way by blackberries and nettles. As a driver she belonged to the Rose Macaulay class and was thus divinely protected. She read the lessons for me, after collecting me every Sunday morning at nine sharp. She read in a magisterial voice, often leaving out some Old Testament barbarity, as she saw fit, and was especially sorry for all the poor Egyptian charioteers drowned in the Red Sea. I now share out the poems she wants read at her funeral between her sons and grandchildren.

The obituaries in the broad sheets are eagerly read by the village, passed on hand by hand, but with no little disappointment. CND, yes, the International Defence and Aid Fund which saved so many innocent lives during Apartheid, yes, and her books and her famous friendships. But what about us at Mount Bures where she lived for thirty years? And the poetry circle where she read all of *Hiawatha*, given a chance? And the visits to the Franciscans? And the lunches at Mill House? And the lunches in the pub? I now see that it is my duty to tell the world of all this. After breakfast I pause to make other funeral arrangements, the hiring of an address system for those who may not be able to squeeze into the little church, the enquiries to see if the field is planted and will not be suitable for a car park, the questions for hospitable Mount Bures Hall re the reception, the words with Michael the vicar about bringing Diana into the chancel overnight, which we imagined she would like, and a thousand other things. Just a simple village funeral, she said. There is no such event.

Diana lived on a windmill site on the high ground between the River Colne and the River Stour, the latter being hers and my native stream. She was born where it comes out into the

sea and its estuarial wonders fed her child's thoughts. She
described it dreamily in her biography cum autobiography,
Partners in Protest: Life with Canon Collins. 'There are
moon daisies, buttercups, dandelions, young red sorrel, and
masses of tiny white flowers; the grasses stroke my bare legs
and arms delightfully. The wind is blowing in my face . . . It
must be early summer, before the hay harvest . . . and I am
running by the river, the magical, mysterious river, the Stour
estuary, which is now at high tide, a huge two-mile stretch of
the bluest of deep sea-water.' She and John caught some of
this airy meadowy-ness, this feeling of water being not
faraway, when they created Mill House. Its hedges were well
packed with birds, and the church spire was aligned up with
the western windows. You could see the Mount itself from
the flat garden and the oak trees clinging to its banks for dear
life. It was the motte of a Norman castle, one of those
wooden-towered affairs which defended border land. But we
had to go up in a glider to see the grave circles which
surrounded Mount Bures. Funerals were being held here
when Abraham sat at his tent door at the heat of the day. I did
once manage to haul Diana to the top of the Mount, all of
thirty feet, to show her the spectacular Essex-Suffolk view.
What a revelation! My last talk with John Collins was at the
level crossing as we watched the Sudbury train rattle past.
When the wind is in the right direction I can hear it at
Bottengoms four miles off. It is the kind of train which rattles
through Proust, and through black and white French movies,
carrying the lovers and the plot.

The funeral arrangements are done and I can sit beside
Diana's coffin in the chancel. On the slab of slate from 2, Amen
Court opposite is John's name and through it floats the names
of Nelson Mandela, Oliver Tambo, Archbishop Tutu and
others, black on black. There is the lectern from which Diana
read, clearly but sometimes doubtfully. There is the ledge on
which she arranged her flower festival flowers like a child.

A Retreat

St Giles, Cambridge, intended to make its parish retreat on the first of February, but it was snowed-off. So here we all are on the last day of May, with the young swimming in the lake and the magnificent Tudor rooms waiting for us to be quiet in. The theme is 'Journeying towards God'. Retreats are very old ways for travelling to God. My favourites are those made by the Australian aborigines. To slip off, to wander to some nice smooth rock, to lie naked on its warm surface – and then dream. Dream for a moon or a month. And to listen to the Pacific Ocean far below. And eat picnics. And get better. And walk home to a welcome, full of desire. At Hengrave Hall I walk in the formal gardens between the talks and silences, and hear the cries and laughter of hidden youngsters, and catch the sound of splashing. The Hall was built by a fabulously rich merchant at the very moment of the English Reformation when, three miles down the lane, the great Abbey of St Edmundsbury was being dissolved. The new man and the old idea in a turmoil of bricks and mortar, stone and glass. I read Sir Walter Raleigh's hauntingly lovely 'As you came from the Holy Land of Walsingham' in which a pilgrimage is not only to the famous and now shattered shrine, but to where two young friends met. Now an old man, he pilgrimages to find her again, meeting – Christ? – who tells him,

But love is a durable fire
In the mind ever burning;
Never sick, never old, never dead,
From itself never turning.

Those who lead retreats are allowed a moment's retreat of their own. So after lunch I steal away to the River Lark on the banks of which both the Abbey and the Hall were built, a fast little steam put out to grass, as one might say. No mills to turn, no fishy larder for fast-days, just a sparkling run of idleness to carry one's thoughts away. Returning, I meet soaking students talking, I later learn, Croatian.

The Seekers

Seeking stories dominate the bestseller lists. I find its precursors, J.C. Powys and T.H. White, more beguiling than C.S. Lewis and J.R. Tolkien and their current followers. To seek involves a quest. The Latin root of 'seek' is to 'perceive scent', the Greek 'to lead'. It was during the Middle Ages, with the spring scents in the air, that our ancestors went off to 'seek a saint'. They might have said, 'It will have to be Canterbury again because Walsingham way will be muddy'. Their motives were mixed, and so they had been from the start. The five thousand returned to the spot where they had fed only to find that the strange provider of the picnic had sailed away. So they too took ship and eventually caught up with him at Capernaum. He knew what they wanted and it was not his teaching. 'You have not come looking for me because you saw signs but because you ate the bread and your hunger was satisfied. You must work, not for this perishable food, but for the food that lasts.'

Years ago I went a long way to seek a seeker, young George Fox. He had scented among the often impure odour of Puritanism something delectable in Lancashire. On a May morning in 1652, although faint from lack of meals and miles and miles of tramping, he had got himself up to the top of Pendle Hill to find, not only a great view but a great silence. I, well-fed by the hotel, did the same. It was pouring, but seekers must never mind the rain. It blew in drifts and wild weather provided intermittent glimpses of Bowland and the River Lune. I was seeing the native land of the Society of Friends, 'the Galilee of Quakerism,' as it is called. William Penn wrote that when George Fox reached the summit of Pendle that 'he behaved as if he had been on a great auditory' and 'became a strong man, and a new and heavenly-minded man, a divine and a naturalist'.

Bunyan wrote his *Pilgrim's Progress* for folk who were no longer able to get away. Times had changed and all the old holidays had been banished by parliament. You toiled, you died, without going far. Never mind, said the author, although you had to stay put,

> This book will make a traveller of thee,
> By its council thou wilt ruled be,
> It will direct thee to the Holy Land,
> If thou wilt its directions take . . .

And so it did until the Bank Holiday was invented. Millions now quest with the *Lord of the Rings* as their guide. Or they follow C.S. Lewis to Perelandra. Or they look up new directions to the Holy Grail. Or they seek refreshment in the blue and yellow lands of the brochure.

More Food

'I am living on raw emotion' says a retiring cricketer on the radio. And so are we, for the long-awaited *Wormingford Cookbook* makes its debut. Brought together by Cynthia at last, though not her fault, more ours for dillydallying with long-forgotten recipes, and resplendent with drawings made decades ago for our village guide by John Nash, it is a gift for the social historian if not for Nigella. Desperation forced us into this foody exposure. A busybody, noting how the churchyard wall bellied a trifle out to the lane, wrote to the papers. Danger lurks everywhere these days. You can't go for a walk without a conker dropping on your head. The wall has behaved like this since the days of Queen Victoria, is interlocked and safe. The bulge is caused, we used to say, by the dead having a stretch. But now it must be what they call 'tied in', which will cost £40,000. The PCC gulps. But then it remembers that the churchyard, if not the church, must be the end place for everyone, if only in a plastic bag. So all must mend the wall. It was then that Cynthia thought of the *Cookbook*. And so here we are, the book on sale, in a tent with the Bishop, the MP, and all of us, launching it, casting it upon the waters. Many of the recipes would appear to speak of six courses up at the Hall long ago or expensive restaurants now, but tucked into them is the fare of the farmworkers under our feet, morsels chopped off with a clasp knife at bait time, cheese, onion and bread chiefly, devoured in a sheltering ditch whilst the plough horses snuffled in their nosebags. My contribution to the *Cookbook* is one for quince jam. I found it scribbled on the flyleaf of a novel and dated 1828. There are Portugal quince trees in the garden, with their dense paper-white blossom and furry fruit, old twisted limbs and breath-taking scent. Take one home for the car.

Spring as Usual

The biggest bean field in the land rolls around my wood. Larks sing over it all day long. Below it the 'bottoms' are covered in buttercups, millions of them, each petal laid like goldleaf. There is watercress in the brook. Once outside it is virtually impossible to go in again. All I want to do is to lie where the sun can touch me. It reminds me of sprawling above the Atlantic in Cornwall when I was a teenager and becoming mesmerised by the blue tumult below, the regular biff of the water on rock, the crying seabirds, the hot sward, the thinking, 'Why ever go home? Why go anywhere?'

On the Ascension I preach on Christ's home-coming, contrasting this King in royal state riding on the clouds his chariot with the dear friend who blessed his followers at Bethany before he vanished in the Cloud of Unknowing. Not that I find much fault with the old hymn-writers' departure language for as Mrs Alexander said, 'Ever on our earthy path a gleam of glory lies.' The essence of the Ascension story is that it tells of a clouded vision.

Ringers' Banquet

I seem to have spent the month scribbling added liturgies to what the lectionary says. Natural and Pentecostal winds blow hot and cold through the Stour Valley. Air balloons float overhead, pear shaped, lazy. Rackety rocks keep out of their path. At evening both birds and balloons are polished up by the sun's last rays. Garnon's Chase glimmers with white campion. The pub bursts with bellringers from all over, for it is our turn to entertain England's best. 'Our' being the Essex Association, founded in 1879 when ringers walked in bands from tower to tower in sociable style and nursing warnings from their wives about such undesirable halts as the Eight Bells at Bures.

Our Pentecostal dinner is laid out at the Officers' Club in Colchester. About two hundred of us sit down after the learned mayor, who is both an M.D. and an historian, reminds us that we are feeding on the exact site of a Benedictine refectory. I say Alcuin's Grace, which goes like this:

> Lord Christ, we pray thy mercy on our table spread,
> And what thy gentle hands have given men,
> Let it by thee be blessed. Whate're we have
> Comes from thy lavish heart and gentle hand,
> And what is good is thine, for thou art good.
> And ye that eat, give thanks for it to Christ,
> And let the words ye utter be only peace,
> For Christ loved peace. It was himself that said,

'Peace I give unto you, my peace I leave with you.'
Grant that our own may be a generous hand,
Breaking the bread for hungry people, sharing the food, Amen.

But what company! I can see George Pipe, scion of the mighty Suffolk bellringing family, and there is none other than the editor of *The Ringing World*, and all around table-loads of the nation's best campanologists and legendary tower captains, 'Youths' from all over whose names fill our peal boards and whose bell music makes the parish air vibrate. A mile or so away would have been the bell-foundry of the redoubtable Joanna Sturdey, the woman bell-maker. As the girls bring the pudding round, I see her delivering our bell for Wormingford, the one which crashes out its sweet note on practice nights and Sundays, and has done so for five hundred years. We should all leave a great music behind.

Cathedral Camps

Writers must have a little outing, even if it pours. London is alternately darkened and brightened as we sit in Southwark Cathedral, and organise Cathedral Camps. We are here to allocate cleaning jobs for multi-racial young people, persuade clerks of works that their Cathedrals need this help, and generally manage this now famous activity. Boats float in and out of view. Downstairs the dust of Shakespeare's brother Edmund lies in the choir, not to be disturbed. He was twenty-seven, a young actor. His is a great role still. The drama of his name when the eye catches it! 'Look,' I tell the Campers when some similar thought-wrenching character crops up among the gravestones and I watch as it momentarily alters their day. Although worshippers may find it impossible to believe, there are parts of our cathedrals which haven't been dusted for five hundred years, glory holes such as Miss Havisham would have tolerated, pigeon and spider empires, splendours covered over with dirt. I feel rather like an orderly officer or one of those grim employers of domestic servants when I pay a visit to a Cathedral Camp. And then I see some treasure made legible, some clerestory (usually the most neglected place) swept just how George Herbert would have liked it. Many of the Campers find their way to this work via the Internet. From all over the world, they communicate in the common language of youth. They take turns to cook and are moderately riotous in the Choir School in the evenings. 'Do the showers work properly?' I ask. 'Has the dean told you the history?' But chiefly I say, 'Marvellous' and mean it. On the whole I do not approve of gardening or of the young campers having to paint yards of railing. I want them to go home after a week's hard labour adding something wonderful to the great interior, seeable glass, sharpened carving, towers spring- cleaned. Roman Catholics and Jews and Muslims are on their knees on an Anglican floor during the organ lesson. The tourists throng, the liturgy goes round like the clock.

After the meeting I walk all the way to Whitehall to fetch documents from the Archbishop of Canterbury's office near Westminster Abbey as the sky blackens and the hailstones clatter, driving the tourists into crannies, banging the protesters to bits, swishing the buses with shot. Through the day I have shivered and steamed in turn. Wandering on, the storm over, I find myself in Ryan's Bar, as do two smart young priests. Enamel ads cover the walls. Players Drumhead, Will's Woodbines, Carrydown Plug, and a young

Irish barman flies about. Scaffolders arrive, office folk, and the wicked clergymen are joined by a lady. Everyone hollers above the din and the barman's beautiful teeth shine. Nearby, just over the road, long ago, at the now vanished Bell Inn someone in a similar uproar penned a letter to William Shakespeare in 1598. They say it is the only such letter which survives. After Ryan's Bar I hurry to the next shelter from the renewed rain, a long dash to St Bride's. Ten listeners stand quietly as a woman pianist plays Rachmaninov, and as a tall soaked waif quietly pads up and down the white and gold aisles, not making a sound. It is London being itself.

Woodland Week

Neil our woodman has to check the churchyard trees for safety and health. A vicar named Chilton planted them in the eighteen-nineties. His horse-chestnuts are about to break into flower with a splendour unseen since last time. Immense, swinging like the great censer of Santiago de Compostella, they will slow down the traffic.

Richard Mabey tells me that he has planted no less than eighty new trees at Mazzards and seen off the grim conifers. He and Polly live on the Breckland, East Anglia's once moor, but still a place of marshes, airy flats and skies which know no limits. It makes me think what an age ago it was since Duncan's men kindly dug holes for my chestnuts, birches and beeches after the elms fell down. England's elms were deeply loved and are now profoundly mourned. They propagated themselves by runners, travelling along farm hedges, and they perished similarly, death running from one to the next until they all vanished. With the strange and wonderful exception of the huge elm on Gravel Hill, now an object of veneration.

At Tiger Hill, a few miles away, elm-death and the great gale of 1987 struck a wild bargain. Hundreds of stricken trees simply fell into the arms of the wind which first rocked them about gauntly, then dropped them to the woodland floor, there to mulch and feed it. Here was my last woodland engagement. It had all unknowingly been my first, for it was here at Tiger Hill that we boys and girls gathered bluebells and blackberries, taking care not to disturb the lady doctor-naturalist in the caravan. She has long gone but we have not. Here we are still, listening to the May nightingales, eating picnics and telling one another that it doesn't seem twelve months since last time. More children splash in the icy stream. Badger setts yawn in the bank as they always did. I think of Mark, that hurrying figure, youthful, swift and to the point, and how well he fits into our bluebell party. 'And what I say unto you, I say unto everyone, keep awake!' The trees and the Tiger Hill birds say, 'Who is asleep?'

June

Magna Carta Day - Get a Life - Trinity - Leaving Home - The Flitting - Sunday Morning in the Highlands - All Flesh is Grass - Singing to God - Beyond Destruction - Taking Liberties in Church - Remembering Evelyn Underhill - Darsham Station - The Haymaker - How to Build a Tower - The Ordinand - The Day after Midsummer - The Divines - Neil's Birthday - The Old Ladies Die

Magna Carta Day

A botanical version of Proust's madeleine experience occurred as I was walking through the just about to be cut long grass. Goose-grass embraced my jeans, suddenly releasing the meadowy toys of old summers. Although why we found it so hilarious for a girl victim to wander about with a strand of it stuck to her back, heaven only knows. Then we shot each other with plantain 'caddies' (catapults) and said Tinker-Tailor as we worked out our futures on a stem of couch, and watched a head of wall barley creep along a bare arm like a little animal. And then of course, the grass-players would one by one go home, and it would become very hot and scratchy, and still there would be a thousand years before tea. And when we got in at last, someone would remark, 'Why, the boy looks all in. It's the sun'. And they would use words like 'listless', which I found interesting and complimentary. I must ask the children at our primary school if they know about the grassy toys of summer, the tangles which wear you out. And they will once again look up pityingly, taking their eyes off their keyboards for a moment, for here is someone who still thinks that a mouse is something the cat brought in. Is there computer ennui?

Haymakers throb all around. Good grass this year. It goes into the machine bright green and comes out pale biscuit. Rooks bounce along behind the haymaker and there is the delectable ancient scent. But no hanging about. The new mown hay is carried off the field in an hour or two. No tossing and turning. No raking and sweating. No children searching for precious quaking grass to set off the bull daisies. No listlessness. Just over the hedge a new house sprouts football flags. And nearby, in Roblett's Way, a pretty hairdresser arrives to give Mr Cummins his weekly tidy-up, but he had just departed, aged ninety-one. So no white curls on the kitchen floor this Thursday. His sedate curtains add nothing more. Such is death in a village.

Pam the churchwarden and I go to Bury St Edmunds for the Magna Carta service in the cathedral. The vast west front is wrapped in plastic like a present, as is the new tower which is still going up. But all else is a sharp blaze of flint which is honed by the sunshine. All the Suffolk mayors and mayoresses, all the D-Day veterans, everybody who is anybody is strolling about. Chains of office and swords and medals clink and glitter. Then the American regimental band arrives and swings 'In the Mood' on Angel Hill and old ladies jive, and old men have rides in jeeps.

In 1214 the earls and barons of England, appalled by King John, swore on St Edmund's altar here that they would make him sign a new set of rules. Magna Carta. He was crazily bad and they roped him in. The old soldiers climb out of the jeeps and into the Athenaeum to receive the Freedom of the Borough whose motto is: *Sacrarium Regis, Cunabula Legis* - shrine of a king, cradle of the law, or as we say, Bury. In the cathedral we sing 'Judge eternal, throned in splendour' and sway along grandly in our robes. The American bandsmen rest among the municipal roses.

Get a Life

Biography has long been among the most dreaded of arts. Thomas Hardy dreaded it so much that he wrote his own. They said that huge bonfires of his papers lit up the Max Gate sky. The life he wrote was sent to the publishers as *The Early Life of Thomas Hardy* by Florence Emily Hardy. She was his second wife and an author of sorts. And she had done enough of the dogsbody work to claim a writer's hand in it. It could give a reputation. But it fooled no one. I treasure my copy. Never will it end up on the flower festival bookstall among the Archers and Cooksons. Hardy's intention was not to deceive or to conceal. And he was far above being economical with the truth. He wanted to present the bare bones of the truth, no more. But of course this 'biography' acted like bait, and the professional biographers have been able to zoom in to the very heart of the great poet and novelist because of it.

We cannot have too much autobiography and biography nowadays, it seems. From the newspaper profiles and ghost writers to the often superb studies of the famous, warts and all, we are in thrall to the genre. It is the current lust. We are like E.C. Bentley who wrote,

> I like biography better than geography,
> Geography is about maps, biography is about chaps.

The scanty biographies of Christ and his circle somewhat baffle us. Why did no one write down what he looked like? What happened to his few possessions after the execution? There is an apocryphal story about St John in old age - how young people would make their way to his door to pester him with such questions. 'What was he *like* - tell us.' But all the ancient apostle would answer, 'Little children, love one another.' It exasperated them. Every now and then in the New Testament the biographical curtain slips to reveal such things as St Paul's nephew exposing a plot to kill his uncle, or that tantalising family visit to Jesus - 'Your mother and brothers are outside.' Yet it was divine genius which ordered what we should know about Jesus and it must have been a perfectly convincing life for so many to have imitated it. There has been little complaint in history about what might be missing, only an occasional and entirely human wonder about what and why so many ordinary things were not said. But then we live in the most documented age ever. Caught in the web we are, from our natal chart to our DNA.

Trinity

The village bakes. Sudden winds fan the heat about and creamy plates of elderflower cense the hedges. Cars are ovens on wheels. Being told that we have only to lift the seed-drill for a few feet to double the skylarks, I examine the Great Field which was many fields when they were numerous. But there are still plenty of semi-bare patches. It is because its ancient dips continue to defy the density levels of seed, and they, plus the tramlines created by the sprayer, continue to provide feeding grounds for these birds. Only this year the crop is beans whose scent was a test for morality in the middle ages. It was thought that girls could not hold out against it, so boys were fined if they made love to them in it. Overhead, invisible now, the larks sing then drop like a stone.

Sunday ramblers swelter past, Sunday gliders cross themselves in the blue, Sunday ringers stay in cool towers where brass knights and their wives can keep an eye on them. I suddenly remember poor young Reginald Heber and his wife in broiling Calcutta, their thoughts on Shropshire. His see was virtually all British India, a land of endless deities and their marigold shrines, of natural excess, torrential rain,

The grasshopper (Le Lavandou) 1990

pitiless sun and exile. He had turned the bishopric down twice but India got him in the end. It drew him into its sacred chaos, into a life of all work, all duty, all brevity. He was a poet who had won the Newdigate Prize at Oxford so he wrote great Christian hymns in the heat. They liked them back home, saw the Church of England triumphing over the heathens, enjoyed their foreignness, their coral strands.

John, scanning the framed Victorian parsons on the vestry wall, wondered what they did all day. Well, there were 'the poor' for a start, those large labouring families which, like Reginald Heber, wore themselves out in the field. They said the Office, they wrote botanies, taught the choir to hold the note in his 'Holy, Holy, Holy' and lived, unlike him, for ages. Then they were laid to rest beneath a flat stone ringed with Latin and harebells. The people would talk of 'Mr Davies's day,' 'Canon Williams's day' as though they were reigns. And they were of a sort. But now we are looking for a 'House for Duty' priest. Whoever decides to live in our vicarage c.1955, rent free, no stipend, will have a famous view. So good that the job could have been advertised as 'View for Duty'. The Stour quavers in the heat-haze. This is the season for Anglican lassitude. As John Meade Falkner wrote:

> We have done with dogma and divinity
>   Easter and Whitsun past,
> The long, long Sundays after Trinity
>   Are with us at last;
> The passionless Sundays after Trinity,
>   Neither feast-day nor fast.

Leaving Home

An essential of crime is the getaway car. Soon I will be on the getaway train, swaying in its sleeper, rumbling north. Leaving Bottengoms Farm has been nearly as dramatic as Emma Woodhouse's seven-mile drive to Box Hill. Our sense of emancipation and freedom is certainly the same. Home and all it contains, including the cats, has not only been left behind but is no more! The summer garden, all mowed and edged for the house-sitter, is little more than a memory when we pull out of Euston. It is different with flying, which has something in common with death, that is the happier side of death when earthly matters drop away and disappear from sight, and nothing more can be done except fly on. Now and then I lift the sleeper blind to wonder which lit city it is, what county, whose bedroom is momentarily staring into mine, or where the stars are. Have I left a forwarding address? Am I addressless at this moment? Curiously, tragically almost, these emotions will be reversed when I leave Rannoch for Wormingford. How will the Highlands survive without me for another year? Sandwiches from the kitchen table will be in the carriage, Perthshire mud too as I glance down at my shoes. The special odour of the great moor will be on my clothes and carried to London.

The Scots of course are notorious home-leavers. How do they manage it, loving Scotland so much? Did they during the nineteenth century flights to New Zealand and Canada hang their pipes on willow-trees and weep by the waters of Otago? Or grow homesick for the Grampians in flat East Anglia, where they settled in droves? Both my farmer neighbours are second generation Lowlanders in the Stour Valley. I must look again into their kind faces for signs of grief for what their fathers abandoned in the bad times, those moors and mountains and burns which I borrow for two weeks a year.

No one lives in the big white house at Rannoch during the winter. Alistair the factor works sheep across its slopes, clangs its deer gates, protects it. Back home, I often think of the birds balancing themselves on its pointed spruces, and of the icy Loch below. I think of the narrow room and its wide view, and of leaving a marker in a book which will be continued next year. Young friends book-up for Tibet or zoom down to Newquay for the surfing, and will hurry from home with a bedroll and the latest shades. Unencumbered with property, they have little to be faithless about. They will not write letters other than C.V.s for jobs and their parents may receive an e-mail or two. Soaring away in cars or on bikes for six months or a year, they say goodbye to me - 'I expect you'll be off to Scotland as usual soon. Have a nice time'.

The Flitting

My regularity out-does that of the handsome French clock which the poet left me in his will and which has long rests between telling the time. But it looks well, and one cannot have everything. I am writing in Scotland. Loch Rannoch fits into the landscape below my window like a blue scarab. The mountains, Schiehallion in particular, stare down on it. As with all deep water, it alternates between invitation and warning. Boys from the school opposite tempt its mood with little white boats. Having done a stint, I walk to the deserted village. It makes me think of Jeremiah's 'heaps'. Jeremiah is the poet of the destroyed home, of clearance. Except, as he says, although everything has been razed to the ground, tell-tale heaps remain, inviting speculation and sorrow, prodding anger. To find Jerusalem a 'heap'! The prophet's heart breaks. Our deserted or cleared or razed village on Rannoch Moor, for which Christopher, Henrietta and myself make an annual beeline, now bakes in the sun. The Moor, now quite empty was once scattered with Sheilings and settlements, now gone, all gone. 'Ours' must have been quite a place and the home of upward fifty Highland families. They think Cumberland's men would have cleared it after the Forty-five. Bread made from meal and cows' blood was eaten here. I climb a house wall to take stock of infields and outfields, wandering paths, enigmatic standing stones, hearths, barns and the clear burn still running its musical route. A harrier is motionless above. A Victorian poet sat here to write:

> By the wee birchen corries lie patches of green,
> Where gardens and bare-headed bairnies have been,
> But the huts are now rickles of stones nettle-grown
> And the once human homes, e'en their names are unknown.

What was called 'the flight from the land' by East Anglian farmworkers caused great consternation before the First World War. Entire villages decamped, as it were, for a better life on the railways or in the Empire. It was 'Join the Army and see the World'. To persuade the farmworkers to stay (at eleven shillings a week) an idyllic picture of rural life was painted by journalists and parsons. Worried, the government commissioned a young Norfolk novelist, Henry Rider Haggard to make an inventory of the countryside. It was all as bad as could be, he discovered. His book, *Rural England,* was prefaced with a quotation from Judges, 'The highways were unoccupied . . . the inhabitants of the villages ceased'.

Empty cottages and tumbledown farms were part of the drama of my childhood. I would raise their latches with a beating heart, terrified of disturbing a tramp. The artist John Nash, when he was young, would search abandoned gardens in Buckinghamshire for rare roses and take cuttings. Everywhere gypsies and other travellers left their brief habitation marks, burnt patches soon to attract fireweed, and evidence of intimacy. I would, being a romantic boy, sit where these people had briefly lived, and wondering what it was like to up sticks and move on, half envying them.

Sunday Morning in the Highlands

The temperature wavers from keen wind to unexpected heat. Loch Rannoch stretches majestically below showing itself first as a water-colourist's palette, all soft greys and muted purples, then as Hector's shield, all flashing metal and gold polish. Monster fish eat their way up and down its length, we are told. On the opposite bank the darker patches are those of the ancient Caledonian Forest which they are now saving from extinction. Swallows, their crops gorged with insects (midges, we hope) loop incessantly above our heads as they summon up courage to feed the gaping mouths over the window. What a bother we are to them, we mere trippers who have come no further than Suffolk, whilst they have flown all the way from Morocco.

Christopher and I find the factor's scythe propped against a stone wall. It has a home-made shaft and a rusty blade. I try it out on the bracken which falls before it with a regretful sound which reminds me of James Shirley's 'Death the Leveller'. I quote it to Christopher who now has the practical business of moving the deer-gate on his mind. How there is no armour against fate and that all of us,

> Must tumble down
> And in the dust be equal made
> With the poor crooked scythe and spade.

Quite so. Scythes and hour-glasses used to decorate

tombstones. Both are still in use back home, the latter as an egg-timer, not a life-timer. We are on our way to climb a mountain – just. This is the rocky cranium which broods learnedly over Kinloch Rannoch, and which is about a thousand feet high. It sports a few trees like curls on a balding head. Christopher beseeches me not to look back until we reach the summit as he wants the full view to burst upon me. But I cannot resist looking back time and time again just to witness every degree of diminishment of the landscape. It is the Scottish Sabbath. There are two kirks below, one surrounded with graves, the other by cars. Two figures are in flight across the stone bridge. A bell tolls. Were the acoustics as sharp as the view might we not have heard snatches of a metrical psalm. 'O set me up upon the rock that is higher than I' perhaps? The burn which brings Kinloch Rannoch its water roars in our ears. Reaching the summit, puffed and happy, we collect stones to place on the cairn raised by other climbers and take photographs as though we were Tensing and Hillary. Straight ahead though not visible lies the holy land of the Lyon and Fortingall where Adamnan brought Christianity from Iona. At Fortingall we observed Mr Carter, a Norfolk thatcher, mending a roof.

All Flesh is Grass

I must be the only person for miles around who has been naming his grass. Timothy, Red Canary, Meadow brome, Marsh foxtail, Nodding grass, Oat grass – I could go on for pages. It rises in the track to tickle the under-bellies of cars and in the set-aside to hide larks' nests. Wind and rain, and concealed infirmities, have brought an ancient crack willow crashing down, and Neil the woodman must be summoned. It always astonishes me how little space trees take up in the air, and much room they take up when they collapse on the ground. There it lies, a Paul Nash tree, huge, horizontal, felled by circumstances. The cats stroll about on its tip with mockery, just as David strolled onto poor Goliath to cut off his head. I have always felt sorry for Goliath, a man exploited by his country because of his size. In a later age he would have been exploited by some boxing manager and ended up with brain damage. The fallen willow soon dies. Its silver leaves blacken. It wilts all over. Ben aged five balances himself on its trunk, shouting, triumphant.

The land goes its mute way. Not a celebratory sound unless one includes birdsong. Weedless fields, rocking hedges, contractors' corn, supermarket onions, unmolested wild animals, bone idle domestic animals, cattle (Lincolns) on the water-meadows once more, Paul's sheep too by the river, all chomping their grass dinners. A hare prays on the hill, balancing on his back legs and crossing his front paws. Swaying, listening, one ear to catch what God is saying, one fearful of us.

Singing to God

What important things one finds when looking for something else. In this instance a tin box of His Master's Voice gramophone needles circa 1936. So out comes the gramophone itself which was first wound up when Bertie Wooster was dancing. Its turntable is velvety and inviting, its arm silvery and promising. In the snapshot album it is playing at the feet of a young man punting across the millpond in his pyjamas, while his wife trails her hands in the water. Here are their records, Schnabel, Toscanini, Geraldo. I put on 'Yours' and expect a whisper but Dorothy Carless belts it out, swearing to love till the birds fail to sing. Wind-up music fills the whole house. We dance round the table. Yours to the end of life's story.

Six o'clock Sunday morning, Fergal Keane on 'Something Understood', that excellent programme. He tells of our history being detected in our singing. It is true. His point is proved by an old homeless man singing of his dependence on Christ, revealing more of himself than he could possibly have intended or understood. Both he and Dorothy Carless had unwittingly 'sung' their life stories, their times. Although not knowing what either of them looked like, I am able to hear who they were. During a Royle Family episode on television the producer allows an Irish pub tenor to sing all the verses of 'I'll take you home again, Kathleen' in order to expose emotions which the deplorable couch-bound family's sub-culture had all but obliterated. Poor old hymns, brash new songs, carry a genetic information. I once stood in a big congregation wondering which girl possessed the fresh lovely voice which made the rest of us sound flat. It belonged to the old woman next to me.

Their own eloquence was sometimes shown to be a drawback for the prophets. But what could they do about it? They complained to God, and He was very understanding, His own voice being so beautiful. He sympathised with Ezekiel - 'Thou art to them as a very lovely song of one that hath a pleasant voice and can only play well on the instrument (of the voice), for they hear thy words but they do

201

not do them'. Jeremiah too tells God that what he is saying is ignored - 'I am their music'. Every now and again through its long history the Church has had a go at knocking the music out of the words, a Sisyphean task where Anglicanism is concerned. I like to hear a country congregation getting its tongue round a language as superb in its way as the building in which it is sung. And I always hear the life of the singer in the notes. Talking about singing the psalms, George Herbert said, 'the heart must bear the longest part'.

Beyond Destruction

Bernard rattles up and down the hill on the haymaker. It click-clacks in the sudden heat. Gnats are out in force, dancing above the stream in insect clouds. I carry scraps of John Meade Falkner round the field edge where they set themselves to the clatter of the machine, the poem in which he thought that the Sundays after Trinity were empty feasts.

He must have worshipped in a nice sluggish Victorian church with nothing to prod him in the direction of SS Peter, John, Mary Magdalen, James, Bartholomew, Matthew, the Transfiguration, et al. But the Anglican torpor of the poem oddly pleases me. It accompanies the laxity, the sloth even, which can still be found in certain country churches, the odour of which rises up, not as incense but as a reminder of the thrill of lifting the latch onto taken for granted treasures when I was a boy, my bike leaning in the lych gate. I still sit in some strange back pew to read a strange parish magazine in which the services wrestle with the rector's requirements, pages full of profuse thanks for this or that, recipes, PCC jokes and dozens of names. None of them disturb the stillness of the ages.

We, Diana, Elaine, David and myself, drive to Norwich to sit in Mother Julian's cell, a more solid structure one imagines than her medieval lean-to. The church which propped it up was reduced to dust and rubble by a German bomb but has risen again as good as new. As for Julian's house, that would have gone long ago. Re-housed, the great writer's spirit might be said to be very comfortable with Norfolk pantiles and her two windows, one to look in at the Mass and one to look out at the world, draught free at last. Oh, that Wensum wind! It was a miracle in itself that she lived to be ninety. Like the Suffolk church, her room is still with an ancient stillness, as if her quietness had returned to furnish it. It makes us feel enclosed, if only for a few minutes. She played down any extraordinariness regarding herself, or even about God, and certainly about her relationship with Him.

There is nothing very special about seeking. It is a thing that every soul can do with God's grace . . . So I saw him and I sought him; I had him and wanted him. It seems to me that this is and should be an experience common to us all.

Time has a way of holding certain great things in suspense and of doing away with signatures. A woman tells us a thousand things about herself but not her name. We feel we should tell her that hers was not the only church to be hit. Ours at Little Horkesley vanished in seconds in September 1940, aged one thousand years. But we change the subject. Did not Julian dwell on the horrors of her day – though not for long? Her crucified Christ flapped on the scaffold like a cloth put out to dry. We tell her that we have driven fifty miles along the A140 especially to see her, hoping to find her in. Her answer is, 'How could I not be?' Outside, her little patch is full of cars and industrial muddle, and signs saying 'This way to the shrine'. She is amused. Her Norwich was a noisy old muddle. She signs off her famous book with, 'So ends the revelation of the love of the blessed Trinity'.

> *Post pugnam-pausa fiet*;
> Lord, we have made our choice;
> In the stillness of autumn quiet,
> We have heard the still, small voice.
> We have sung *Oh where shall Wisdom?*
> Thick paper, folio, Boyce.

Taking Liberties in Church

Country ladies frolic amidst the sun-warmed tombs like Herrick girls. It is lunch break from oasis, from swaying on steps, from snipping and arranging well-bred jungles of flowers. No hasty sandwich. They do themselves well with wine and paté and fruit and coffee, and their laughter carries into the trees. After the show is over, they will all appear once more with a packed lunch to demolish their fantasies. Extravagant bouquets will leave the font for long-dead neighbours. 'I'll put these on Joan's grave — what do you think?' In between there is the mighty display, the visitors, the happy clink of Quota money in the big glass jar. It once fell to pieces under the weight of copper and silver, so best notes and cheques. Birds and bees soar into the aisles and out again. The ancient doors gape. Will Shirley's flaming arrangement last over Pentecost? Will people actually come to see what these Herrick women, and their slave-labour men, are providing? Is the Tombola under the yew a sin?

Rural churches are liberty halls these days. 'Please, sir, may we sing a carol?' pleaded Parson Woodforde's congregation one Christmas morning. 'Certainly, but wait until I am out of the church'. I am reading the wonderful short stories of A. E Coppard written during the nineteen-twenties. There is one about a village boy who becomes entranced by the interior of the church and watches the vicar's servant arranging flowers. 'The boy heard the rattle of a bucket handle and saw the maid place the bucket beside the altar and fetch flowers and bottles and pots from the vestry. Some she stood upon the table of the altar; others, tied by pieces of string, she hung in unique positions upon the front and sides, filling them with water from the pail as she did so; and because the string was white, and the altar was white, and the ugly bottles were hidden in nooks of moss, it looked as if the very cloth of the altar sprouted with casual bloom.'

The boy, the son of a free-thinking cobbler, knows nothing about church and becomes curious and entranced. He gets accidentally locked in over-night and to keep himself warm he dons a few choir robes, has supper off the scraps of bread and wine which he discovers in the vestry, and lies down and falls asleep. He wakes up to a nightmare. The vicar is dragging him from the building by the ear and screaming . . . 'Beast . . . Beast!'

Songs of Praise with Pam Rhodes at Long Melford. A burning day and a coolly aristocratic church. Having told Pam a tale of my coming here on my bike as a boy, the BBC has reconstructed this episode with a little fair lad who, a) is too young for perp and dec, and b) could not by any feat of the imagination be the earlier me. However, we play our part and I hold forth on the grand architecture, having learnt much since then.

I then wander off to pay a courtesy call on Edmund

Blunden's grave. I knew him slightly. He once gave me his lecture notes in his exquisite handwriting. He was slight, bird-like, the strength of his poetry neither visible in his face or his frame. He liked a pint in the Bull before lunch. He lived a few yards from the pub in the old house which Siegfried Sasson had given him. He had taken the poems of John Clare to the trenches, to Oxford, everywhere he went. As I stand by his grave traffic spins along the pilgrim road to Bury St Edmund's like glittering beads from a snapped necklace. The huge green is empty. My teenage self cycled to

A tern feeding its young (1) 1983

the fair which suddenly grew up on it once a year, the roundabout with its mirrors and lights and mad music, the swings with the girls' skirts flying and voices screaming, the passionate glances from strangers, the sordid sideshows, the strange excitement, the moonlit majesty of the vast church above and the Tudor palace below. And then, after only three days, the fair all gone. Just wounded grass and sawdust from the coconut shies.

Remembering Evelyn Underhill

Summer rain – the first summer rain. It drenches the small Suffolk market-town and polishes it up. The dentist talks of the Algarve. His drill hisses painlessly. What a blessing he has been to me. I would tell him so if his fingers were not in my mouth. The Algarve – has he read my favourite book about Portugal, Rose Macaulay's *Fabled Shore*? Did he know that the newly-wed Gainsboroughs lived just opposite his surgery, Tom beginning to make a living from painting the squires? I wander on but the drill sticks to the point, then stops, and the dentist says, 'There …' Rain patters the window. I am thinking of William Sansom's hobby in *Who's Who* - 'watching'. That's me, I think, watching when not actually spying. At the bus station I watch three men devouring fish and chips in the downpour, and talking amiably. Soon I am watching familiar fields between the clicks of the windscreen wiper, wet sheep looking like loofahs, the pitted surface of the Stour and finally a water-logged partridge legging it down my track.

I see that we are asked to remember Evelyn Underhill – St Barnabas and Evelyn Underhill, a piquant couple for Trinity Two. Barnabas had the task of convincing the nervous apostles that Paul was one of them. Was he sure? Saul, that monster? Remember Barnabas, herald to St Paul, Son of Consolation. Remember Evelyn Underhill who, apparently wildly efficient herself never demanded efficiency in others. She said that she 'loathed pushing souls about'. Her book

Mysticism (1911) was a coherent statement on a subject on which the Church itself was rather woolly. It would become a primer for the new translations of the English mystics, Julian, Rolle and the unknown author of *The Cloud of Unknowing*. She wrote it in her Thirties, which must have been about the same age as Julian when she began to write her *Revelations of Divine Love*. Evelyn was not some holy tyrant driving her reader ever forward and upward, no matter how short of breath (or understanding) they were. She was simply saying, like Julian, 'Here is an interesting old path to God which people used to take. It might interest you'. Many people between the wars – and through them – found her 'useful'. 'Here is the mystical way', she would say, 'and here is the latest guidebook to it'. Mysticism told one how to travel that amazing journey which a Norwich woman had mapped out seven hundred years earlier. I watch, historically speaking, the Norfolk rain pattering on Mother Julian's leather curtain, on her violent city, and she all cosy within, her cat on her lap, her Saviour by her side talking to her, her fire lit even if it is June, for He did not tell her to be uncomfortable.

Darsham Station

En-route to the literature festival at Southwold I alight at Darsham Station. Such pauses breed notoriously reflective thoughts, like those of Edward Thomas when his express train 'drew up unwontedly' at the non-stop Adlestrop. My train drew up as arranged in the timetable. Soon a car will arrive to take me further. Meanwhile, Darsham provides me with all the necessary conditions for reflection, a fading yellow brick grandeur in the form of the Stradbroke Arms, an ambitious stretch of platform with valerian thriving in its cracks. And here, once long ago, would have waited an old friend, Peggy Somerville, after a day in London but looking as fresh as a Renoir all the same, bright face, Horrocks cotton dress and her voice a seabird's wail as she catches sight of me. And here, just up the road in the churchyard, she remains. Have I time between train and taxi to make a dash to her? No. Best to watch the wild flowers flourishing between the lines and to imagine her painting them. Or setting pastel drawings of them, first giving a petal here and there a little finger smudge as I so often saw her do. Death is such a strange business. One goes but never leaves. Artists and poets in particular will hang around at halts along the line. Peggy was a dab hand at the milky light of coastal Suffolk. We filled her coffin with primroses. Her studio was in a small orchard which in retrospect is in perpetual blossom. I stand quite still and glance around, for the waiting-rooms of old country stations have a Buddhistic air and are temples to pause.

The Haymaker

The white cat worships water. It leans over the stream by the hour, looking in. Should it be indoors, washing-up water will do. 'In water face answers face', says the Book of Proverbs. What question does the white face with its green eyes ask? Both John Bunyan and Thomas Traherne would stare into puddles, Bunyan in the hope that they would miraculously dry up at his command, thus proving the existence of God, Traherne that, like Alice and the Looking-glass, he could step into the reversed world which they showed. He believed that

> below the purling stream
> Some unknown joys there be
> Laid up in store for me:
> To which I shall, when that thin skin
> Is broken, be admitted in.

I advise the white cat to take care as she leans over water and remember what happened to Narcissus. But she never listens, being lost in reflections. Larks sing a hundred feet above us. The lawn steams after the downpour. Bernard makes damp hay. His machine drones all day on the top field, releasing scent, squelching on the turn, making geometry of the cut and the uncut.

As with almost everything on the farm these days, haymaking is a one-man rite. Whereas it used to be every able bodied woman's rite, and old photographs show sweaty girls with huge wooden rakes and pitchforks tossing grass in blazing sunshine. Bare arms and shoulders, but a bonnet of course. Bernard has finished when I take the field. Only a triangle of purple budding thistle is still standing, and harriers are wheeling over the blond stubble. Hay wisps hang in the hedge. Horses, their heads deep in still-growing grass, have their eye on them, and soon it will adorn their mouths like whiskers. Hay once had to be made when grass was full of growth, and sappy, then left and thrown about, and only when it was as dry as a bone made into stacks. Wet hay in a stack would heat up until it became an internal oven setting fire to the lot. The River Stour water meadows were hay-kingdoms when we were children, but now corn and potatoes flourish to the water's edge. The hay was as much wild flowers as grass and their chopped stems would scratch our legs and make painful walking. The air would be heavy and overpowering, and a feeling of lassitude would run through the landscape, causing it to droop. George Herbert, being a consumptive, avoided river valleys in summer, disliking their baked plants and aridity, and finding their water unrefreshing.

At St Edmundsbury

In the petitionary prayers I sometimes include one for 'those who are undergoing difficult treatments'. Many operations may now be routine, though never to those having them. The old friend was her customary elegant self as she drove to Bury St Edmunds to have her cataracts removed but was less so as she waited her turn. Some blind men had to make a tremendous row in order to be heard above the crowd as Christ passed by. 'Sir, we want our sight!' The friend's name was eventually called in the waiting silence. The moment had come. Two lots of drops, the curious blow of the needle, her name being spoken as though the surgeon was her guest at lunch, then a mighty swab stuck over her 'done' eye. The other next month. And soon bright day, bright text on the page. I thought of brave old Mr Brontë, quite blind now, under Mr Wilson's knife in Manchester. No small blow from the needle. 'The feeling . . . was of a burning nature', he explained. He laid in a darkened room for a month, bandaged, prayerful, bled with leeches, in lodgings in Boundary Street, his daughter Charlotte beside him writing *Jane Eyre*. Then the marvellous moment when they unwrapped his eyes and he could see like a boy.

Bury St Edmunds is a favourite sight. Rather like going to Cambridge, it is one of those towns whose glory is invisible until one is at the heart of it. However, by 2005 the Cathedral will have its 150 feet Clipsham stone tower to make an exciting point from a distance. The gridded streets laid out by an Italian abbot in the twelfth century are low-lying and quite out of sight until one is walking them. Bury is a town for strollers, for gossiping on corners, for lolling on benches, for running into people you know. Everything is of the very best, town hall by Robert Adam, an Athenaeum, a church by the builder of King's Chapel, the flinty wreckage of a vast Abbey, once among the wonders of Christendom, a River Lark, and municipal carpet-bedding of such lavishness that folk stand in awe. The site of the Benedictine Abbey which contained St Edmund is littered with fragments of holiness and history. The rearing West Front is domesticated with pleasant Georgian houses stuck into its wall like pain-stopping fillings in once perfect teeth. I would cycle to Bury to find King Edmund when I was a boy, the saddle-bag packed with his legend. I thought of him as a river prince, crowned at fifteen, murdered at thirty, who had looked across the river to where my house now stands, Edmund, King, Martyr. The locals loved him but not his colossal shrine, which they eventually used as a stone pit.

I amble around the Great Churchyard where the Georgian headstones lean conversationally this way and that. All these people who danced and diced at the Athenaeum, drank at the Angel, gazed at the wooden seraphs, went to school with Edward FitzGerald, made love among the ruins. John Baret's cadaver reads, 'From erthe I kam and on to erthe I am browht'.

How to Build a Tower

Dean James, the master mason – Tony – and myself are carried aloft in a flimsy wire cage like carefully trapped birds. The cage is similar to those which lowered miners to the coalface, rattling up instead of down. The tower is at the halfway mark. Half a dozen young masons, their arms pollinated like bees' legs with stone dust, are at work in a cat's cradle of scaffolding. No transistors. It is hot and breezy and extraordinarily quiet, just the soft tap of mallet, the chink of chain, the occasional 'I've got it', the flap of plastic and the completed silence when golden stone meets golden stone. It could be 1303 in many respects. Far below, looking like pegs in some ancient cribbage-board, rise the flint cores of aisles and the stacks of freshly carved Clipsham. The Dean, Tony the master-mason and myself, stare down and bells chime. Close-to the tower stone reveals fossils, shells and sea creatures. Section by section are swung into place by a kind of expanded scissor which can be closed when they meet mortar. One day soon Bury will be visible miles away.

I have lost the shears, the expensive long ones, put down where I was working, I thought. They must be found before I go to bed. So out to where the trees are massing into blackness and the wild animals are calling, and the garden has withdrawn its companionship, for it has a life outside my own. The corn, just made out, heaves like the sea as though something or someone is passing through it at root level.

213

There are minute cries and scufflings. I remember Nicodemus's furtive walk through the sleeping city to the young teacher's house. How embarrassing it would be found consulting such a person about one's soul. Writers don't have to be respectable. Here is one climbing the big hump in Duncan's meadow at gone midnight, his head muddled with God, his ear full of badger grunts. And what will be his answer if accosted? That he is looking for his lost shears, or was, but it was so lovely outside that he just walked on.

The Ordinand

The night's storms are 'decaying', says the weatherman unexpectedly. He puts the noun in quotes. How it rained! How the thunder crashed and reverberated all the way to Lavenham! I rose at three in the morning to shut the windows and met the cats clinging to one another with 'wondering, fearing, doubting, dreaming eyes' (Poe). The old rooms trembled from the onslaught of lightning as it shivered the pictures.

The heatwave storm was brewing when Lee and Elizabeth arrived for lunch the day before. She from Idaho, he from Manchester, and both on their way to Mirfield. They were all of twenty-one and en-route to marriage and ministry. Their happiness commandeered Bottengoms Farm, took it over. We eat malformed strawberries, sweet and local, sharp and delicious. Lee heads for the library the minute lunch is over. He has reader's lust and has already taken Elizabeth to Hay-on-Wye to break her in for what will be expected of her, a husband turning the page. I think of my old friend Alan when, at the wedding, his mother looked compassionately at the bride and said, 'Poor girl. I hope she knows what she is letting herself in for – books everywhere'. Lee and Elizabeth politely enquire as to the churchmanship of Mount Bures, Little Horkesley and Wormingford. Well, who is to say what it is – I mean exactly? I mean in words that will make sense in Idaho, or Mirfield if it comes to that. We then drift towards the Quakers and I tell them about George Fox climbing Pendle Hill and walking the Trough of Bowland. Have I, did I, cook enough food? Theology makes ordinands ravenous. The young have a way of bringing their unknown future into old lives.

To Little Glemham Hall to read in a marquee which has been left over from a wedding and which is being put to good use for the St Elizabeth Hospice in Ipswich. I read poems and bits of my journal, and the Leiston High School Musicians play. Classic English parkland, settled these several centuries, the crack and pull of canvas, and sheep heading off for a bit of quiet. Nearby the pretty church in which a previous owner of the Hall sits in a Grecian chair, a marble squire at his ease with God. His name is Dudley North and he is to be admired because he befriended George Crabbe our realist poet. It is midsummer, the solstice of lunacy, but the moon over Glemham looks sane enough.

The Day after Midsummer

Proof-reading in the garden, the pages fluttering, the cat sisters rolling in a flower bed, alert now and again when they see the flycatchers. I am trying to forget some of the daft things I may have said during the great PCC debate on the lavatory. Should it be in the shed or should it be a Perp loo in the church itself? For eight hundred years we have gone to the bushes, I may have said.

Mr Sycamore arrives to slice off the rise in the track. Winter rains have run gullies on either side of it so that the middle has become the terror of drivers. Tall grass waves from it like a Cherokee's haircut. Mr Sycamore takes his horizontal knife to it. His machine sounds like one of those treadle dentist's drills. The ancient surface of the road is exposed and I think of all the women and children who picked these stones from the fields, generation after generation mending the parish tracks. Boys' work, girls' work, mothers' work, these flints once in their warm hands.

Travellers have made a camp on the wide green bend above Sandy Hill. Vans, dogs, brown children and a crowded clothes-line. They were there when I was a boy, when John Clare was at Epping.

> 'Tis thus they live – a picture to the place;
> A quiet, pilfering, unprotected race.

I protect them from the slander of Clare's 'pilfering' whenever they are mentioned, even now. I remember their Colchester protector, Grattan Puxon, a solicitor's son who helped to legislate for gypsies and travellers generally, helping to force the Caravan Sites Act through in 1970. Not that these freedom-loving folk cared much for concrete parking places and the adjacent loos, to be honest. But in a property-dominated society it pleases me to see their indifference to our now sacred bricks and mortar. Not for them the first rung of the nightmare. A real gypsy caravan appears at the flower show, a painted vardo with shafts and an enticing interior. I step inside for the first time. It is gaudily private.

The Divines

When I was twenty I would often find myself staring hard and long at a tall old clergyman, not because he wore the full Tractarian dress of soutane and shovel hat on the town bus, plus a red wig, but because I had been told that at Oxford he had known Walter Pater. I was then in the grip of my Victorian period – my French period would be next – and Fr Gilbert Newcomen had become for me a living witness of what I could only read about. It was 'And did you once see Shelley plain?' I was studying the celebrated literary style of Pater's *Marius the Epicurian* and his *Renaissance*, and here in the High Street, upright and 'well preserved' as they said, was a pupil of his. Fr Newcomen had been Canon Henry Carter's curate for as long as anyone could remember, refusing all preferment to be with him. Never parted, they had shared the hard work in a poor Colchester parish, had enriched its ancient church with Tractarian art, filled it with music and ceremony, and cared for everybody. They had lived too in the terrifying legal climate which prevailed around love such as theirs until 1967.

The Oxford historian Richard Cobb and I would eventually correspond about Gilbert Newcomen and Henry

Carter. Cobb's grandparents had lived opposite St Leonard's church at the Hythe in a fine house, now destroyed. They and all the local gentry called them 'the Divines'. All around were mean streets, small pubs, small works, and alleys running down to the landing stage on the River Colne where Roman galleys had landed supplies for Camulodunum, the first city of this country to have a written record (by Tacitus). Fr Newcomen was ninety when at last I was introduced to him. We sat in the George Hotel, he with his library book in a fish basket. Looking back, I can see now why I did not bring up the subject of Walter Pater. It was because, close to, I could observe only too plainly Fr Newcomen's battle with old age and making him talk about Oxford in 1880 would undo what he clearly believed was a successful attempt to remain his more youthful self. So we drank sherry and ignored the seventy years between us. They said his aunt was Lady Londonderry – they said all manner of things, but with affection. About this time I also met two Religious women who loved one another and who, too, were saints. Anyone with any experience of the Church who has not observed such love, true and lasting as it is, would have to be blind or ignorant. Theirs has always been a special ministry through the ages.

A southerly gale sprang up all unannounced. Softly devastating it was, bashing the rose garden with its zephyres, throwing the birds about the sky and pushing over an ash tree until it held itself against the telegraph wires. Although I sawed away as much of it as I could, it was 'Ring for Neil'. Ring while there were still wires. He and Paul, his mate, arrived with their woodmen genius and the toppling ash wavered, shook all over, let go and met the ground like Goliath, surprised, saddened. 'No trouble at all', said its slayers.

Having the ritual tea, we discussed our surnames. Mine apparently comes from the Suffolk river and hundred, Neil's – Catchpole – from a Norman tax collector who would take chickens in lieu of cash. Catch poule. Neil takes R.H. Reaney's *The Origin of English Surnames* out of my hands to see if I am making this up. Then we visit the fallen or cracked willows. How gaunt they are, one sporting a blackberry bush in its cleft. The last of the farming went on beneath them, the final harvest of Bottengoms, the last sheltering of the plough horses in their shade. On a hot day like this elder branches would be tucked around their tossing heads to see off the flies. Led to the pond below them, they would have gulped the world dry.

Neil's Birthday

A scorcher for Peter and Paul and their patronal at Little Horkesley. Who names this church? Meriel has brought me to it in a car which has the kind of mesh gauze fixed on some of its windows which meat safes were made of to keep the sun off her sleeping grandchildren. The boot is stacked with already arranged flowers for the altar. Bells clash through the lopped limes. The choir, all grown-up, refuses to robe saying that it might faint from the heat. I corral the minute congregation into the chancel, but when I emerge properly robed myself, it is to find that it has escaped back into its scattered pews. We sing, 'We love the place, O God' and I can smell mock orange and sweet peas. I talk about church dedications in the neighbourhood and we all go home to Sunday lunch through the quivering heat.

It is not only Peter and Paul's day, but also Neil the

woodman's birthday. He is forty-eight. So we all meet in his meadow by the river, the entrance to which is piled with tree trunks and logs. He has mown the meadow and set up shady pavilions, and we have lugged garden chairs, rugs and cushions to where a purple cord marks out the stage. There is a bravura display of sun hats and great anticipation, for although no curtain can go up we are about to watch a performance of *Much Ado About Nothing*. Nobody in Wormingford has ever celebrated such a birthday. Can the golden girls and boys, and the well-lunched old men in their boaters sit through it? Before they all come to dust? I stroll to the Stour to pass the time – all of twelve yards. The dressing-room tents heave with actors. I find a marvellous hollow ash, quite enormous about eight feet in circumference, a barkless theatre box. All around there are stands of teasel, the plant whose spiny seed heads were set in frames to tease out the wool before it could be spun into cloth whose profits in their turn were spun into wool churches. Behind me the groundlings loll impatiently in various stages of undress for the first sight of Leonato, Hero and Beatrice. Are we really about to see an entire Shakespeare full-length play down at Bowden's Farm? The hum is partly anticipation, partly incredulity. The curtain goes up. That is, Leonato steps over the hay and says, 'I learn in this letter that Don Pedro of Arragon comes this night to Messina.' Well, all five acts can only follow after this but there is something extra – Shakespearian in seeing one of his plays on a summer field, with Dogberry behaving like a lot of people we know, and the ladies sweeping about in their long skirts like bridesmaids after a wedding, and others having all the time in the world before them. Some players are memory perfect, others shamelessly read their parts. Claudio gets halfway minus a script then catches lines which appear to be written on the palm of his right hand. Hero's shocked collapse when she is told that she is a bad lot is worthy of the National.

'Done to death by a slanderous tongue indeed', and in Wormingford of all places. It is all strangely beautiful, strangely moving, this comedy in a meadow on Peter and Paul's day. Neil the woodman brings us birthday wine.

The Old Ladies Die

The silences of faith. 'There was silence, and I heard a voice saying, shall mortal man be more just than God?' (Job). 'I was dumb with silence'. (The Psalmist) 'There was made a great silence' (Paul, with a wave of his hand) and of course, 'There was silence in heaven about the space of half an hour'. (St John the Divine).

In the garden at Bottengoms. Total silence, according to most callers, though not so. What about the bullfinches, the Stanstead planes, the far tickety-tick of the Sudbury train, the poplars clapping their leaves, the water-splash, Elspeth's bees, a girl calling a horse, the yells from the playing-field, the sound of squirrels tumbling from bough to bough, and sometimes the mere whisper of a piece of history falling into place, and which Shakespeare called 'noises off'. I once tried to make a friend hear this kind of sound. He listened hard and said, 'Peter's onion-lifter'.

The old ladies continue to leave us, to our unutterable sadness. Funeral follows funeral. They leave such large spaces in a little church. They were girls hereabouts. The jolly undertakers carry them in and out of the chancel with grave faces then the shell from which their spirits have fled rides grandly off in a glass coach and the mourners go about the streets wondering what to do about lunch. One old lady, a Franciscan, has commanded us to sing the asterisked verse,

> And thou, most kind and gentle death,
> Waiting to hush our latest breath, Alleluya!

Yes, take away this asterisk, I say, for we need to get rid of the horrible 'terminal illness' and reinstate 'dying'. Let us sing our dying as our days run out. George Herbert sang his morning hymn on his death day. Hymns were paired. There was one for when you woke up and one for when you went to sleep. You sang them at your window.

I walk to the village shop and note the arable weeds, hedge mustard, mallow, traveller's joy. Someone in the shop asks me who wrote *Mehalah*? Answers on a postcard. Swinburne reckoned that it was as good as *Wuthering Heights*.

I tie-up wanton roses, Madame Alfred Carrière, Cardinal Richelieu, Leda, William Lobb who supports the oil-tank, and Duke of Wellington who supports the roof. Then to Mount Bures, which is heavy and drowsy with funeral flowers. Our little district nurse has gone to God and the door arch has been wreathed in the manner she used to wreath it, the blooms tracing its Decorated line. I preach on the Comforter and the handful of us do what we can with the *Veni, Creator Spiritu*s.

July

A July Agenda - Frail Children of Dust - A Trip to Taunton - Garrow at the Font - The Silent Village - John Clare at Stratford - Before the Coming of the Trees - Woodland Trust - The Summer Ploughman - Lewis Carroll at the Synod - Ricky and Titus - Helpston Pilgrimage - The Day we Walked to Stoke-by-Nayland - Say Love, not Charity - On the way to School - Idol hands - The Barley Harvest

A July Agenda

Having begged Jean to beg Mr Bradshaw to beg one of his men to cut back the sides of the farm track, I now rather wish I had not. Towering stands of thistle, ragwort and tansy all the way, forests of blackberry and jungles of wild parsley scintillating with glitzy insects of every kind, and all this rich muddle giving off that old, old smell of summer from boyhood. The young postman doesn't mind brushing his van through the tangle, in fact spins through it at such a rate that he can only glimpse a passing goldeness en-route. Friends are another matter. 'Your track . . .' they say. When trimmed just before harvest it returns to being a Saxon M5.

Off to Houds Farm for a PCC. Selina, Countess of Huntingdon endowed her chapel at Fordham with this farm. The chapel is now a nice cottage with a crop of tombstones in the front garden. How hard she toiled to bring Methodism to the upper classes, how nigh impossible it was for her to breed dissent in the squirarchy and among the peerage. So here we all are, a mostly non-dissenting dozen of us, at Houds once again, drinking either Harold's grape or Donald's elderberry, Pam in the chair and our papers in hand. We sigh over the business of the leaning churchyard wall - it has leaned like this since about 1880 and due, it used to be said, from the dead having a stretch - and we pass over the Interregnum and the House for Duty, but go all out for the creation of a 'Friends of St Andrew's', the success of the

Wormingford Cookbook and other fiscal matters. The Countess's farm parlour grows cosy with our resolutions as we listen to the tree-surgeon's report on the churchyard trees, dizzy pines and chestnuts planted by a Victorian priest but still as good as new, given a rain hole here and there and a bough fingering the tower. Grace is said.

Frail Children of Dust

A jack hare races before me, every sprint ending with a backward look of terror. How can I tell it that I am not hunting it, simply going its way? Ken reads about the lean kine and the fat kine at evensong. Must he read it all? Yes, because it is a story with a finish. It is an age since I last heard it, and what a tale! The Nile fails to irrigate the delta during what the *Book of Common Prayer* would call 'A time of dearth and famine.' Mighty rivers overflow or dry up and the river people pray for 'seasonal relief.' We pray for Bangladesh and its flooded folk. We sing 'Disposer Supreme' to 'Michael', an old French hymn by Jean de Santeul and this makes me wonder about the hero of Proust's unfinished novel *Jean Santeuil*. But soon I am concentrating on –

> Like clouds are they borne to do thy great will,
>   and swift as the winds about the world go;
> the Word with his wisdom their spirits doth fill;
>   they thunder, they brighten, the waters o'erflow.

A member of the John Clare Society rings me up to tell me that the poet's birthplace in Helpston is for sale. 'How much?' 'Nearly half a million.' And to think that his poor father paid the Michaelmas rent with apples. The house agent's board is by the plaque which Edmund Blunden unveiled in 1930. When Clare was made to leave this cottage for a far better one in the next village, his mind began to leave him. Should the Society put in an offer and turn Clare's home into a kind of Dove Cottage? There is irony in the question. Remembering the poem he had 'muttered' whilst ploughing, he would hide in his room under the thatch and write it down. Once, when it became too dark to see, he pushed a bit of thatch aside to let in the evening light.

The garden blazes with hyperican, St John's plant. Our ancestors thought that it was given a double dose of sunlight. Mourning his cousin's ghastly death, Jesus said that he was 'a burning and a shining light.' I have always believed that this bereavement caused Christ the worst suffering he had experienced as 'man'. He would have remembered how the crowds surged down to the river to stare at John, avid for sensation, and how he had rebuked them - they were there to *see* a prophet, not to listen to him. John had cried, 'Look who approaches, the Lamb of God!' How they stared then.

Dick arrives from the Ipswich company which looks after my well. It is what is called a spring-fed well and only Dick understands it. So welcome, welcome. He is large, calm and he has my Suffolk grandfather's voice. Our conversation is all about mud and flow, pumps and pressures, ladders and plugs. The huge round tank is uncovered and Dick descends. It is just like Herod's cistern into which that burning and shining light was let down and down. Or maybe a little like the other John's salt mine, a shaft so deep that he could look up and see Heaven. Dick makes a splash, gives a triumphant shout, finds 'the trouble', mends it and ascends. Both of us quite filthy, we eat bread and cheese. Later we walk to the back of the wood to take in the marvellous view and are waist deep in beans and nettles. 'I will put you on our computer,' he promises, 'and give you a look once a year.' Those who are on the mains know nothing of these joys and terrors.

A Trip to Taunton

The field edges are being cut for the combine to go in. I pick raspberries, holding up the laden canes to find them. Chagall horses stand still in the pasture, whisking away each other's flies. Then an outing to Taunton to present the Threshold Poetry Prize. They have all been printed and put into a book called *Elephant Pie and Monkey Love*, and what a sight all the poets were gathered together in one palatial school. Long ago, I told them, and not all that far from where we are at this moment, two young men walked the Quantocks at night making up poems, composing on the hoof, if you know what that means. Walking and walking, rhyming and rhyming, making it up under the Somerset moon. What were their names? Yes, Sam Coleridge and William Wordsworth. Those were the days. My six-to-elevens listened but when was I to get on with real genius, about *Monkey Love* and about *Johnny's Tiger*? I read all their poems aloud and parents burst with pride, and myself with enchantment. Earlier I had walked round Pitney to see old apple orchards and green lanes, and St Stephen Hardinge in the church window. He was the monk who drew up their 'Charter of Charity' for the

Cistertians in 1119. William of Malmsbury called him 'approachable, good-looking and cheerful in the Lord' and said that everyone liked him.

It would be hard to say what Bramfield, Suffolk called Mrs Applewhite when they read her tombstone for the first time. 'Between the remains of her brother Edward, and of her husband Arthur, here lies the body of Bridgett Applewhite, once Bridgett Nelson. After the fatigue of a married life, borne by her with incredible patience for four years and three quarters, bating three weeks, and after the glorious freedom of an easy and unblemished widowhood for four years and upward, she resolved to run the risk of a second marriage-bed, but DEATH forbad the banns, and having with an apoplectic dart (the same instrument with which he had formerly dispatched her mother) touched the most vital part of her brain he must have fallen directly to the ground (as one thunder-strook) if she had not been catch't and supported by her intended husband, of that invisible bruise, after a long struggle for above sixty hours with that grand enemy to life (but the certain and merciful friend to helpless old age) in terrible convulsions, plaintive groans or stupefying sleep, and without recovery of her speech or senses, she died on 12th day of September in the year of our Lord 1737 and of her own age 44 . . .' Epitaphs are an ancient literary form says the *Churchyards Handbook*.

Garrow at the Font

We baptise Garrow, that is Michael makes a watery cross on his brow and I read him a poem. The christening is wildly unpunctual due to there being Irish guests, including a Godfather who plays a tune on the flute. No, it is a tin whistle, and wildly musical it is. The church is cool and the churchyard is baking. Garrow is a year old and sports a rosary. He lolls on Michael's arm like a Florentine Christ-child, serene, forgiving, turning his full gaze on us as we applaud the tin-whistler. An uncle passes him to me to hold. I am astonished, having no idea that Christ-childs weigh a ton, well a stone. He stares past me, looks past all of us to see what only babies see. We all drift outside to talk among the graves, and Garrow passes from strong man to strong man, bringing them a mite of his holiness in turn. Over the churchyard hedge the lane rustles where the graves stop.

Back home the farmhouse is locked into its four hundredth July or thereabouts according to those who list such buildings. Its inhabitants came and went. 'Every exit is an entrance somewhere', says Tom Stoppard. Trapped butterflies are shown the door via a glass and postcard. Having to work on a short story, I get the lawnmower out, a mechanical job being the best jolt to the imagination. Garrow has gone home to cake and wine. Traherne is the singer of Infancy, a favourite word and state of his. 'He in our Childhood with us walks, And with our Thoughts Mysteriously He Talks.'

The Silent Village

A packet of family papers has arrived to prove that we have relatives at Kensal Green, in Kensal Green to be exact.

> For there is good news yet to hear and fine things to be seen,
> Before we go to Paradise by way of Kensal Green.

Irish writers are drawn to pubs, English writers to country churchyards, and real aficionados of the crowded place to cemeteries. When you think that the average old churchyard has been the scene of the greatest human sorrow for a thousand years, the most heartbreaking acre of a community, it is strange that one can walk through them and not feel upset. They contain both rare wild flowers and rotting cultivated flowers, noble monuments and naïve monuments. Here is a Victorian colonel with six names. Here is James, 'Jimmy' in brackets. Here lies Canon Smith, five up on the Incumbents' board, covered with stained marble chippings. Here is Terry, a schoolfriend, aged twelve, winged, half-naked, looking up, his small white feet perishing cold. Here is Somebody, Armiger, his name scrubbed out by two hundred years of rain. Here are all the neighbours whose funerals I took. Here are plastic sprays which are forbidden. The older stones are more literate than the latest stones and sometimes tell the reader what the dead man did, which is interesting. A little Gehenna of wreaths smoulders away by the tap. After awhile headstones lean over to talk to each other and footstones give way to the mower. Is it really twenty years since Joan went, since Mr Spicer stopped ringing?

Farming is going through a funny old time. A period like none other. During every previous agricultural recession the people looked desolate. But now, while bank balances might look starved, neither the farmers nor their fields show the least hardship. Vast machines take to the land twice a year, and that is that. Not a stroke of work otherwise. And no country voices except in cars and lounges. No fancy work to show off. No boys and girls at play outside, no swimmers in the river. Wormingford might be Hamelin at times, with all the young danced out of sight. Preparing a reading of John Clare's poems for Stratford-on-Avon, I am struck yet again by his faithful recording of noisy Helpston, its daily hubbub, his need to escape from it at times. The shouts, the songs, the animals, the curses, the games, the drunks, the wild life ever calling. Here the feeling is one of inertia rather than what is called by townees 'peace'. A jogger speaks into his mobile. In the school bus the pupils sit demurely like the painted passengers in a toy bus. But then, the concourse at Liverpool Street Station is a whispering multitude, a patter of gentle feet, thousands of them making no noise at all. Not nearly such a row as one of our drinks parties.

Clare at Stratford

The train drags to a halt in rural Oxfordshire so that I can gaze on as fine a patch of ragwort, fireweed and teasel as one could hope to find by a railway line. In fact it has been ragwort most of the way, this persecuted plant has found refuge in the railway system. The poet John Clare honoured it and seemed not to have heard about its horse-poisoning properties. He thought it burned 'so bright and glaring' that it paled the July sun. The young lovers opposite see nothing but each other. We part – for there has always been a strange relationship between fellow passengers, even if they do not exchange a word – at Stratford-upon-Avon where the wide streets are curiously quiet, considering they are filled with

Bees in a lily 1992

what at first glance seems a million walkers in search of Shakespeare. What a handsome town it is, a town from which a man might well rise in the world, should the fancy take him. The Avon so broad and smooth, so complete with swans and the two theatres peering into it, the trees so opulent, the church bells so used to drowning the camera clicks. And what journeys these pilgrims have made, these Shakespeare finders from every land. I peer down on them from the hotel window, and on the Guild Chapel opposite where he and his classmates trooped in daily for Reformed prayers. The old Dance of Death paintings would have been hiding under the whitewash. He remained canny on the subject of his own religion. How little we continue to know of him. To have written so much and for his life to have remained speculative to this scholarly day, well that is a kind of genius in itself.

To four baptisms and a Eucharist in his parish church on Sunday morning. It is packed. Daisy, Eleanor, Jack and Charlie are passed one by one into the motherly arms of the Reverend Jenny, not without some dismay, and join the Church. Is it not odd to be christened the diminutive of one's name? Just imagine the indignation on that spring day, and on this selfsame spot, had the glover and his wife insisted that their son should be baptised Bill. Or even Will. But now we have Prince Harry. I kneel before Shakespeare's grave to receive Communion. He looks over all our heads from his high position, quill in hand, and more like the local town clerk than the greatest author in the world. Before the chalice arrives I sneak a glance at the famous doggerel and wonder what bones *he* moved in order to claim such a coveted grave space. And how young he was to have retired from being a genius in order to become a gentleman – to climb down from Olympus so that he could loll comfortable-like in Chapel Street, Stratford. Outside, at noon, his words seem to pour through the universe. Small Japanese ladies have them on their lips. Tall German boys duck their heads in his bedroom.

And then to Marie Corelli's house to present another poet altogether – John Clare – but one who read deep into him.

Estelle Khiler and Michael Pennington from the Royal Shakespeare Company speak Clare's Words. They are closer to Shakespeare's than our words are to Clare's. During the interval I think of Marie Corelli and dip into her novels and imagine her butler creaking about her house, and her Venetian gondola being punted up the Avon. Clare, who always had his eyes about him when he left home, would have stared hard at Stratford-upon-Avon.

Before the Coming of the Trees

I am in seigneurial mood, having just been made patron of what will eventually be one of the largest new woods in Britain by the Woodland Trust. Alas, I will have long been with God before its trees could cast their shade on me. Or on the five hundred acres of Essex farmland which it will cover. Richard Mabey, Roger Deakin and myself walk the wide-open site in the July sun, following dusty tracks between the last potatoes, the last rape. Over three hundred thousand trees, tonnes of wild flower seeds, new grass, old birds, all are on the way. We have lunch at the Thatchers' pub, sitting outside in the suddenly not quite warm enough afternoon, taking in the great view, a cool breeze fanning our fish and chips, and mull over maps. The new forest-village, Fordham, is at this moment a mixture of ancient Saxon settlement, Tudor farms, Poundbury commuters and lovely sweeps of Colne Valley meadows. Soon, i.e. half a century, it will once more be what it was, a forest community.

We wander through the already emerging wetlands to the river itself, where I promptly trip over a wire and fall flat at the brink. An extraordinary sensation, to fall and then go on falling. And to bury one's nose in a river bank. And to be heaved up and dusted down and to say that one is all right when one is not at all all right. And people go on talking about trees, but not how they fall, either in parts or altogether, one great plant simply coming down to earth. I surreptitiously examine my ribs and touch my nose, wobbling it about to see if it crunches, and wipe off a bit of mud. 'Are you all right? asks Richard. 'Are you all right?' enquires Roger. They don't really care. They are saying, 'We hope that you aren't wanting to be taken home'. Victorian soldiers said, 'It is only a scratch, sir', to their colonels, before falling dead with a sabre cut. Then as fast as it took me to fall I am perfectly well again and we all three banish the horrid business from our minds. It will come back to me in bed, the dismissed ache, the nearly busted bone. But to get on.

The Colne is golden brown and studded with water lilies, and less than three yards across. And yet a dozen miles downsteam it is a tidal river which brought the Roman galleons up to Colchester. But here, marking the boundary of the forest to be, it is a stream waiting for Millais' Ophelia to spread herself in it. A blackcap sings in the medieval wood up the hill – Fiddler's Wood. Was there a Mr Fiddler? Or did the Fordham wives send their musician husbands to it to practice? Or did the fiddlers choose it for its nightingales, which like a bit of noise? Retracing our steps, we enter the ancient barn which has hoarded the hard-won crops from the forest clearings which we are about to plant with oak and ash. How dumbfounded the farmers would have been to know that one day the trees would be back, not stealthily in the form of suckers and natural seedlings, but with full ecological legitimacy. Nothing furtive. The corn barn is immense, still and weather-boarded, with seven bays. It is completely empty and the afternoon sun glitters through the knotholes and slats, turning the black walls into a kind of interior midnight with stars. There are chalk marks and scratchings where the last loads were totted up after the last harvest. Like so many East Anglian barns, it looks flimsy. Its doors are crumbling biscuits, its rafters are sticks. Yet it is woodland architecture at its most durable and will stand nobly in the new wood when it grows, maybe for five more centuries. All Saints Church stands companionably by, and Roger notes that the holiness of both buildings is enjoined. We may be living at a time when little is sacred but barns such as this speak of a time when everything was sacred. The latter was the time when patrons fell left, right and centre – if they didn't look out.

Woodland Trust

Liz, the Regional Development Officer from the Woodland Trust arrives and off we go to walk again the farm which will be a forest. The heatwave is blown blissfully around us by one of those southern winds which make heatwaves blissful. Pippen field, Silk Cobs, Ramson Pits, Muttone Meadow, Slatenways, all will soon disappear, along with many other fields and become Wrens' Wood. Wrens because the donor was in the WRNS. We lean on the new bridge over the Colne and watch sticklebacks and sand-dace darting across our reflected faces. The weed is the kind in which Thomas

Hardy's victims drowned, their hair dragging in the current. We can just about make out Colchester on its far hill, the sunbaked buildings from this distance might be in Eritrea. The Fordham acres are saying, 'What are you going to do with us?' So do some of the Fordham folk. Forests are not all trees we tell them. You will be able to see out. Already, left to their own devices, the only recently ploughed fields by the river are becoming marshland. Mace-reed is advancing across a once sugar-beet field like a pike regiment.

'Swithun' comes and goes with not a drip of rain. In church I tell them about John Keble, who nudges St Swithun in the Lectionary. There they are, side by side, the Saxon rainmaker and the modest author of 'New every morning', which we sing commemoratively. The hymn echoes school assembly before we settled down to the common task of maths. Keble College, Oxford is the patron of Mount Bures, our, I like to think without any evidence, especially sacred little church which Keble would have fitted into. The locals like people to fit in. When newcomers arrive they are supposed to fit in. But now the parishes are full of people who don't make the least effort to fit in and who don't know what fitting in means. It is all very awkward, not to say bad mannered. And then there are those who are too odd to fit in but don't know it, which is a blessing. They are held up as examples of local tolerance, even sophistication. 'It wouldn't do for us all to be alike,' they say, bending understanding to the limit. Writers and artists are not supposed to even try to fit in, and are best when outside in some kind of celebrity. John Keble accomplished two things, one of them sensational, the other as quiet as could be, the Assize Sermon at Oxford which fired-off the Tractarians, and a book of gentle meditations entitled *The Christian Year*. A small shy priest, he did not like Swithun have a struggle avoiding preferment, because only one came his way – the Archdeaconry of Barbados, which shows how daft the

Church of England can be when it tries. So he remained in his parish and wrote a handful of lasting hymns.

Untwining bindweed, I suddenly think how unpleasant it must be to be prayed for by the self-righteous. Though enough of this. Irritants are a concomitant of religion. Perhaps my presence in the big field irritates the skylark, and is thus the source of its song. My irritation is sudden and then gone. Should I sting, I am metaphorically rubbing a dock leaf on the source of my irritability before he has had time to close a surprised mouth. All is forgiven before he has worked out what to forgive.

The Summer Ploughman

Drenching days. Even when the rain stops the wind shakes torrents from the trees. Soaked animals are extra friendly so that they can share their sopping coats with me. Tall plants cannot hold up and the new ploughing shines with water. Having so often deplored farming inertia I am now suddenly quite excited by the ploughing of a field in July. It is the set-aside field which used to be Hilly Holt Land, Shoals, Ten Acres, Three Acres, Two Acres and so on to the hedge of Garnon's Chase. A vast multi-shared plough is lumbering up and down it and chopped hay is being folded into it like some pale addition to a rich dark mousse. It is real spectator stuff and the ploughman waves to his audience. But he must think me a lunatic to watch so.

At Diane's we eat bread and blackcurrant jam and watch

about a dozen chaffinches flashing about in her briar roses. Then we are off to Bures to open the Carnival. I sit beside Colonel Probert in his 1928 Rolls and he drives it very slowly behind the boy band. 'The trouble is, it will boil if we go too slow.' I am now a grand version of the ploughman, cabbed and waving to familiar spectators. Over the bridge we go, from Essex to Suffolk in slow seconds. A mile away, the new bridge is for walkers only. Some young men are dancing on top of the church tower, and bunting is drying out. I make a speech in the Playing Field then do what openers have to do, become a big spender. I buy a Jubilee mug and Sylvia Townsend Warner's life of T.H. White for a pound, a jar of pickled cabbage and a flutter of raffle tickets. Children shriek on the bouncy castle and a hopeful author nobbles me with his manuscript.

On Sunday a note left in the vestry by the vicar says, 'Bring large coloured umbrellas next Sunday as he intends to talk about St Swithun at the family service.' I preach on St Paul's inward voice telling him, 'First Jerusalem then Rome'. I imagine it raining on the sea at Aldeburgh, 'prinking the waves,' as Thomas Hardy put it. Paul has been shipwrecked on Malta where it too is being rained on, coming down for all it is worth in fact. The Maltese could not have been more welcoming. They rush around collecting sticks to make a nice fire, the apostle giving a hand. Only three days away lies the Italian coast which, of course, will be in bright sun. And gathering at Puteoli after walking the Appian Way will be the friends from Rome to meet him. 'Quo vardis, Paulus?' Whither indeed.

Lewis Carroll at the Synod

I am writing my umpteenth presidential address to the John Clare Society. Helpston, July 13th, the poet's birthday, is my favourite literary outing. I re-read him, make notes. Can I not repeat myself? If I do, will the members notice? If they do, will they forgive me? Soon I am in the great meadow of his language. It is now dried up and blazing hot. Sheets and pillow cases bleach on the lawn. Cats take cover, corn rustles and raspberries flop into colanders. After Clare comes – Swithun. Can I repeat my Swithun sermon? Will they notice?

They have Lewis Carroll's confession of faith in the Diary column of *The Independent*. He tells his friend, 'I am a member of the Church of England, and have taken Deacon's Orders, but did not think fit (for reasons I need not go into) to take Priest's Orders. My dear father was what is called a "High Churchman", and I naturally adopted those views. But I doubt if I am a full "High Churchman" now. I find that as life slips away (I am over fifty now) and the life on the other side of the great river becomes more and more the reality, of which *this* life is only a shadow, that the petty distinctions of the many creeds of Christendom tend to slip away as well – leaving only the great truths which all Christians believe alike. More and more, as I read of the Christian religion as Christ preached it, I stand amazed at the forms men have given it, and the fictitious barriers they have built up between themselves and their brethren . . .'

The general Synod sits and its members will be passing to and fro in the Yorkshire sun. From this distance they are like figures in the margins of the Book of Kells or, more geographically, in the Lindisfarne Gospels, hierarchic and ordinary at the same time, pointing to words. Perhaps they will have a moment to be like figures from *Alice*. 'I wish I

241

could manage to be glad!' the Queen said. 'Only I never remember the rule. You must be very happy, living in this wood, and being glad whenever you like!' But then, as we know, when the Queen was Alice's age she had been able to believe in 'as many as six impossible things before breakfast', and that is not a recipe for joy.

I finish my John Clare address, which is about flowers becoming weeds and fields turning into tyrants, and about toil and loneliness, and then find hymns for Swithun. *Lamentations* may be read, I see. The sad singer in this book ends his song with, 'Turn thou us unto thee, O Lord, and we shall be turned, renew our days as of old'. John Clare was usually in the woods or by the River Nene on Sundays, hiding away to write, turning away from Glinton church spire not because of any quarrel with God but because the girl he loved, but who was forbidden him, lived near it. Unable to be her friend, he made her his Muse.

Ricky and Titus

Dawn, Sunday morning. I can hear Fergal Keane talking about water and larks, also the telling silence of starving cats. The windows are wide and the curtains are waving to the valley. In Perthshire, seen by me once a year yet seen all the time, the cold burns will be running down to Loch Rannoch and the sheep will be complaining on the hills. The radio runs out of Fergal Keane and into farming. My disordered thoughts now turn to Thursday and the long bus-ride to the cathedral. Old men get on at Sudbury, holding out their fare money like children to the young driver. 'Return to Bury Hospital, old mate.' The fields in which my grandfather worked appear and disappear in the landscape. Some forty at a guess swans have climbed out of the river near Andrew's house to take up monumental positions on the Croft, which isn't a farm but a grassy slope on which also sits a stone Saxon bishop, his back to the churchyard wall. The bishop looks east, the swans look everywhere, their orange gaze turning in all directions. Old ladies are set down precisely at their cottage gates by the boy driver. 'You all right?' Not at all all right, but then who is? At Bury I run through a squall to the Chapter House.

Later, Ricky arrives from the next village to fix the new cooker, accompanied by his wife. The old cooker would catch the wondering glance of friends and even I, fond of it as I was, could hardly not be aware of its antiquity. It would take its time to warm up and when it did there would be not only the smell of the present meal, but of meals long ago. Two plates no longer heated and recently the oven door fell off when guests were present. What a tale to tell the neighbours. Ricky unhitches this emeritus cooker and bumps it out into the garden, reassuring me that it is 'going to a cooker heaven where it will be this size' – his hands shaping a brick. 'It is off to the squasher', explains his wife. We have some tea and admire the new cooker, black and grey and opulent. We talk about their son who is a Black Belt at thirteen. We talk about the need for rented property in their village so that young couples don't have to emigrate to the town. At seven the new cooker produces its very first dinner, grinning blackly, and with alarming speed. It is facing the great brick structure in which for centuries a joint would twizzle or a pot would dangle. Their smoky odours would bring men and children galloping in from the farmyard. Ricky presses an instruction book into my hands with earnest insistence that I should read it. The new cooker gives me a glassy wink.

But Titus. Discovering him between Timothy and Philemon, I remember Joseph Poorgrass in *Far from the Madding Crowd* - 'And I was sitting at home looking for Ephesians, and I says to myself, "'tis nothing but Corinthians and Thessalonians in this danged Testament," when who

Butterfly rasping across the floor

should come in but Henry there: "Joseph", he said, "the sheep have blasted their selves".' No such disaster interrupts my reading of Titus, the letter in which the birth of Church organisation begins to emerge, the titles of 'elder' and 'bishop' at that moment being felt for rather than grasped. Titus has been sent to Crete to ordain elders. They are to have the unenviable job of rebuking 'sharply' their own countrymen, famous as they are for being 'liars, evil beasts and slow bellies'. A bishop, goes on Titus, must be a lover of hospitality, a lover of good men, sober, just, holy and temperate. He himself became the first bishop of the difficult

Cretians and his see ran from Nicopolis to Macedonia, a vast area. I imagine him in his ship, dipping and weaving his way through the Aegean, youthful, austere.

Helpston Pilgrimage

A day never to be missed when the John Clare Society descends upon his village, Helpston, the centre of everything he cared for. Like an insurer against such evils and misfortunes that may come, the poet put his own price on what Helpston contained for him, right down to trampled grass and fragmented birds' nests. One loves what one touches, smells, knows intimately. Thus Alan, Jane and I drive through the early morning counties of Essex, Suffolk and Cambridgeshire as we have done many times, past toadflax, paper-boys, dogs giving their masters an airing, country shops at opening time, flags saying something on church towers, tousled women opening gates, flowering potato fields, table-level corn, notices to fayres and flower festivals until, quite suddenly, having skirted Peterborough, here we are where Clare walked.

This year my presidential address is on 'The Poet and the Nest'. Afterwards we lunch at the Blue Bell pub where Clare worked as a lad. Then we go to the Exeter Arms to have some beer in the room where he lay in his coffin, and in a kind of state with his face looking up through a small glass window let into the oak, the famous son brought back to his parish for burial after all those sad years in the Northampton madhouse, his name for it. After which we cross to the churchyard to stand by his lozenge of tombstone on which is written 'A Poet is born, not made' and around which lies a carpet of midsummer cushions made by the Helpston children, flower heads stuck in turfs. Lichens soften and obscure the lettering. Nearby lie his parents, 'the Lame man' and his wife, and his twin sister, though her grave is now lost. A boy tugs his mother's attention to his midsummer cushion and she says, 'Very nice, dear'. All over the churchyard we see the pact which limestone has with botany. I look for the stone of Mr Gregory, the landlord of the Blue Bell who gave Clare various tasks, fetching flour, ploughing a little bit of land, cleaning the pub. There he is, young for death. And then my annual homage to Royce Wood where John Clare, scarcely daring to breath, came close to a sitting nightingale and wrote the great 'Nest' poem which Ted Hughes read at Westminster Abbey when we put Clare into Poets' Corner. No nightingales on this July afternoon, only unidentifiable bird cries as I crackle through the blackberry bushes. At Westminster Abbey we sang Clare's unsettling hymn 'A stranger once did bless the earth' in which he sees Christ as 'An outcast thrown in sorrow's way' to 'Surrey' by Henry Carey, Ted, myself and a muster of writers from all over. I could see my midsummer cushion, a turf from Bottengoms Farm stuck with Stour Valley flowers, and a surprising weight on the train. Ted unveiled the memorial. It was next to Matthew Arnold's. The sculptor had made play with his name and placed a sprig of clary (Salvia verbenaca) in a bird's mouth, unaware that it means clay, and I had written the inscription. Clare himself, in a tragic moment, had ordered a kind of milestone for his grave on which was to be inscribed, 'Here rest the Hopes and Ashes of John Clare'.

The Day we Walked to Stoke-by-Nayland

Michael and I sit at the kitchen table allocating harvest festivals in a lordly way. The three congregations will as ever be divided up between those who knew what it was like to bring in the harvest and those who have never clapped eyes on them – the real harvests, that is. The back-breaking, triumphant cutting and stacking of the corn, the brutal clubbing or shooting of the rabbits and hares as they fled from the ever decreasing shelter, the great annual accomplishment of beating the weather, the classic tiredness and celebration. On the sideboard the old clock chimes just as it did in France when Millet was painting *The Angelus*. It keeps poor time, often no time at all, but its enamelled face shines, and painted cherubs continue to knock out a good tune on their tambourines. 'Is that the time?' ask friends, panic-stricken. Our labours accomplished, Michael and I close our diaries. Outside, the garden reaches for the sky. The hill opposite is grass where it would have been corn. Corn for ages. I am now enclosed in meadowland and have to take quite a walk to see barley. The damp summer has brought luxuriating ditches full of meadowsweet and cresses, stately hogweed and teasel through which running water glitters. The rain has gone now and the days are fair.

After lunch Alan and I wander up Gravel Hill to Stoke-by-Nayland. Here the intensely blue alkanet is in flower and greenfinches accompany us, swooping and going chup-chup-chup. The tremendous tower of Stoke-by-Nayland church comes and goes in the hilly landscape, now you see it, now you don't. Now it is a hundred feet high, now just pinnacles.

We pass the elm – the one which has mysteriously survived the elm death. It looks abashed at being such a rarity and is reminding itself of the time when men assessed it for coffin wood and floorboards. 'I'm a common tree', it insists. We stand looking up at it. Soon we are standing under Stoke tower, gazing up and up at the perfect muddle of its materials, orange bricks, grey flints, sarsons, any old thing which came to Tudor hand. It is rubble raised to glory. John Constable, Cedric Morris, John Nash, Alfred Munnings, all painted it, and Suffolk boys all climbed it to find out if it was true that one could see 'Harwich water' from the top.

Say Love Not Charity

'Please read 1 Corinthians 13', requests the new widow, 'but say love, not charity'. Summer rain soaks the mourners and the churchyard birds sing a littler louder, as they do in a downpour. In his letters to the wild Corinthians Paul needs to stress what love actually is – needs to use all his literary power to show its transcendence over everything else. *Caritas.* He peers at what we can only humanly make out where our future is concerned and sees dark shadows for the time being. Never mind: one day it will be face to face! Total clarity, full recognition of ourselves and of God. The funeral is for John, who was no age at all and who played squash and whose face shone.

On the train to Devon via a million bull-daisies. They sway elegantly in the suddenly moving air. Thunder-daisies they are called in the west. Youthful friends sit opposite, reading and half-smiling with caritas. He is reading *The Gramophone* and, without looking up from the page, he grins widely as she teases him. I read *What Maisie Knew,* which of course was far too much for a teenager. As we hurtle through Dawlish I can see people behaving as though it was 1880, making sand-castles, dashing back from the slapping waves, giving happy shrieks. If only Maisie could have given Society the slip and paddled at Dawlish and watched the trains go by. Could have bought an icecream for that bare young man with his dog. However, what would have become of the plot?

At Dartington I sign-in at the 'Ways with Words' literature festival and then make straight for the grand garden, the kind which Henry James admired and believed to be one of the proofs of English civilisation. Terraces, statues, herbaceous borders of an heroic nature, glimpses of distant moor and river, flight of steps, a medieval tiltyard, oak gates which go clunk and in the far distance – Cornwall! Literary folk pass to and fro, nodding kindly. I have to talk on the literary nature of the sermon. *Sermo* = talk. *Pulpitum* = platform. Talk from a platform. Although to be precise I tend more to read than to talk from Wormingford pulpit, breaking into my prose now and then with asides which have just occurred to me. I have little idea what preaching means. It sounds too professional for me to try to do. I shrink from the memory of the confident preachers of my boyhood, their passion, their stirring it up. But mother would return home, elated, thrilled, their words ringing in her ears.

On the way to School

Nervously filling in the time before seeing the dentist, I re-walk the way I went to school in the Suffolk country town. So much having changed, I imagined I would pass sites and developments, the usual thing. But there they still were, the cottages-turned sweetshops, the modest terraces, the cuts and alleys, the pubs on the corners, the monkey puzzle trees, the letter-boxes with V.R., the doorways, the coping stones where we sat and swung our legs. I could hear, though this time in my head, the clang of the shop bells on the C-springs which brought Miss Scott, haunted, silent, unwelcoming to serve us boiled sweets, or Mrs Gilder, a floury Juno, to hand us doughnuts. Miss Scott carried the exactitude of weights and measures to the limit and would, they said, have halved a toffee. Mrs Gilder knew nothing about weights and measures but everything there was to know about hungry children and sent us off with more than we durst expect or could have paid for. Both ladies in their neighbouring shops emerged from inmost shrines in their premises, the curtained rooms which Thomas Hardy described as 'penetralia'. How enormous they seemed as they leaned towards us over the tiny counters, huge Alices bearing down on their child customers, Miss Scott without a word, Mrs Gilder with her 'dears'. She had two floury sons and a kind heart, and is without a doubt in paradise.

And there is where the blacksmith's should have been but a new road has pushed it over, and there is the Patty-man's shop, so small, however did he get into it. He had a double life as potato-cake seller and town crier. The handsome Suffolk white-brick terrace where the sweep lived, and the Miss Willises, 'Dressmakers' on a swinging card, did their expert business, has come up in the world, and would not be below the consideration of the local commuters. The Miss Willises were identical twins who wore seasonal weights of the same clothes, tweed in winter, silk and serge in summer, black woollen stockings and strap shoes. A single bow or raised hand did for the pair of them. They grew pansies and ferns and went to Evensong, and would measure you up as soon as look at you. At home they wore pin and needle necklaces and knew the size of every woman for miles. Silent now their Singer, vanished their twinned decorum. The pity would be, they said, that one must outlast the other. But not for long. If a school cap was raised to them there would be a double Mona Lisa smile, fleeting, transforming. Not so Miss Baker at Pont's Palings – the artist Dupont, Gainsborough's handsome nephew, had lived there – she would croquet conkers at us through the iron rails with unbending skill but never a smile. For her the lovely horse chestnut which dominated her street garden was an annual penance demanded of her by God. She shrank from boys and wondered why they had been made and turned her face from us as she batted us conkers. 'I hope you were polite to Miss Baker', our mothers would say. What else could we be? There was a time when every country town was an armistice of old women and cautious lads, with neither side caring to come too close.

The dentist is pleased with me and praises my brushwork, and I am grateful to him, for he has in the past worked mighty things for me, giving me, as he said, a good smile. We talk of his Scottish home. Then I continue my home-town tour by walking to the river, from which fifty or more swans have landed to sit on the Croft, waving their necks and fixing humanity with swivelling eyes. By the church wall, very upright, sits a Saxon bishop who died here in A.D.791. He is worn and lean. A mitre topples on his brow as he tugs a warm cloak around his slight frame. Just behind him in St Gregory's vestry, ghastly in its niche, is the decapitated head of Archbishop Simon Sudbury, murdered during the Peasants' Revolt. The Stour slides under the bridge, green, blue and glassy. And there we are, or were, ages ago, with our white feet in the water as we gorged on Mrs Gilder's buns.

Back to Wormingford. I have to choose ten pieces of music for Michael Berkeley's Radio Three programme *Private Passions*. No easy matter. Some Bach, some Schubert, some Britten, a great hymn sung by a cathedral choir, some *Belle Epoque* songs, Butterworth, Couperin . . . John Wilbye . . . Ella Fitzgerald . . . my friend Peter-Paul Nash? Books and CDs pile up. The trouble is that I will have to enthusiastically justify these choices when I meet Michael. There is music which one can remember hearing for the very first time and there is music which seems to have got into one's head prior to memory itself. The music of the spheres, maybe. Totting-up my choice, it adds to twenty, so who to throw out? It is agonising. This is where the private passion comes in. Hildegard von Bingen's passion only for Christ fills the kitchen. *O ignis Spiritus Paracliti*, sing the Benedictine ladies, their voices winding like white swans' throats. 'The structure of Vespers is used in a plausible context' reads the label. In bed I listen to the stream splashing and the valley owls calling as they low-fly where the mice run for their lives.

Idol Hands

A neighbour shows me his grandfather's chair. It stands gauntly by the telly, a worn rebuke to the viewing sofa. The chair has two simple wooden arms, one of which is a mere sliver of its earlier self due to grandfather whittling away on it after work. He carved dolls, catapults, Noah's Ark animals, walking sticks - 'Anything you fancied', says the neighbour. I am reminded of Gabriel Oak's proposal to poor young Bathsheba Everdene in *Far from the Madding Crowd*. There they are the pair of them, in their twenties with the world before them, and he is telling her that after they are married he will be whittling away, as it were, by the fire of an evening, and 'whenever you look up, there I shall be – and whenever I look up, there will be you'. He promises her lots of babies and that he will learn to play the flute. Music, constancy, children, what more can a farmer's wife want? She is not able to tell so she turns him down flat. For she sees all too plainly how soon the young husband by the hearth will be the old man by the hearth, whittling on the arm of his chair to the end of his life, his muddy boots drying in the fender.

Isaiah would not have minded the carpenter carving toys and pretty things for the house when his work 'proper' was done, for craftsmen cannot sit still. What worried the prophet was where imaginative, as against utilitarian craftsmanship could lead to. So he takes a carpenter and a blacksmith to task. They are an essential part of the economy but what happens when they are tradesmen by day and artists by night? Is there not danger when the maker of useful objects, in his spare time, is able to make purely aesthetic objects? And this at night! Table and chairs and horseshoes and pots and pans, hinges and nails, yes. But supposing the same skills go into creating a carved man or a metal man?

Supposing, like Gormley's *Angel of the North*, a man copies his own divine form – models for what is his own personal image of his Maker, then what? The old Jews had made the huge discovery of there being but one God, whereas all around them 'gods' proliferated and had, being so many, to be made recognisable by images of them, thus requiring the services of those who knew how to fashion wood and metal. Moses, as soon as he had met a recognisable one God, hastened to make all 'other gods' unrecognisable. 'Do not make graven images because, if you do, you are bound to lend them some of my holiness (wholeness), and thus revere what you have made.' Isaiah would beseech the blacksmith and the carpenter to stick to their trades, and why? It was because he knew that they had the skills to go further, skills to move on to what is sacred or what we call art.

Isaiah traces wood right back to its first usefulness and its first appearance as art. He says that man begins by being a forester, using mighty trees for fuel - 'Aha', says man, 'I am warm, I have seen the fire'. He then sits by it when his work is done and, seeing a bit of wood lying about, whittles away at it with his knife. He thinks of his own or his wife's – or his calf's form – and shapes it. How beautiful it is, this carving. He places it on a shelf and, well, you know the rest.

Barley Harvest

Dashing from one matins to the next, Diana's small car hurrying round the big bend of Sandy Hill, I am suddenly reminded of a thrilling cry from childhood, 'They are cutting at Wilson's!' Because there on the right is a freshly mown barley-field, level as a new carpet. Its gold beats against the windscreen and burnishes our faces. Only the old thrill to the news of 'They have been cutting!' To that old excitement of the first cut, to that heady confusion of hard work and play which was 'harvest'. The barley fields can have long stalks for thatchers but mostly they are short-stalked with top heavy heads. They hiss and gently rattle with elfin applause. So much barley this year. It cancels the lines where the hedges were and ignores parish boundaries. On and on, it is barley where ever you look. Make the most of such a wavering sight because next year it could be beet. Years ago there would have been a rush to make the first loaf from it for Lammas – Loaf Mass in the early English church, celebrated in thanksgiving for the harvest – on the first of August. Barley has grand antecedents in scripture. Christ's own family first took root in a barley field when farmer Boaz fell in love with the widowed girl he had allowed to glean. And it was barley loaves which fed the five thousand, symbolically satisfying the world's spiritual hunger. The barley at Bottengoms is delicately harsh to the touch as I trail my fingers through it. Who will see the reaping of it next week? No one. Who would have watched it grow? The contractor and myself. Who will miss it when it has gone as we once did a summer cornfield? No one.

The fields of Bottengoms Farm were once in the kingdom of Cymbeline or Cunobeline or Old King Cole who reigned just up the road. His coins surface now and then, each stamped with an ear of barley. The Romans went on using this emblem, for what better sign on a penny than one which spelled bread? This king was contemporary with Jesus.

Light rains fall on the waiting barley field, too light to soak it or to darken the dusty surface of the soil to any extent. Summer rain which dimples the river and makes the wilting growth sit up a bit. It continues to past midnight and falls on me when I shoo a bat from the house. July creatures are apt not to know where they belong when windows and doors are wide open. I walk in it to the edge of the field where the barley is counting the hours. Farmers – what are left of them – commuters, broken up for the summer holidays children, Marcia from the shop, the vicar and his family, are all abed. And here I am, barley, come to visit you with a little of the old thankfulness.

August

Sandlings Flowers - Crowded Days - Rain, Rain - Elecampane - Ivor Gurney - The Way to Akenfield - At Hadleigh on John Newman's Birthday - Recollecting Barbara Pym - Job and Ely - The Applicant - Woodcuts - The Shutter Falls - The Big Green at Mellis - Another Water-side Party - Looking Out - Rat Run - Son of Tolmai - The August Dragonfly - A Voyage

Sandlings Flowers

To Westleton to give a talk at the Wild Flower Festival. It is one of those wide to the skies villages on the Suffolk sandlings with a broad green, a white windmill, an airy church and a whiff of the North Sea. The wild flowers make a shy show and unlike most such exhibitions there is a touch of reticence. These grasses and blooms from the local fields and ditches invite us to get to know them - to actually *see* them as we see only a few of them, primroses, bluebells, etc. Wild violets are one thing, *Mentha aquatica* another. Wood dwellers, marsh dwellers, one group is eye-catching, one holds back. The annual Westleton Wild Flower Festival brings an entirely little noticed flora to the fore. It speaks to us from unambitious arrangements and in a mixture of learned and simple tongues.

The pulpit having been turned into a thicket, I take my stand on a carpeted dais. In front, dear familiar faces and unknown faces. After which a long drive home with a retired Baptist pastor from the Forest of Dean. So of course we talk about Dennis Potter. 'I would like to ask the people of the Forest of Dean not to be too offended about some of the things I have to write . . .' he said in his first book. It is something which most local authors ask. Potter said that the Forest of Dean was 'an important part of my own life' and that he was 'alternately attracted and repelled by it, rarely unaware of its power'. Here again we have the 'home' writer's dilemma. Readers like their regional books to be a paean of praise.

I take Margaret's funeral at Wormingford. Her son Barry has written her life story for me to read. How well I know it, having seen what she saw, heard what she heard, walked where she walked. We lower her into the grave on the eve of the Transfiguration and the bell-ringers rock the tower.

Crowded Days

Blissful summer rain. It falls straight down like a hissing curtain, and is too good to miss. I stroll about the garden in it and it softly sticks clothes to flesh. The stream finds it all too much and chokes its way to the river. Sopping wet squirrels start nutting. It is very hot and every now and then the horizon shudders with lightning. I hip-hop from task to task, finishing nothing. Then I sit in the open doorway and read a novel. It is Colm Tóibín's *The Master*, an exercise in walking where angels fear to tread, and quite marvellous. There are times when holding back can take one straight to the truth.

Then to the little thatched chapel of St Stephen at Bures to give an address to the magnificently named Guild of the Servants of the Sanctuary: Chapter of St Felix and St Fursey from St Edmundsbury Cathedral. This Chapel is faintly visible from the back of Bottengoms, an historic smudge on the hillside. The guild has lit it with a hundred candles and misted it with incense. The De Veres lie all around on their grand tombs, hands together, feet on alabaster animals, countesses by their sides, vetting our Latin.

Rain, Rain

Wet Augusts raise terrors in the farming mind. It is now over a century since the great rains washed away British agriculture, flooding its poor labourers into the towns and out to the Empire, reducing the fields to what the land agents called 'sporting interests.' Yet the memory of this disaster floats into the consciousness of rural England whenever it 'comes down', as they say. As it is doing at this moment, coming down for all it is worth. The papers call it climate change now.

My neighbour John who has the loveliest fields in Wormingford, with their surprising heights in what is popularly known as a flat country, has given me the obituary of a farmer who died in 1930. This obituary is in the form of one of his fields saying farewell as the cortege passed, the coffin on a flowery wagon, the Suffolk punches be-plumed.

'I have been a field for nigh on a thousand years, and I know men. Some are clever, some are kind, but very few are clever and kind, but he was, and I am sorry that all the other fields of England - who need him so much in these days - will have to go on without him.'

Sunday afternoon was visiting time for a field. I have no idea how to introduce our many newcomers to a neighbouring field. 'Swallings, Stony Hollow, meet Mr and

Mrs Commuter. Have a word with them about your long life. Tell them not to mind the water in the ruts. Let them on a better day find a fresh view from your headlands.'

Contrary to what might be expected, the cat likes a bit of rain. She is in fact a weather cat and given to long spells of contemplation by the waterfall of a blocked gutter, watching it for hours, enjoying its sound. I find her now and then drinking from the brook like a lion, delicately poised on a stone, lapping deliciously, looking sideways for elephants. Should it bucket down she will often prefer a rainproof shrub to a dash inside the house, somewhere where she can smell and taste the downpour without being soaked. The horses too, one of them in genteel retirement from Newmarket, allow the rain to shoot from their shiny backs. I was about to find time for the Apostle Bartholomew but he was rained out. Bartholomew, son of Tolmai, what can you tell us?

Elecampane

More so than for any other approaching change of season, Autumn lays down the odours of its time. With almost a month of summer still in hand, not to mention Luke's and Mark's supplements to it, on this August day I catch a whiff of rotting foliage as the butterbur leaves fall flat on their faces and grow black. The seven a.m. morning is a mite sharp and at seven p.m. migrating birds line up on the wires. Between these hours I am digging up Elecampane from the flower-beds and planting it where it really belongs, among the wild flowers. George Herbert would have grown it in his physic garden as it was said to cure everything, asthma, the hip-gout, worms, the plague and was able to 'quicken the sight'. Geoffrey Grigson admired it. It would, he said, 'outlast house or garden'. It was certainly good horse medicine up into living memory, this and comfrey. Once it takes root in some fanciful flower-bed, no plant could be more confident. It towers up handsomely and spreads luxuriantly, halting those who are not familiar with it in their tracks. Might they have a bit? East Anglians who went to New England were careful to take it with them – maybe from Bottengoms Farm. I can envisage the check-list before the wagon set off for the coast. Feather-beds, the pewter, the Holy Bible, the seed-corn, the spinning-wheel, grandmother's chest, the dogs, the children – and the Elecampane! It rules the Massachusetts and Maine highways to this day, this beneficent sunflower which will still be thriving back home at Wormingford when my house is no more than a stain in a field. So I enter *Inula helenium* into my Wild Flower Society register with a flourish. Who needs the National Health Service?

This mid-August Sunday I preach on Sufficiency and Limitation. The first, says St Paul, is of God, who reminds us that there is such a thing as enough. Enough sense, enough to eat, enough everything. 'Not that we are sufficient of ourselves to think anything of ourselves', adds the apostle witheringly. Meaning that God alone has our full dimension. Christ could be enigmatic, daunting generations of interpreters. Sometimes his words run through human history as clearly seen as pebbles in a brook, sometimes they are puzzles. Do not be too worried regarding such obscurities, Paul told the Corinthians. They were to become ministers of the *spirit* of Christ, not followers laying down the letter of his law, 'For the letter killeth, but the spirit gives life'. Theology was being warned.

We drive back from Matins among the grain trucks. The Gliding Club is winging about the blue sky and could be seeing prehistoric grave circles in the stubble. I have called banns for those who did not come to hear them, have said some ancient prayers and some of my own, have put the brass cross away, put down the collection in the register and observed the first dead leaves of autumn chasing each other along the path. And now I shall sit on the garden seat and read Peter Ackroyd's *Blake* and drink sherry. 'Ah, Sun-flower! weary of time, Who countest the steps of the Sun . . .'

Ivor Gurney

A single bloom of my rare Anne of Denmark carnation has opened. It is a flopper and must be lifted up and staked. Its scent over-powers me, as it over-powered the smelly gorgeous gowns which Anne wore. Carnations flower but once a year and then are gone but their scent hangs around in my head for ever. The Child and his Mother in the Raphael are drowning in Pink perfume. It is said that carnations began to be neglected from the 1850s on and some of its varieties vanishing then. Might this not have been due to improved hygiene? But cottage gardens remained full of pinks. I sit on a little wall and sniff my incomparable Anne of Denmark without picking her, as half a dozen more buds cling to the one which has opened. Flowers are among the more direct experiences which we share with our forebears. Mowing the lawn, I carefully miss a corner filled with dandelions and tall grasses because it is exactly as Breughel painted it.

I am writing an essay for the *Ivor Gurney Society Journal*. It is a year overdue and its editor Kelsey Thornton has – quite properly – borne down on me, he must be six foot-six, to ask, 'What about it?' The procrastination of authors is shocking. I imagine the Chief Musician of the Temple bearing down on David and wailing, 'But you promised me a new psalm last Nissan,' and the dilatory poet-king guiltily shutting himself away to compose 'O sing unto the Lord a new song'. Ivor Gurney belongs to the asylum poets, those terribly sane voices which sang from the madhouse. For it would be their songs alone which would continue to contain the sense. Much of what Gurney said outside his 'song' was 'disturbed', as they called it. Gurney had the city-dweller's vision of the surrounding countryside, his city being Gloucester, and it is quite unlike a villager's picture of the land. It is a distinction which is not sufficiently understood by those who separate town and country.

Ivor Gurney was born in 1890, the son of a tailor of Gloucester. A local clergyman guided him into the sumptuous sphere of Victorian Church music. His student friends were Herbert Howells and Arthur Benjamin, and their teachers were Charles Stanford and Vaughan Williams. But in 1915 it was the Western Front and in 1922 it was the City of London Mental Asylum at Dartford, Kent, an inevitable conclusion for many young men driven insane by war. From Gurney's boyhood until his death on the feast of Stephen 1937 there had been genius and confusion, long walks by night, poverty and uncertainty, odd jobs – and a great sequence of music and poetry. He was truthful when he said, 'There are bright tracks where I have been'. I follow his tracks in the Cotswolds, in London, in the trenches, in the bin, and bright they remain. When Helen Thomas, widow of Edward, visited Gurney in the asylum she brought with her her husband's maps of Gloucestershire, spreading them out on the bed, and guiding Ivor Gurney's finger along the lanes he had once walked, and seeing him smile once more as he recognised 'home'.

The Way to Akenfield

Barefoot at dawn during the heatwave. The garden is seeding and tall. I water the cucumbers then the onions, carrying pails from the stream's overflow. How the Israelites lusted after these vegetables, and so would I have done given their parched land and diet. All the same, I am one with God in his dislike of complainings and whinings. He had given his people manna and they longed for – cucumbers. Mine are doing well. They glisten on the earth and are gathered with a gentle severing twist. I weed them after breakfast, take up new potatoes and listen to the old battery Hacker. Moist dirt and grass clippings pack my toes. The pigeons call to Mozart. Overhead, silver crosses steer to Stanstead with only a faint noise when they approach my trees. Bernard's harvester begins to thump and the horizon to shake.

Later, we drive to Charsfield. How could it have got so hot in four hours? It is an auction of promises outing and I have promised to lead half a dozen parishioners round the scrap of Suffolk which I called 'Akenfield'. Here is my old farmhouse by the edge of the Roman road, there is my study window squinting over my hedge. Alas, all the elms have gone, the elms that made it so beautiful, which gave it a little grandeur. The house looks depleted, less than it was. We cannot slow down because of all the traffic behind us, so seventeen years of habitation are over before one can say knife. We visit Peggy Cole, the doyenne of our village life, in her famous garden where fruit and veg and flowers and grass flourish in the old cottage order. We walk her ruler-straight paths and see that everything is better than anything we can do. Her husband Ernie Cole and myself were churchwardens at St Peter's several heatwaves ago. 'Several' in Suffolk-ese is a non-committal number. 'Were there many there?' - 'Several'. The church has a fiery-red Tudor brick tower on a medieval flint and stone base on which the Virgin's monogram is let in, an elegant crowned M.R. I slip away to call on the dead, Ocean the gipsy woman, Peter who helped me with the hay. Across the lane the children buzz in the school like bees, and the playground bakes.

On we tour to Hoo, for me the simplest, most sacred building in my personal guidebook, rubble walls, Early English windows, more Tudor bricks, an altar like an hospitable tea-table, a brick floor like a larder. I take a look (as he would have said) at Mr Buckles' grave. He was a devout farmworker who 'lost himself' in scripture and who would suddenly pause as he read the Lesson, looking up to explain, 'That was very fine, I'll read that again'. His wife would pack half a dozen eggs into my bicycle basket and say, 'Well, come again but not too soon'. And so on to ducal Framlingham Castle from which Mary I rode to unseat poor Lady Jane Grey, to stroll round the walls between the candy-twist chimneys and stare down at the deep dry moat. I am accompanied, not only by the promise-winners, but also twenty years of residency in these parts and people they would never know.

It is the weekend of the Transfiguration, enchanting, inexplicable, convincing. All these things. Upon the mountain the full glory of Christ. Down below the complete humiliation of some of his followers as they attempted to miracle-heal an epileptic lad. Alongside Jesus, the sharers of his vision. And the word itself, Transfiguration, how perfect. How disturbing that this feast was entered in the calendar to celebrate the victory of Christians over Muslims at Belgrade on 6th August 1456.

In the New Testament the Transfiguration story is told by three men who were not present but with agreement if not with the same similes, which somehow increases belief in what happened. Each agree that Jesus' face shone like the sun. Matthew writes, 'His clothes became white as light', Mark that 'they were whiter than snow' adding, 'as no fuller on earth can white them', and Luke that 'they were white and glistering'. So Peter, James and John, who were there, had provided incandescent accounts of this marvellous event in spite of Christ's order that they should tell no one. Diana Collins, who has just died, told me that she climbed to the traditional site of the Transfiguration to discover a little plateau covered with spring flowers. It was where the three closest disciples had fallen to the ground in terror, not of the whiteness but of hearing God's voice. Jesus had asked them, 'Who do men say I am?' and God had given the answer. No wonder they collapsed. When they stood up 'they saw Jesus only'. Herman itself is snowcapped, rising nine thousand feet between Palestine and Syria. I find the story mystical and at the same time rational. Life is a grubby business, half-lit, unclear, yet it should shine, if only now and then. 'Anoint and cheer our soiléd face with the abundance of thy grace.'

Richard Bawden has come to paint the garden. I see him shifting around to find the right spot. He is one of that host of artists who prop up easels in flower-beds, who put August into frames, whose beards tousle the summer growth and who hope that soon I will be making coffee or popping a cork. The garden seat is covered with resting butterflies, satiated after their business with the buddleia, a bush named after a Mr A. Buddle, a botanist who died in 1715. Let us give thanks for him and other men who domesticate enchantment. Later, I watch Richard painting far below as I cut ivy from the roof where it likes to weave in and out the pantiles, dislodging them, heaving them up and bringing them down. I remove it from the brick bread oven and clip it in a neat line. Ivy dust smothers me and the silver ladder burns in the sun. The radio says that it is the hottest day.

Late in the evening Joachim telephones from Berlin to tell me that the Constable in the National Gallery there looks just like Wormingford. He sounds excited and happy. His voice is infectious and I catch his delight in things, this time a Constable landscape which has been behind the Wall for most of his life and which now spreads a familiar view before him, the Stour Valley where he has walked with me. He is an East Anglianophile. 'I am washing-off ivy dust', I tell him. 'Ivy dust . . . ?' he repeats, suddenly lost.

At Hadleigh on John Newman's Death-day

Keith's handling of the 'murderer', as the old farmer dubbed the new hedge-cutter, is obvious to us all. No longer a trail of frightful amputations and lane-litter, but a kind of desperate art as it scoops from the tall roadside trees a lofty proscenium through which we can see the small drama of Cockrell's farmhouse. Once it was a pair of men chopping and laying, chopping and laying, and conversing all the way, and looking up when we passed. What they achieved would take weeks where the murderer takes hours. The wounding is great but

Spring will heal it. Often it is done at the wrong time, just after harvest, destroying all the berries in the haste to be tidy. I am a voice crying in the wilderness where such matters are concerned.

It is the eleventh of August, the day when Newman died in his ninetieth year. He was only sixty-four when he wrote *Gerontius*, his old age masterpiece. He came into my mind suddenly as we drove through the back lanes to Hadleigh, for it was at the Rectory there that Fr. Hugh Rose held the

Insects on hogweed

conference which laid the foundations of the Oxford Movement. Newman wasn't present. He was making his way home from Sicily after the little group of friends had separated, and feeling as one does at such a time, abandoned and lonely. Nor did he seem to be a very practical traveller and soon he was sailing uncomfortably from Palermo to Marseilles in an orange-boat, very low and sick. And there was another journey to make when he reached Oxford and the decision as to whether or not he should set out on this tore at him. Hence the young clergyman so wretchedly ill in the orange-boat trying to write 'Lead, kindly Light'. At this moment four other young Anglican priests had gathered in Archdeacon Pykenham's spectacular gatehouse to talk about the state of the Church of England, to raise its worship and to bring it closer to Catholicism. It was from this very same building that the Rector of Hadleigh, Dr Rowland Taylor had in 1555 begun a journey which led to the stake.

Hadleigh bakes in the August sun. Housing crescents bear the names of Protestant martyrs, Suffolk weavers who died for the reformed religion, Rowland Taylor's pupils. We stroll down Angel Street along which Taylor rode back to front facing the tail of his horse and wearing a dunce's cap to the bonfire, that learned man. Women emerge from Mass in the Catholic church and walk on to the supermarket. House agents' boards loll from gardens on Gallows Hill. Then to the other end of the straggling town, Benton End, where we remembered all the many days we spent at Cedric Morris's and Lett Haines's art school, Cedric painting irises, Lett cooking and drinking behind the Newlyn-blue door, and artists all over the place, the botanical talk and, below, the River Brett shining in its shallow bed. It often struck me that there was more humanity at Benton End than in all Hadleigh's Christianity. Its wide street must be among the best parades of domestic architecture in England. It burns in the sunshine and there is that lassitude which brings back the weariness of children on long summer walks. I remember an old woman telling my mother that I looked 'listless'. August had worn me out.

Recollecting Barbara Pym

Butterbur flops, pigeons mourn, Stanstead planes beeline for
home, balsam-seed patters onto motionless leaves and a bat
escapes from the unlit dining-room into the outside darkness.
I preach on Wisdom to sunburnt faces and we sing 'Light's
abode, celestial Salem', omitting verses four and five. I have
never discovered why organists rush to leave out an
asterisked verse. I was actually looking forward to singing
about being beautiful and resplendent, full of health and
strong, free, full of vigour and pleasure. Outside the church
cars are carefully parked where honey-dew from the limes
won't mark them. It is a time of visitors and a family from
Maryland join us. Father Episcopalian, mother Quaker,
children saintly, sit in a row. We all sing about the man who
'shall be satisfied with the pleasures of thy house, even of thy
holy temple'.

Will Barbara Pym enter the Lectionary? I have been re-
reading her, sitting in the shade, turning the familiar pages.
She is the doyenne of Anglican novelists and twenty years
after her death there is no one to hold a candle to her,
parochially speaking. Had she been an order of architecture
I suppose she would have been called Transitional, for her
stories bridge the late twentieth years of liturgical change.
Her heroines, if this is not a too magnificent description of
them, have good degrees in anthropology or English, her
men are unenthusiastic about sex or God, if it comes to it.
They get under the feet of their clever wives, especially in
the rectory. It is the pre-Delia era and the meals are terrible.
There is no central heating and the water-bottle is carried to
bed like a lover. It is also the pre-family service time and the
grown-ups can worship in peace. Below the light touch lies
a profound understanding of English Christianity.

Notoriously, Pym was dismissed by her publisher in 1963 as a middlebrow nobody. They had published six of her wonderful novels and now did not want any more, thank you. A few years later they were having to eat their words when she was voted one of the best writers of her day and the most underrated.

We wrote to each other a few months before her death about a contribution to an anthology I was editing, and she sent me some entries from her diary called 'A Year in West Oxfordshire', her home. It was August 1979 – her last August. She mentions a walk round Ditchley Park, the home of the poet Rochester, and notes that he writes hymns for girls. 'My light thou art, without thy glorious sight/My eyes are darken'd with eternal night'. So he wasn't all wicked. She notes that among the family memorials in his village church there is none to him. Which is what happens when you write hymns for girls.

Job and Ely

Poor Job of Uz and his miserable comforters, what a poem they make! It is the rising and falling of a man who would not blame God. Job's wife, reduced from riches to rags by her husband's obdurance, takes one look at him, horrible as he is with boils, and tells him to curse God and die. Three old friends, the comforters, arrive to spread their platitudes, as folk do when faced with another man's misfortune, but being characters in a great work of literature they do it eloquently.

The tale is a long one. Every now and then come words which we know by heart because they have been uttered during centuries of funerals. 'Naked came I into the world, and naked shall I leave it. The Lord gave and the Lord hath taken away. Blessed be the name of the Lord.' Bildad, one of the comforters, is the most comforting, the most philosophical. And a good poet. He tells Job, 'For we are but of yesterday, and know nothing, because our days on earth are but a shadow.' The Satan of Job is the Satan of Compline who walks up and down the earth. 'Your adversary the devil prowls around like a roaring Lion, seeking someone to devour'. God then does a deal with Satan. He can try Job to the uttermost but he must not destroy him. Job wishes that he had been stillborn but he does not attempt suicide. The book ends with classic storytelling. Job gets better, gets richer than ever and lives to the age of a hundred and forty. The language of mortality is unequalled.

After Matins the congregation goes home to lunch then goes on the annual Farm Walk in the Middle Eastern heat, with garden Evensong and tea up at the Hall to follow. I stay at home to get ready to go to Ely as Patron of Cathedral Camps, rising at dawn to feed the cats, fetch the milk from the top of the track so that it doesn't grow sour in the sun, rip through the post and eventually catch the train to Norwich and then the Liverpool train to – Ely. It snakes through a harvested East Anglia, shorn fields all the way. And through the black Fens until, as fair as the towers in a medieval missal, Ely suddenly rises on the flat land. Lunch in a pub with a fan twisting in the beery air and beautiful Indian ladies in saris drinking coke at the next table. Then up what goes for a hill in Ely to the cathedral in which tourists halt in their sightseeing for the Lord's Prayer. The Campers are all over the place, up scaffolding, lying on their tummies to clean brasses, in a courtyard scrubbing a Victorian canon's huge side-table of its wines and roasts, and in the Triforium, a glory-hole of discarded furnishings, books etc. which still might come in handy. There are fifteen Campers including an American. 'What else have you done?' I enquire, awed by their industry. 'We have cleared the garden for the new Dean'. Are they comfortable in the Choir School? Properly fed? Hard done by? Burser and Conservator then arrive to praise them. The leaders tell me about their jobs, their homes, their hopes. Next time, maybe, the great stone screen. Until the invention of Cathedral Camps there were bits of these immense buildings which were never cleaned, carvings never seen to their ancient advantage, some tomb which had been passed without a glance for generations. How youthful the hands are which bring-up its ponderous Latin, which dust its cherubs, how unmarked. I am taken to see a few yards of the original cathedral floor, the tiles on which its founders had trod and which were a soft red from careful washing, a girl bending to see if it was still damp. Then the walk to the station and the tiny city shutting up shop all the way.

The Applicant

'Here I am my dearest love quite safe and well . . . I am just out of the coach and my hands are benumbed . . .' scribbled John Constable to his wife back in London. 'You will be pleased to hear that our friend the Rev. William Hurlock succeeded in his election to Dedham as lecturer – a good house and garden and a good six hundred a year . . . He is quite worn out with anxiety, and had it gone against him must have been very serious to his peace of mind.' Mr Hurlock was the youthful rector of a Norfolk parish who wanted to live in Dedham, as who would not in 1818? It was a grand place. Unlike parsons, who could put a curate in where they themselves did not wish to reside or toil, artists had to live in London if they wanted to get on. So John Constable had to make regular forays to his native Dedham and East Bergholt on the Blue Coach from Ipswich to acquire headfuls of inspiration to take back to Soho. If only he could have stayed put in a good house and garden with a good six hundred a year, and his boys being taught by kind Dr Grimwood at the Grammar School, and his girls riding with his sisters, and all of them coming to Dedham church on a Sunday to listen to the new Lecturer.

The Dedham Lecturers were ordained stipendaries, although sometimes laymen. Being Puritan country it had attracted some pulpit firebrands in its time. But Mr Hurlock sounds lacking in fire if he could have gone to pieces should he have lost the vote, which was eleven to six. It had been ranting lecturers in churches who had driven George Fox to search for silence. Twenty-nine years old, he climbed Pendle Hill in Lancashire and had found how to respond to them. Discovering 'Seekers' like himself, he mounted a haystack and preached his first sermon, saying not a word. It resonates to this day. Perched high in Mr Hurlock's pulpit at Dedham I give a talk on the local painters, Munnings, John Nash and Cedric Morris. His lecturing would have required a loud voice, given the big nave, plus gestures. A microphone allows me to stand still and talk. The Greeks described 'church' as 'a thing which belongs to the Lord'. Christ saw church as architecture in progress, he the corner-stone, we the variously useful stones which make up the sacred structure. I think of John Waters, the first name on the Incumbents' Board at Mount Bures – John Waters 1301. Did he rant about Purgatory, frightening the wits out of the peasants? Was he Franciscan, standing up there against the north wall for a few minutes or so and pointing to a face on the window to tell them, 'Love is he, radiant with great splendour, and speaks to us of Thee, O Most High'.

Woodcuts

Because of the pattern of farmwork, even now farmers are bound to fall into certain timeless attitudes. Take Duncan watching Lower Bottom meadow being mowed at this moment. He, the man on the mower and his setters, and a scuttling rabbit or two, have all assumed the attitudes of figures in a Bewick woodcut, the machine notwithstanding. Dogs and humans are engrossed by the circling cutter and are even correctly turned-out for black and white illustration, Duncan in his white shirt, dark braces and cap, the abstract man in the cab, the glossy creatures bounding in the foreground. Falling thistles provide most of the action. Like children who will eat all round what they dislike, the horses have grazed up to the thistles and left them standing in small forests here and there. The stream which wriggles through the pasture has been wired-off to prevent sheep and horses getting stuck in it. Should I shout, 'Duncan!' and shatter the woodcut? Better not. Let one man labour and another stare. Let dogs not look up. So I go inside to remind myself about Thomas Bewick, founder of the modern school of wood engraving. A Northumbrian boy, he taught himself to draw by chalking pictures on the church flagstones. His sketches were made with pen and blackberry ink. His woodcut books have a skill and fidelity to the countryside such as had never been seen before, and here are Duncan and the haymaker and their beasts in the Georgian meadow, just as I imagined.

Until he married, when his wife put a stop to it, Tom Bewick slept naked throughout the year, wrapped in a single blanket with the bedroom wind and the snow sometimes providing an extra covering. He walked in all weathers, waded across rivers without drying his clothes afterwards, and believed that boys and girls were 'harassed with education before their minds were fit for it' and would have liked their early years spent 'running wild by burns'. How he would have spurned today's test after test, or central heating for that matter. His *Memoir* is a printed burst of fresh air, cheerful, funny, accusative and with some breezy notions of the Church.

Will rain hold off? is what we are asking. Because harvest will have to be held off if it does not. The wheat is dry enough to scratch my bare legs, yet the ears still hold moisture, I notice – are quite heavy with it in fact. So the combine stays in its den. At midnight the first quarter of the harvest moon rocks in the oaks. At Matins we read from that master of dryness, Ezekiel, whom God addresses as 'Son of man, can these dry bones live?' Jesus called himself Son of man. 'Son of man', God instructed the Temple priests, 'these are the ordinances of the altar'.

Bewick surveyed Georgian Christianity with conventional respect. But 'Wagon loads of sermons have been published . . . of no importance either to religion or morality . . . How could they stem from the 'beauty and simplicity' of what Christ taught? How could these teachings have become 'distorted and disfigured' by the various sects? They should be 'compared to a mathematical point a point of perfection for all men to aim at, but to which none can fully attain . . . As far as I am able to judge, all we can do is to commune with and reverence and adore the Creator . . . I know of no better of which is called serving God than that of being good to his creatures'. Bewick's Franciscanism had begun when he was a schoolboy. He had caught a hare in his arms, had stoned a bullfinch. 'Struck with its beauty I instantly ran into the house with it. It was alive, and looked me piteously in the face; and, as I thought, could it have spoken, it would have asked me why I had taken away its life. I felt greatly hurt at what I had done and did not quit it all the afternoon. I turned it over and over, admiring its plumage, its feet, its bill . . . This was the last bird I killed.' Let the hunter reach the fox before the hounds get at it and hold it in his/her arms and read from its dying eyes, 'Why have you taken away my life?' For fun, is their answer.

The Shutter Falls

At last we are harvesting. That is the occasional grain truck rolls from a dusty field to block the lane, and bale rolls and oblongs are beginning to make Paul Nash shapes in the landscape. I note that lots of the August wildflowers are tangling with blackberry and seeding grass. Combines rumble and so does thunder. The young postman crackles down the farm track in his red oven dreaming of a beach. I visit an old friend in the nursing-home, passing wide open doors, catching degrees of senescence and the occasional greeting. The sun is a strange glaring black. Pretty oriental nurses, cheaper than ours, bring round tea. I sit on my friend's bed and unload novels. She wants to hear all the village news. Her life has been so drastically reduced, I don't know how she can bear it. But she does, with a kind of exalted commonsense. Has she not lived in wonderful places, had wonderful friends, done wonderful things? I say yes. Well then.

This evening I fall prey to the secondary nature of the black and white photograph, whose first nature is to provide the image selected for it by the photographer. A figure, a view, both. Having achieved this, the photo cannot help doing much more. Who is that man with the rake behind the sitters of 1963? Who are the unknown guests at the picnic given by my friends? Here is a German boy in a Hamburg studio wearing a sailor hat with ribbons, like the tempter in *Death in Venice*? Bismark was living when this studio photograph was taken. Here is my house long before I was born – the same windows and doors. The same trees casting the same shadows. And a different cat – one who loved lights. In the vestry on Sunday evening they show me the party pictures, shiny, richly coloured, slipping like ice, perfect in their way though not with the haunting perfection of black and white, which preserves both the likeness and the dream. It took a Box Brownie or someone with a velvet cloth over his head to catch the likeness and the dream.

The Big Green at Mellis

The weather breaks. I can hear its change of tune as I pick the broad beans. From listless summer to soft turmoil. The trees which have stood stock-still like leaden trees in one of those farmyard sets we had as children are thrashing about, and shaking the collar-doves out of them. Harvesting continues to throb in the fields like heart-beat and in the lanes the commuters are amazed to be held up by monster machines. I sit in the doorway waiting for the downpour. If the clouds get any lower the spire will puncture them.

Death 'the ruffian on the stair' is hanging around, upsetting the holiday plans, and maybe he will give us a miss. When he does arrive the Church will pull out all the stops for him. 'Death', it says, 'meet Life'. Although its language, so perfect for the occasion, will make us all cry. Friends under sentence of death talk to me on the telephone. How strange it is. Could I do with some plums? Theirs are so weighty that they have broken the bough and they must prop it up next year.

To Mellis to see Roger Deakin's moat. Roger swam up and down in his moat before setting off to swim round Britain. There is Mellis church. Pevsner, prying into it, saw 'no indication of the Renaissance'. That's Mellis for you. It has a vast green still governed by Anglo-Saxon rights and with old houses all round it, so that for generations the natives have been able to sit comfortable of an evening and watch what was going on, games, goats, courting, somebody going into Mrs Smith's, somebody sneaking out of Lizzie Brown's, young Fred coming home after midnight. Ancient folk going mad. And animals chomping up and down and boys being wicked. The usual thing. Mellis hasn't quite done with summer, I notice, and the splattering of rain will do no more than make the roach rise. This is de la Pole country, that romantic north-western Suffolk family whose castles and manors lie scattered around, and whose shields are fixed to flint walls.

May we go to Eye, to Wingfield to meet the de la Poles and look at their leopard's head badge and see their possessions now the corn has been cut? No, we are here to see what Roger has been up to, which is writing a book about wood – wood as material, which is what medieval Suffolk saw it as. Everybody went around keeping an eye on the growing trees and marking a future shaft here, a house-beam there. Everybody walked with a pocketful of acorns to push into the damp earth wherever there happened to be a space. Carpenters made wooden angels so that when you looked up in church you thought you were in heaven. Woodland hides Roger's farmhouse and, should his neighbours look up from television, they will not be able to watch him naked in his moat. We lunch on its bank and hear the invisible Norwich train scream by.

Another Water-Side Party

The Church Commissioners have lost twelve million pounds. Or maybe it is only eleven million, people do exaggerate. I ask the vicar, wildly, 'suppose a young man turned up in a village and called the inhabitants together to tell them, "I am a priest of Christ and will minister to you in return for a little home, food, clothes etc. No money, just the usual human necessities. What do you think?" Suppose a young man imitated a Saxon saint as well as Christ, what would Church House, not to mention the parish, do?'

But to move on from frivolity. My swallows are all lined-up on the wires to take off for Algeria. Not so fast, dear birds. Tall globe artichokes sway beneath them. A cat gives me a

Moth coming towards me

dead shrew. Such kindness. I do not give Billie and Donald a thing on their Diamond Wedding. 'No presents' says the invitation, although some guests do, and it looks like Christmas in their hall. On the way to them I pass the site of a timbered farmhouse which was shipped to the United States during the great period of taking as much of the old country across the Atlantic as a ship could manage. Numbered beam by beam went Bowden's farmhouse, to leave a haunting space in a muddy lane. A farmworker was also shipped to Botany Bay from the same spot for being a unionist, or trouble-maker, or simply desperate. Coming close to the Colonel's, I can hear a sound like angry bees. It is the entire population of Wormingford come to do him homage in his riverside garden. The rain says, 'I will soon put a stop to this', but doesn't. I carry my glass through the orchard to the Stour and along to the iron bridge which fastens Essex to Suffolk. Grey water reflects grey sky, as it must. Billie's prize sheep trundle towards me, still chewing. The wedding party now sounds like Fortinbras on the last mile to Elsinore. The air is wonderfully warm and I can smell roses, also hear the Colonel making his speech. It is 1941 again and he is a long way from being what he has become, a grandfather, retired. He is a boy on a bike - 'and an old grid at that' anxiously courting the prettiest girl for miles around, a young regular with other battles ahead. A middle-aged son proposes the toast. Will it pour – surely it must? At eight-thirty precisely the rain falls but there is no stampede. When it strikes into the river's surface like silver nails we head for the cars.

Looking Out

It must be all of a year since the kitchen curtains were taken down for painting the window-frames and never to be put up again. Ian has stuck some fragments of old stained glass here and there on the panes and from now on the window has performed as an early morning oblong for meditation. I drink tea and just look out. The view remains the same yet endlessly different as well. It reminds me of Proust's morning window:

> Meanwhile winter was at an end; the fine weather returned, and often when Albertine had just bidden me goodnight, my room, my curtains, the wall above the curtains being still quite dark, the nuns' garden next door I could hear, rich and precious in the silence like a harmonium in church, the modulation of an unknown bird which, in the Lydian mode, was already chanting matins, and into the midst of my darkness flung the rich dazzling note of the sun that it could see . . . Presently the nights grew shorter still and before what had been the hour of daybreak, I could see already stealing above my window-curtains the daily increasing whiteness of the dawn.

Exactly. When I used to take John Nash his morning tea he would say in the darkness, for the light must not be switched on, 'Draw the curtains just an inch, old chap', for the actuality of a new day had to be broken to him gently. Then, 'What is it doing?' Raining, shining. Nothing in particular. Silence in the streak of light which fell across the bed. As the world is divided between those who bring morning tea and those who receive it, myself being the bringer, I find that I never really mind what it is doing outside as long as I can sit watching it, sipping and thinking, for an hour before the house is plunged into breakfast. The uncurtained kitchen window contains the landscape contours which it has framed for centuries, humps and hills and dips which were the work ground of the farmers who lived here for twenty or more generations, and the food patch for countless wild and domestic animals. I just look at them, no more. Weather plays tricks with the contours – turns them into a meditative base. 'You were up with the lark!' say the guests, bringing down their cups.

Rat-Run

The *Today* programme rings up to ask me to join in the Council for the Preservation of Rural England's protest against the increase of traffic on minor roads. Being a non-driver and living a mile off a road I had not noticed this. Asking around, I am told that many small lanes and little roads which until a decade ago were part of a hinterland of quietness between the A routes are now ferocious short-cuts to the station, and nippy parts of the school-run and the supermarket pilgrimage. For young drivers their ancient twists and turns were a challenge to their nerves, and for old drivers their once promise of peace after the terrors of the motorway is no more. As for people who until recently could walk their dogs up the lane or tell their children to keep to it when they went for bike-rides, or who could let their cats out at night, all this is no longer possible. The minor road was now a major hazard. Supplied with these facts, I sit in a studio and hold forth on the iniquity of its abuse.

The number of cars outside our three parish churches on a Sunday would suggest a religious revival to the passer-by. Roughly speaking, a congregation of thirty will arrive in twenty cars. Should a wedding or funeral be taking place cars will, in summer when the ground is dry, fill acres of meadow, or in winter trail bumper to bumper for miles. As for the clergy-drivers, I once gave a talk to the Norwich and Norfolk priests on their 'car isolation' and recommended that instead they should like me walk or bike, and there was great amusement. I told them about the ministry of nineteenth century clergymen such as William Barnes and Francis Kilvert, of how much was achieved on the hoof, and imagined them thankfully clutching their car-keys. Could they offer me a lift?

Son of Tolmai

August for scything the orchard. I slice down the marestail and nettles in grandiose swoops, partly to clear up, partly to get at the greengages and the first pears. Across the hedge unseen riders talk softly to their horses. Then Colin arrives to tell me that they are having a Seventies fancy-dress party and that he is going as John Travolta and what do I think? Then Tony arrives to say that he has been to a barbecue and isn't feeling too good, and no wonder. Then comes a friend who says that why haven't I got a sit-on mower? I sharpen my blade and swish on. My hair is full of dust and my legs full of scratches. Towards evening the orchard is filled with irritable screechings (grey squirrels) and pure singing (blackbirds). As it grows dark, the outside light is crazy with hornets and the garden grows sumptuous with the scents which the heat has drawn from it. It would be nice to sleep outside.

We have to think about Bartholomew. His hymn, 'Saints of God, lo, Jesus' people' is an acrostic on his name. Some of its lines are a bit of a puzzle too. Bartholomew was his surname and means 'son of Tolmai' but we now think he was

Nathaniel from Cana, which makes him the right saint for what they are calling a vintage year. It is strange how much we know (or feel we know) about people whose biographies are minimal and how little we know about those whose lives fill volumes. Think of Mother Julian, then of some of today's political autobiographies.

Lee and his wife Elizabeth come to lunch to tell me about Mirfield. Married for just a few months and in their early twenties, their crowding eager talk wakes me up. They are at the moment being youth leaders at Walsingham, so I hear all about the Pilgrimage of Gypsies. I tell them about Ocean the East Anglian gypsy woman who walked Suffolk and Norfolk until she was ninety, a proud and famous person whose grave I saw being dug, although alas I never glimpsed her. Imagine, I said, 'To be named Ocean, to have walked the eastern counties for nigh on a century, what a life!' I could see Lee and Elizabeth imagining her, their young faces all future, all what will be, not what was. We have cold chicken and salad and raspberries and cream and wine and coffee and Lapsang Souchong tea, and much Anglo-Catholic conversation. Did I know that Ninian Comper designed sixteen churches? I certainly did not. They stand on the brink of what is best for them, which is the best place to be. My faith, I tell myself, is like some baggy old garment compared to theirs, roomy without being comfortable exactly.

The August Dragonfly

The dragonfly returns again and again to the open page, alighting as though it was a helicopter-pad, sometimes at the top, then at the foot, as the book rests on my lap. I clasp it stockstill. The dragonfly's wings are colourless and translucent, and I can read Binchester and Yatterdon through them, so no prizes for guessing what this book is. It shifts to *O qua juval*. It is a darter, a creature of speed and pause. I am a creature of sloth, and thus a scandal to Harold's bees as they assault the balsam. My garden-chair is like Cleopatra's burning throne and very soon I must muster enough energy to carry it into the shade. The stream is at its mightiest flow because of all the rain in the night, providing delicious fresh water for both darters and honeybees to sip. Over my head a green woodpecker knocks monotonously on the willow to see if the grubs are in. 'Yatterdon,' asks the dragonfly, 'isn't that in Berkshire?' It reminds me of Fanny Burney and her aristocratic husband, M. D'Arblay sitting on the lawn at Camilla Cottage waiting for the second Napoleonic wars to begin. They were in 'retirement'. It meant something quite different in their day, an exquisite withdrawal from the fray, just as I am at this moment pleasantly withdrawn from the goings-on in Wormingford. Dragonflies are *Odanata*, carnivorous creatures who begin as maids and end up as Darters. Or Hawkers or Damsels or Demoiselles. I must brush up my Odanata.

It often takes a late August afternoon to hear the minimal voice of nature, the sultry popping of seed, the whisper of dried petals, the scuttle in the vine. Such energy. I gently kick Conrad's *Letters* into the shade with a bare toe so that the cover doesn't curl. When the telephone rings from the sitting room I think how foolish of whoever it is to imagine that I would have the strength to get up and answer it. Over the hedge, a girl is talking to her horse under a tree. A hundred years ago Conrad was writing *Lord Jim* at Pent Farm, just off Romney Marsh and giving his literary agent Mr Pinker what for, reminding him that 'there are other virtues than punctuality'. Photographs of Conrad at work reveal that he would also give me a piece of his mind if he could see me in nothing but a torn shirt and shorts writing in a garden. He wore, even in August, a splendid suit, cravat and polished boots at isolated Pent Farm, as befitted a Polish gentleman. Moreover, inside, there was Mrs Conrad who could type, that marvellous style of his curling from the keys. My ballpoint does its best and now and then the dragonfly makes a sudden landing on a line. 'O English summer day,' it pleads, 'as it is my only day, last as long as you can'.

A Voyage

John Constable when a boy would have taken rides on his father's barges. I am riding in James's skiff, a pretty little Edwardian boat straight off a Tissot painting. When it sailed the Thames at Henley its name was *Speedwell* but now that it is sailing the Stour it has no name, I cannot remember why. It rides low in the evening water. The air is suddenly cool, the sky banking up to hide Mars, the swans fretful at being disturbed. We lie back on cushions whilst James rows and the willows trail across our bodies. Not another soul about except the young fisherman who is throwing bits of bread where he hopes to land a chub. Chubs are first cousins to dace and much sought after by coarse fishermen. We exchange river pleasantries as we pass through the tunnel and out of Nayland. Wissington ahead. Delicious watercress which nobody eats festoons the oars. I nibble a bit. It is peppery and good. It is not gathered these days, I have forgotten why. It is the same as swimming in the river, or not harnessing its power. Nobody does any of the things which river dwellers used to do any more. How powerful the Stour is. I can feel its pull, muscular and surprising. It is saying, 'I am not just a pretty face'. Rivers are disconcerting in the way that they present their own version of landscape. Walk along the banks, and it is the familiar account of the local landscape, get into a boat and foreign country is floating by. As well as patches of cress and weed, the surface is dimmed with combine-dust from the harvest until we reach the stony shallows which herald the millrace, then all is flashing brilliance. The water falls in a continuous glass sheet and is roaring with all its might. Ahead is the white clapboard skyscraper which is Wissington Mill and some of the tallest river-side trees I have ever seen. We debate as to whether we should let the friends who live in the Mill know that we are bumping about outside. No, we must return. An argosy of three watery miles has to be made if we are to be home by supper, and so more cross swans, more trailing alders to ruffle our hair, more corn-dust, then the chub-fancier, then the exposed gardens with their fashionable decking, then the currents into which we must not plunge and, all the way, 'the scenes which made me a painter' – John Constable. Although for him it was a toilscape, work all the way for men and boys and horses.

It is sad to disembark, to gather up the cushions and oars, and to walk the few steps to what was the miller's fine house, to feel our land feet. No bankside trees and bushes in Constable's day. The towing-path must be kept clear. But dozens of skiffs and scores of rods belonging to the Stour boys, the artist's 'young Waltonians'. And the familiar drama of 'The Leaping Horse' when a whistle would make a great Suffolk Punch jump over the little fences which kept the cattle from straying. Commuters cars are homing-in on the village. Showers and dinners and soaps await. Overhead the passengers will be buckling their belts for the Stanstead landing. In the church Constable's 'Christ presides at the Last Supper'. James's arms ache from so much rowing, ours with idleness.

September

In Whodunnit-Land - Castle Boterel - The Retable - Fieldwork - Two Singers - Michael Vanishes - Dwindling Landworkers - A Lost Reality - More Gatherings - Colin Marries Zoë - At the End of the Day - Cousin Winnie Blythe - Being Young, Being Old - The Hog Roast - The Arrowhead - Monkshood - The Mad and the Sane - Fordham Wood - Persian Suffolk - At the Charterhouse - At Discoed

In Whodunnit-Land

Duncan from Maltings Farm arrives to return my Keats from which he has read *On Autumn* to Rotary. Then a *Thought for Today* man sits on the fence to tell me of the pros and cons of hunting, quoting St Aquinas on the one hand and Jesus on the other - his formidably caring words about the fall of a sparrow. And where do we hunting protesters stand on factory farming and devouring animals etc? The white cat looks up at me from the ironing-board and we both feel very uncomfortable.

And then to the Margery Allingham Society at Writtle Agriculture College near Chelmsford, Jean driving and the traffic mad. I do so enjoy literary societies. There is almost one for everybody. This one is dedicated to a genre of which I am very nearly illiterate, and I confess as much, adding brightly, 'But I did once meet Dorothy L. Sayers!' The Society sits up. What can I do but promise to meet Albert Campion too? He is of course Margery Allingham's well-bred sleuth and he appears in its magazine, the enormously readable *Albert Memorial*. After a lunch during which her devotees follow her hero around inter-war Essex with amazing skill, a wreath is laid on her grave at Tolleshunt D'Arcy. Now where else could a Whodunnit queen be buried? Photographs show a dedicated face, one perpetually bent to paper and fountain-pen. Back home I go to the neglected green Penguins and there and behold are half a dozen Allinghams, all waiting to convert me. I take out *The Fashion in Shrouds* (1938) and begin, having faithfully promised the Society to make amends for my ignorance. But life is so brief and how can we ever read all we should? But then I think of young John Keats at Winchester and seeing his last Autumn. I read Psalm 126 - 'Then was our mouth filled with laughter and our tongue with joy.'

Very ill people write to me. What to answer? What can it be like to be very ill? My friend Rosie who runs our local Hospice, the St Helena at Colchester, wants some musical instruments so that her music therapist can do her work. I manage to gather in for her some recorders, a guitar, an Albert Campion-period mouth organ - and a psaltery. You see angels playing psalteries high up in spandrels or leaning from roofs, plucking with long white fingers, making no sound. But I have a go on the mouth organ before handing it in to Rosie. It wails sadly. It is making the sound of an epoch. If Albert Campion was passing he would have tossed me a sixpence, being a real toff.

Craig Taylor, a youthful Canadian writer, comes to see me and we talk about Alice Munro, that peerless short-story countrywoman of his, because he is writing short stories. Neither of us can work out how she does it, nor how Chekhov did his. We splash our way to the village to look at John Nash's grave and to buy Whiskas. On the tombstone the words I chose some quarter of a century ago are scarcely decipherable. I read them out from memory to Craig. ' For, lo, the winter is past, the rain is over and gone, the flowers appear on the earth, the time of the singing of birds is come, and the voice of the turtle is heard in the land.' He listens and writes it down. His little notebook is damp and our toes squelch in the churchyard grass. He tells me about Clapham on the way home.

I note that St Bernard of Clairvaux and Catherine and William Booth share a day. All three were hard hitters,

Bernard when it came to anti-semitism, the Booths when it came to poverty. They called Bernard the 'honey-sweet teacher' and the Booths all sorts of things.

Castle Boterel

In all the words about the Boscastle flood there had not been one about this Cornish village's unique place in English literature. For it was at St Juliot just above Boscastle that Thomas Hardy met his Emma, the inspiration and the plague of his life. He courted her in the Valency Valley from where a minute stream joined two others and drowned what lay below. After Emma's death in 1912 Hardy went back to Valency to write what many believe to be the greatest sequence of love poetry since Shakespeare's Sonnets.

I was often there with writer friends, James Turner, Charles Causley, Richard Mabey, Peter Ford, drawn to this rivulet and its steep glades by these lovers. Either of them at that time would have been thought youthful, neither of them were beautiful. I was trying to make out what had happened during that long marriage. The courtship was totally set out in *A Pair of Blue Eyes*, Hardy's poetic novel. Unknown to him until the morning after her death, Emma too had recorded this passionate prologue to what lay ahead. With her body lying above, Hardy matched his wife's words with his. Then he returned to Cornwall for the first time since their meeting there and the amazing poems followed each other in succession. There he mourned the girl from St Juliot rectory, not the formidable mistress of Max Gate. He saw once again through forty long years the mesmerising rider who so recklessly galloped the dangerous slopes above the sea as he did the usual damage (restoration) to the ancient church. Once, returning there after a few weeks to see what had been done he asked what had happened to the medieval pews – they were missing. They had been burnt and new ones were to be fitted because, said the foreman, 'It was a pity to spoil the ship for a ha'p'orth of tar.'

Later he wrote, 'The shore and country about "Castle Boterel" is now getting well known. The spot, I may add, is among the furthest westward of all those convenient corners wherein I have ventured to erect my theatre for those imperfect dramas of country life and passions . . . The place is pre-eminently (for one person at least) the region of dream and mystery. The ghostly birds, the pall-like sea, the frothy wind, the eternal soliloquy of the waters, the bloom of dark purple cast that seems to exhale from the shoreward precipices, in themselves lend to the scene like the twilight of a night vision.'

Flood damage is not food for contemplation. The muck of it can scarcely be faced, nor at this moment Emma and Tom's pretty stream grown ugly. He would have known how to deal with it, the dirty torrent, the vehicles bobbing in the harbour, the calamity.

The Retable

We are off to see the famous retable at Thornham Parva, twisting and turning in medieval lanes and once humiliatingly for locals having to stop for directions. The fields provide a strange sight, the harvest being almost medievally late. Some are just being cut, others ploughed, some are stubble, and in them, still or moving, we see a strange display of pre-harvest and harvesting, and post-harvest machinery. The air is milky with corn dust and is skirling with rooks. And soon we find the retable in its thatched casket, all beaten gold and sacredness, some say the finest thirteenth century painting in these islands. A Dominican altarpiece which holds the gaze like a lovely child, or a perfect flower, or a dancer, or a great poem on a page. How we stare. How we trust that no one will read to us from the guide. Let us - look. Let all mortal flesh be silent to let the painted flesh speak. Here is something perfect into which the followers of Christ poured their wonder in the 1330s. The figures are Dominicans all, even the Christ. The simple church is chilly and field-smelling, and has a pale picture-story running round it of the life of St Edmund. The artist has used the hump of the north door as Stratford bridge over which a Suffolk cart carries the body of a martyred king to London for safety. The cart is a sketch for Constable's *Haywain*. It is how St Edmund's trip to London would be painted in Wormingford School at this minute. Following the fresco round the nave we experience a kind of early religious delight. These Thornham pictures bring us closer than language ever could to the medieval mind. Gloriously advanced as paintings, the saints on the retable bend and sway towards each other in continuous conversation from which we are excluded. The central figure is the dead, speechless Jesus. He flops forward wretchedly, half-wrapped in a rag. To the left is Dominic himself, the brilliant Castilian founder of the Order, at the far end, holding a book and covered in blood, he stands once more as martyr. The saints in between sway against a chequerboard, the pattern usually followed by East Anglian masons when they decorated their towers.

But we must get on, get into the burning car. Nobody stays very long at a shrine these days, and when they do they worship art and not saints, read brochures and not missals, see masterpieces and not God. But what an outing. The tall, long figures continue to sway in my head as I pick pears that evening. 'You must learn our conversation,' they say 'and then you won't just stare.' The pears are cookers and unassailable by human teeth when raw. But rabbits, hares, foxes and deer have had a nibble. The poplars accompany me with a soft hullabaloo and the white cat with evident pleasure.

Fieldwork

Just to remind me of our earthy Suffolk childhood my Australian brother has reminded me of our now scarcely believable way of earning pocket money, such as singling-out sugar-beet and stone-picking, and of our aching backs. Talking about this in the pulpit at harvest festival, I am careful not to catch Peter's blue gaze, knowing that he too, at Framlingham long ago, had tested his boy strength in the harvest field, heaving up the stooks and getting what we called 'bushes' (prickles) in his small hands. Old soldiers have their reunions and maybe there should be a last coming together of those who actually did what we continue to sing in the harvest hymns. An annual meeting of the last true harvesters. Stacking the hymnbooks after the service Peter and I exchange grins - the smiles of those who garnered, though inwardly wondering if it really could have been us who followed the binder as it reduced the circle of standing corn, to the terror of the rabbits and hares.

The Great Field behind Bottengoms is not being ploughed this autumn, just having its previous crop of beans harrowed-in before being sown with winter wheat. The bean hulm is black and glittering after rain. Huge September sunsets fire the village. We pick blackberries before the devil spits on them, i.e., before the spumes of foam which the nymphs of frog-hoopers produce makes them unappetising. In church we read the *Book of Ruth*, a great favourite. It is about a young farmer and a young widow seeding the Lord's family-tree. How Thomas Hardy loved this story and the *Books of Kings*, just as a poet he loved the pointing of the Psalms.

A trip to Discoed, a minute village on the Welsh border where my old friend the poet Edward Storey has created a little arts festival. I have among other things to plant a medlar tree (*Maspilus Germanica*) in memory of the composer Trevor Hold. This is Bryansground, that marvellous garden by the River Lugg. A girl oboist plays a Hold sonata in the open air. I tread the medlar in, blessing it and Trevor and all of us. A heavily wooded rise known locally as Elephant Hill cast dark shadows. Tea with David and Simon, the makers of Bryansground. Planted all along this England-Wales countryside, flowering at regular intervals, are George Herbert, Francis Kilvert, Henry Vaughan and Thomas Traherne. The views are enormous. On the wall of the shepherd's church at Discoed is Isaak Griffith's memorial of 1789. It reads, 'Christ's preference makes eternal day.'

Then in Anglican contrast, to Lambeth Palace for our reunion, plus a dash to the Garden Museum where I note that the scythe I use at Bottengoms is in a glass case. Escaping the learned throng at the Palace, I wander through the long corridors to look at poor Laud, Tait, the Temples, dear Ramsey, Benson, Runcie, Cranmer, searching them straight in the eye, seeing them in the everlasting light. Their robes rustle as I pass. Outside in the huge beds, Lady Runcie's michaelmas daisies and departing birds.

Two Singers

September, when Cuthbert may be celebrated instead of the twentieth of March. I like these lordly permissions in the Lectionary. His shrine makes travellers want to jump out of the train at Durham on what suddenly becomes a sacred journey. And then, what with Anthony Gormley's *Angel of the North* and Lindisfarne itself, a watercolour wash through the carriage window, the entire route turns into a swift pilgrimage. I tell the Evensong congregation about Cuthbert. It is good of it to have turned out, what with Queen Victoria and John Brown on the telly and the remorseless rain. The latter has turned the new stubble into paddy fields. So Cuthbert's name is heard in the nave. It is said that when he was a boy making funny faces he was seen as a future bishop. He minded sheep in Lauderdale then walked on to Melrose where the prior said, 'Behold a servant of God'. And thus it began. He was a tall, strong young man, although never exactly well due to an attack of the plague. The sweetness of his personality played havoc with the Rule. I remembered this when the Lectionary said that we could read Ecclesiasticus instead of Jonah, lines which Cuthbert himself might have written:

> Wisdom lifteth up the head of him that is of low
> degree, and maketh him to sit with great men. Commend
> not a man for his beauty; neither abhor a man for his
> outward appearance. The bee is little among such as fly
> but her fruit is the chief of sweet things.

Cuthbert was the most unwilling prelate that ever was, much preferring the seals and fishes and gulls of Farne Island to the Northumbrian people. He wrote no books but simply was – a man who expressed in his solitude the sweetness of Christ. What he would have made of Durham one cannot imagine, although he would have loved the splash of the Weir below it.

Back home, half soaked, cassock steaming by the Rayburn, I have a whisky and read my friend Stephen Varcoe's *Sing English Song*, which astonishes me. I once asked him, 'Stephen, what is it like to open your mouth and have that beautiful sound come out of it?' And now he answers me. Chapter two. 'Shut the door, open your mouth, and make the loudest noise you can'. The cats forbid it. And so I move on to how to sing Gerald Finzi, Ivor Gurney, the madrigalists, Britten. 'How far should the singer go into dialect?' Stephen asked me, thinking of settings of Hardy and Clare. Not very far, perhaps. I thought of Jesus singing the psalms in the Temple or some Palestinian holy song on the road, his voice like Stephen's.

Michael Vanishes

It has continued to rain all the week and the trees are asway with their drenchings. Harvest dust has been washed from hedges, birds, roofs and flints. Falls shine in the orchard grass, bedraggled creatures splosh around. 'Nice rain', they say. It holds off for a bit as I walk to the village hall to judge the fruit and veg at the Flower Show, with Harold as my assistant to stick the blue, yellow and red dots on the winning entries. What I have to remember is that big is neither necessarily best nor beautiful, nor indeed edible. Every now and then I consult the Rules, frightened of exposing my ignorance where parsnips, say, or cherry plums are concerned. Harold of course knows everything but when I whisper, 'What about this?' he says, 'You're the judge'. On the next trestle a lady judge is holding up a bottle of the Colonel's elderflower wine with contempt. Five silver cups go to Harold. I was not allowed to enter, being a judge. Which is a mercy as most of the fruit and veg at Bottengoms is waterlogged. Why isn't Harold's? How come this perfection? The lady judge is slicing into Victoria sponges to check if they are being held up by scaffolding. Gordon her assistant sticks on dots and is thrown a crumb now and then. I recall what Plato said - 'Refrain awhile from setting yourself up as a judge of the highest matters'. I do better with the children's handwriting, painting and decorated biscuits entries. Outside, Wormingford is playing – who? A roaring shouting side, anyway. The goal posts gleam in sudden sunshine.

The following day, Trinity thirteen, the vicar retires – leaves, goes, vanishes for ever from our sight. He celebrates his final Eucharist, is given his presents, has some wine with us in the now drying-out churchyard, and walks to the vicarage to await the pantechnicon. O seat of desolation, O void of habitation, to whom will the diocese let you? Well, we shall see. Meanwhile we must paint Michael off the Incumbents' Board and off the Notice Board, hold a PCC and choose the hymns for next Sunday.

The intriguing St Theodore of Tarsus has a date in September, that Asiatic Greek sub-deacon who was consecretated Archbishop of Canterbury in 668 and who more or less single handedly created most of today's diocesan and parish map of England. He travelled the whole country. Tarsus bred mighty organisers, but who would have thought that a middle-aged sub-deacon from there would, to quote Bede, 'Unify the English Church and establish the metropolitical authority of the See of Canterbury?' The sub-deacon sat on the lowest seat in the sanctuary after presenting the chalice and paten to the priest, which is what I have been doing for Michael these eight years, and now he is winging north.

Dwindling Landworkers

A vociferous week in the countryside, although it always amuses me when farmers bewail the remoteness of government when half of Whitehall seems to commute from farmhouses, barn-houses and restored cottages. The popular image of the farmer is that of a stolid man not easily stirred

In the time it has taken me to draw this the shadows will have moved right round and the sun will have finished its course

to wrath, whereas the truth is that he is likely to be an emotional and somewhat lonely chap now having to involve himself with many things which go against the grain. He lives on a hundred acres or six hundred acres with only beasts for company, all his men gone, and without the old sociability of market-day in the neighbouring town and scores of other things which came to a halt in the 1960s, never to start-up again. A contractor zooms up and down his fields twice a year and his sons can't tell a coulter from a shovel. Hodge and his master have at long last parted company.

We pore over the old photograph albums, picking out faces, fashions, machines, wide views of small expectations. Here is the wrathful grandfather who threatened to hang the government during those huge farmers' rallies on Newmarket Heath in the Thirties when things could not have been worse. Here he is fighting the Church during the Tithe War. Here are Brownie snaps of quite unbelievable poverty in the tied cottages, the tin bath dangling on a wall, the arrested faces of the children, the bike against the woodpile, brief views of quite amazing poverty, of rural beauty not quite masking rural collapse. The history of agriculture is a roller-coaster of heart-stopping plunges and brief peaks. Apart from wartime subsidies, no government has been able to steady it. But one triumph over what used to happen is that although plagues continue to sweep through the cows, pigs and chickens just as they used to from time immemorial, for the first time in farming history there is never corn failure.

At harvest festival the new commuters sit in the ancient pews and the old farmers walk to the lectern to read about Ruth gleaning and then temptingly resting at the foot of young Boaz's bed, and about Christ's seed parables, nodding comfortably to the altar en-route. There is a home-made loaf on the altar and some especially grown long-stalked wheat to make a proper sheaf. And a positive supermarket display of fruit and veg for the churchwardens to take to St Saviour's, Hackney for the, to us, puzzlingly homeless. In the pulpit I do my best to reconcile agri-business, as they now describe it, with yesterday's reaping, binding and stooking. There are still quite a few folk present, widows of horsemen, daughters and sons of the last classic harvesters who ran around the crowded fields to watch the poor rabbits and hares trying to escape the dogs as the binder reduced their cover, to see that I get the facts right. We sing the 65th psalm in which God 'providest for the earth' and crowns the year with his goodness, and its elemental language strips away all the agri-tech, if only for a moment.

Then a walk to the river, to see how it is getting on, as they say. It is swollen with rain. Later, a waning harvest moon casts its watery light on dripping tombstones. Grain-dryers thud in the barn, so not to worry.

A Lost Reality

Having to convert the old village realities into some kind of convincing contemporary spiritual experience is never more difficult than during harvest festival. The now quite unimaginable toil and the ruthless analogy of the gathering-in of the corn with the reaping of the harvesters themselves, both quite lost. Ubiquitous flower arrangements take precedence over the old hard truths and symbolism. Plenty is what Waitrose is for. I find myself looking for just a few michaelmas daisies on the window ledges and a whiff of the barn plus holy things.

Yet weariness still haunts the faith – that sheer bodily tiredness which resulted from physical work day in, year out, as people once experienced it. At harvest it had its greatest reward, its most visible acknowledgement. Christ the wanderer knew it. Tramping, teaching, healing, homeless, he saw the fieldmen and the fishermen at their tasks, the fieldmen at it from dawn to dusk, the fishermen spasmodically toiling and idling. Theirs was the most commonplace sight in any land, by any water but it was attended with ceremony. Thus the understanding invitation, 'Come unto me, all ye that labour, and I will give you rest'. Thus the speaker's own fragility, that pushing himself sometimes to weakness and tears. In George Herbert's poem *The Pulley* God loads man with every gift except rest because

> Let him be rich and wearie, that at least,
>   If goodness leade him not, yet wearinesse
>   May tosse him to my breast.

Writing my Harvest Festival sermon, carefully omitting country customs and farming practice, both subjects having been aired so many times, and trying to take myself back to the body-breaking fields of my childhood, I stop to catch a play on ITV. I catch too the ads. They are all for sofas.

More Gatherings

Heavy rains have given us a good scrub. Then dry winds have carried lime from the harvested fields to the surrounding blackberries and damsons. Then more torrents to wash them shiny once more. Big leaves flop. Butterbur blackens. Fruit bumps down, more than one can eat or freeze.

At Mount Bures we dance on the dirt floor of a medieval barn to the Hot Club de Pebmarsh, or something like that while the Countryside Marchers put the wind up London, or so they hope, although the divide between village and city has never been smaller. All those MPs commuting daily from the shires, all those early morning trains packed with workers from remote rural communities earning their mortgages in EC1. Tourists will gape at the massed tweeds and hunting horns in Hyde Park. Meanwhile, Vulcan, the Turkish boy au pair who has come to look after a friend's son, arrives at Bottengoms, where he follows the swinging squirrels with lustrous eyes. 'England!' he exclaims.

Rose reads from Tennyson's *Ulysses* at the memorial service for her father the Colonel, and I think of the poet on the Isle of Wight watching the shipping in the Solent which provided him with the imagery of the final departure. Having struggled not to go, Ulysses comes to accept that everything he has achieved in this life is no more than 'an arch where through/gleams that untravelled world . . .' And so we all pass on, Victorian sails billowing, and pennants streaming, longing for Rosie not to end. We sing John Newton's 'See the streams of living waters/springing from eternal love' and I think of the old man's relish for a good solid tale when he read the Lesson, one from the Books of Kings. The gaps made by silenced readers in a country church are often impossible to fill. We go on hearing the dead voice for years and years. At last they join the readers on the monuments who go on saying 'Here endeth' and mean it. The Colonel was harvested alongside his own wheat but Tennyson has the dying Ulysses smiting 'The sounding furrows' with his oar.

I judge the children's section at the Flower Show. The prizes are for the best handwriting for a poem by Edward Thomas. Crayoned butterflies and bees swarm in margins. Who can accurately name the winners? Neat letters, wild letters. An infant's page from the Book of Kells. Cats and

cars and dinosaurs. A bird hiding its head. The village hall is
painted cream and raspberry and the floor shows signs of
line-dancing. There is an ambitious collage made by the now
defunct W.I. of Wormingford itself although my farmhouse
is off-page I grieve to note. Harold wins half the silver cups
for his plums, roses and onions, etc. and goes off with them
like a burglar in a comic and I get a first for a monster pot-
plant. It is not at all Ulysses' scene. He said, 'Though much
is taken, much abides'. I tell the dead pear-tree this as I lay a
bow saw to it. How tall it has grown, how barren it is.

Colin marries Zoë

A dash to Cambridgeshire to open the Annual Booksellers'
Dinner at which I learn with satisfaction that in spite of the
chains there are no fewer than seventy small booksellers in
East Anglia, and here they all are, mostly youngish couples
with a noticeable streak of idealism in them. Hard on the
heels of this outing comes the marriage of Colin the book
conservator, young friend and old neighbour. The marquee
cracks in the wind at Dairy Farm and the barn is laid out for
a feast. Colin repairs precious books to a near-perfect state.
Colleges and cathedral libraries place their tattered treasures
in his hands. Zoë his bride is Belgian and has written out the
Order of Service in both English and French. She shows it to
me. *Moi, Colin, te prends, Zoë, pour éspouse, pour te
recevoir et te garder à partir de ce jourve et pour le futur;
pour le meilleur et pour le pire . . .* The pair of them exists in

a world of craftsmanship, which is among the best worlds ever. When I take stock of a community and find in it a craftsman or two, all my fears vanish, for there is no one as stabilising as a blacksmith or a carpenter or a bookbinder. A Chinese poem about the marriage of true craftsmen is read at the wedding. The poem describes the clay figures of the bride and groom being broken up, moulded together and made one.

> I am in your clay.
> You are in my clay.

We sing Jan Struther's 'Lord of all eagerness, Lord of all faith, Whose strong hands were skilled at the plane and the lathe', myself with feeling, for I can hardly knock a nail in straight. Belgians are everywhere. And Scotsmen. *Moi, Zoë, te prends, Colin, pour éspouse* . . . And the farm dogs whirl around and the horses give us a glance, and the Belgians dance.

After the reception at Higher Dairy Farm barn, where the Union Jack and the Belgian flag hang together in new found drapes, I walk back home, mildly dizzy from drink and toasts and kisses, to sober up under the Victoria plum tree where the fruit bends the branches to the grass, gathering pailfuls for the deep freeze. A heady day. It is still very hot even after the morning rain and the land has a touch of sierra about it, a blond dryness which belongs to the plain. Gnats zizag frenetically by the river. Hanging over the warm rail I can hear the plop of invisible fish. The following day says, 'Summer is past, heat or not heat'. Stumps are drawn from the playing-field. A red bus packed with Sixth Formers on some history lesson creeps through the village filled with faces looking out. The nifty little aeroplane from a farmer's airstrip crackles over the garden. Boys and girls should be swimming, boating, walking, playing, climbing but it is the age of the imprisoned child. 'When did you last run in a meadow, splash in the river?' Don't ask. Of course they could retort, 'When did you last surf the Internet? Got you there!' September wears away like a stone in a stream, imperceptibly.

At the End of the Day

'Lord, we are few, but thou art near' we sing, not without satisfaction as there is just enough of us to fit comfortably into the chancel for Evensong, the ringers, the Wardens, the Colonel and his wife. I say the prayer of St Chrysostom whose feast-day lies just ahead. When they made him Patriarch of Constantinople he decided to clean-up the city. They said he was quite dazzling as a preacher but quite lacking in tact and in the end, like his Lord, they ran him out of town. The manner by which they executed him was very strange. Seeing how ill he was, they forced him to walk in bad weather until he collapsed. He was aged about sixty and had fallen foul of the Empress Eudoxia. His name means 'golden-mouthed' – from his beautiful preaching. His prayer says all that needs to be said to a small congregation - 'that when two or three are gathered together in thy Name thou wilt grant their request. Fulfil now, O Lord, the desires and petitions of thy servants . . .' Cranmer chose it from the Litany for Chrysostom's day.

The ringers give up, having attempted a peal and failed. I talk about the many towers of the Old Testament as a sliver of late sunshine cuts through the west window, Saxon may be, and no more than a sliver itself. Babel, of course, and the towering God of the Psalmist. The ringers, tower-men all, prick up their ears, having climbed them all over England. We walk down to the Stour. The river is black and deep in thought and Samuel Palmer apple trees on its bank yellow like Samuel Palmer paintings. The temperature tumbles in a little rush and we rub bare arms. I imagine every Wormingford face that ever was looking up at its owner from the dark water, Normans and Victorians, and the boys on the war memorial, all these likenesses bright and exact for a moment then flowing away. My features wobble on the surface, briefly defying the current, and are gone. An unseen creature joins the flow and it makes me think of those William Blake angels who watch over animals and who

> Look in every thoughtless nest
> Where birds are cover'd warm:
> They visit caves of every beast,
> To keep them all from harm.

Let us hope that they make the Countryside Marchers uneasy. Blake was writing about the spiritual protection of a spiritual creation. No one exceeds his love and pity for animals. The crass language of the blood sports lobby becomes illegible when it runs into his words.

> O lapwing! thou fliest around the heath,
> Nor seest the net that is spread beneath.
> Why does thou not fly among the corn fields?
> They cannot spread nets where a harvest yields.

Cousin Winnie Blythe

Some of the last words of the Old Testament are about the Lord coming when it is 'not day, nor night . . . but at evening time.' At Bottengoms I have to climb from a hollow if I want to see the sun set. Celebrated they are in East Anglia, these sunsets, blood-streaking, raging, lurid and glorious by turn. Westering rooks head into them. Drivers are blinded by them. Should the curtains not be drawn, television screens are little more than shifting glaucus oblongs when a sunset hits them. Horses' eyes run gold and have to be turned away when our suns go down. Cut harvest fields offer a stringing-out of this gold, the stubble lined to infinity and shining out of sight.

Yesterday I was walking in Little Cornard at sunset, where Martin Shaw composed 'Hills of the North, Rejoice!' and Thomas Gainsborough painted *Cornard Wood*, and I wandered with mother in childhood, picking wild flowers. Here in the churchyard is a sailor named Charles Constable, John's cousin or uncle – the artist's family had spread itself along the heights of the Stour Valley for centuries – and I see that Charles has what at first glance is a Roman emporer carved on his tombstone, although, since he died just after Trafalgar, must be Britannia. The familiar cupola on the church is first ignited then put out by the dying sun. The evening has always been a time of contemplation, an 'abyss of wonder'.

The next day to Long Melford for Cousin Winnie's funeral. It takes place in the 'strange' (Pevsner) Lady Chapel, a rare medieval shrine room annexed to this vast parish church with its parade of glass and flint donors and its march of tracery, and its holy palace splendour. It was in the strange Lady Chapel where Winnie lies that there stood a *Pietà* which was like a Suffolk version of Michaelangelo's grieving, nursing Mother 'having the afflicted body of her

315

dear Son . . . lying on her lap.' A *Pietà* is among the most physically complex works of art imaginable. For where normally would lie a child, lies a full-grown man, and where even a baby's liveliness relieves the strain, there is adult deadweight. But nothing remains of this burden and its bearer. D.H. Lawrence must have thought about it when he wrote *The Miner's Saturday Night*, the *Pietà*, the tragic second bearing by a woman of her son. The washing of his injured body, the arrangement of his limbs, the view of his nakedness, its coldness and rigidity. A clumsy pattern of humanity and poignant beyond words. Where stood the *Pietà* in the strange Lady Chapel? Up there near the Georgian multiplication tables, when the Long Melford children came to school here? By that arch? There are tennis racquets and Slazenger balls arranged against the altar, and pews filled with Wimbledon folk, and an umpire to tell of Winnie's fame, and a gentle priest and weeping sisters. I see too my dead cousin, a thin dark girl dashing about on the Suffolk courts, only not yesterday. Our grandmother Martha Allen, a Long Melford child, was confirmed in this church by having a purple-covered board carried over her head, and those of hundreds of other boys and girls, the churchwardens, the Bishop of Norwich in between. Up and down went the board and the Bishop under the eye of the medieval aristocrats, the children nodding, the tea calling from the marquee outside.

Being Young, Being Old

Today I preach on the young men who have the nerve to raise their voices against the old men, my favourite being Elihu who broke into the sterile debate which surrounded poor Job with, 'I am young, and you are very old; wherefore I was afraid, and durst not show you mine opinion. I said, Days should speak, and multitude of years should teach wisdom. But . . . great men are not always wise, neither do the aged understand judgement.' The Job poet then puts into the mouth of young Elihu some of the most wonderful distinction between God and man ever written. So captivating are they that God himself has to add a rider to this boy's argument. All this in the golden chancel with old friends.

This week my priming the pump book has been Italo Calvino's masterpiece *Invisible Cities*. I read it before work, just a few pages, and feel the morning translating itself into words. Marco Polo is telling Kubla Khan about his travels even though 'the emperor of the Tartars does not necessarily believe everything the young Venetian says'. Neither can we, the readers of this great book, for what we are told has to go beyond our ordinary understanding. This is the function of inspired writing, to push against what are taken to be the limits of possibility. Calvino's cities of the high imagination contain street maps of Birmingham, say, and of Jerusalem of course, for they have to be both civic and sacred. They are to help us to find our way about what we call 'civilisation'.

Through the study window I watch wrens picking away at the heads of dead marguerites. I can see the hide which the rabbit shooters built on the set-aside field. It has been set alight and smokes rather wearily, having outlived its function. After lunch I wait for Elizabeth who is en-route from Idaho to Oxford to take a course. I show her Stoke-by-Nayland church and our church here. She sees faces, not

317

architecture, not perp and dec but all the unregarded angel faces looking down from the string-lines, human faces uplifted in Victorian glass, rude faces spouting water from the leads. 'So many faces, Mr Blythe.' More than I had noticed. She takes the bus to the station and her face in profile becomes that of a passenger on the red tin bus of childhood, a girl ever in outline, travelling on and on.

The Hog Roast

The wind blows surprisingly cold. Laggard swallows whirl around the wires, screaming about take-off. Bernard ploughs and harrows the stubble in one go and the usual army of gulls descend on the pickings. At the Mount Bures harvest festival Andrew reads from *Ruth*. 'So she gleaned in the field until even, and beat out that she had gleaned.' Poor woman, she would have had a thin time in Bernard's field. It is Duncan's fifty-first harvest and, he says, his second worst. Winter flooding, spring flooding, ponding, last minute drying-up. But we have to celebrate what there is, hence all these well-fed young Boazes and Ruths filling their plates at the hog-roast. A brass band blares a heart-rending arrangement of the *Last Post* and *Now the Day is Over*, the trumpets crossing the hymn. In the barn another band from Pebmarsh swings in the hay loft and we take to the earth floor. Two rosy sisters on leave from an H.E. Bates tale dole out hog and salad, apple pie and cream, and there is pressure at the bar. Agriculture may be having one of its turns but a meadowful of glittering cars and a barnful of folk who could not look more prosperous if they tried, or less physically exhausted after all has been gathered in, display an absolute break with the past. A poor harvest nowadays means just a bit less in the bank. And what happens in the August and September fields has been totally abstracted from village experience. The hundred and fifty or so of us are being good mannered to Providence, happily miming the old gratitude, the old relief, the old customs. One thing is certain, farmers' children all over East Anglia do not want father's acres and the contractors are doing the family work.

The Arrow-head

Waiting for a lift to church, I see the arrow-head. It is cushioned in a furrow and is like a jewel in a velvet box. It is perfect and has been fashioned, not from flint but fossilised shell, and is dangerously sharp. It lies in my cassock pocket all through the service and I hesitate to feel for a hanky. Preaching on God's 'continual pity' for us, I am careful not to draw blood. The arrow-head calls out to me. It says it is born of a sea creature and a human creature, of a cold mollusc and a warm hand, and that it could have brought cold death to a warm body. It might even have started out as an arrow of desire. I touch it delicately with the tip of a finger as we sing, 'There let it for thy glory burn with inextinguishable blaze.' It is the last week of summer. Back home I lay it alongside conches from some Empire shore in which I have heard the rise and fall of the Indian Ocean.

Empty pews here and there in church. The Countryside Alliance is at its beano in Hyde Park, a comic army which believes that rural life will faint right away without a regular injection of animal blood. It must have been the new contract ploughman who turned up the arrow-head. I walk in his tracks after church to see if there are any more, stumbling about, picking up sharp implements which turn out to be nothing more than flints which have been split by a plough-

Man with saddleback pig

share. Again I think of the flint artist chipping away out of the Neolithic wind, perhaps in the sheltered corner where the farmhouse now stands. A few yards from where I am searching the soil for arrows are the last tied cottages to be given up by farmworkers in the village. Bernard and Keith have left the land to find another life in their middle age. The absence of their men has left the farmers lonely. Although the relationship possessed an historic complexity and awkwardness, to find themselves without it is causing farmers to feel a bit lost. The question lying dormant is of course that of subsidy. It rolls around like a bomb in a pit, always there, never going off, too dicey to touch. No one says what must happen.

There is too the problem of urbanisation, of comfort and guilt for being normally comfortable with TV, supermarkets, cars, foreign holidays, clubbing, computers, central heating, etc. when living in 'the countryside' where things should be different, and better and above what townspeople have or strive for. Scything the orchard, I come across a myxy rabbit. It trembles and has opaque eyes, and is the victim of rural management. High up on the balancing scale the white cat swings after squirrels as they screech through a pear-tree. The last of the farmworkers may have gone but never the rooks. Phyllida said that she watched miles and miles of them – it is not possible to exaggerate about rooks – crossing the early evening sky like a bird river. We pray that the lapwings will do the same. The huge philosophical joy of rural life stems from the sudden revelation of timeless happenings. Take colchicums, for example. No leaves to warn one where they lie and then, yesterday, a dozen of the purest most virginal white stems were cupping through the earth and looking more untouched by it than any other flower. The sensuality of purity – can there be such a thing?

Monkshood

Before the corn drill was invented broadcast seed was occasionally harrowed into roughly straight lines. Ideally, the farmers liked it to fall into autumn or spring dust. Dust therefore had its moments and was praised by rural poets. At this moment David – call him that – is driving a monster machine up and down the enormous field which has been set aside these last four years and turning it into a dusty Bridget Riley. What was once all bumps and weeds will soon be a green geometry. Harvesting is now so early that, further up the lane, winter wheat is already inches high and gently overcoming gold-leaf straw. Nearby Jean is snipping branches of a fruiting hedge, blackberry, sloes and damson, to decorate the Baptist Chapel in Bures, our tin chapel having gone years ago. It had been built from farm labourers' pennies in the 1890s. The symbolism of this Victorian festival gets harder and harder to recreate. Stacks of tins for institutions which do not want them, prayers for the starving nations we glimpse on television. Elaborate flower arrangements screen an absence of conviction. As for the tragic metaphor of ourselves as an eventually reaped crop, 'Christ's golden sheaves to garners bright elected,' we no longer see life and death in such terms. Yet many of the old harvest hymns deal chillingly with things like Time and Tares, good and wasted seed, refusal and its consequences, and their tunes are plaintive rather than joyous. Perhaps the Church has to deal again with the roughness of feeding ourselves, with the reality of an untidy sheaf, with the sight of perfect fruit on the turn, with the evidence of spiritual hunger.

Monkshood is in bloom where my friend John Nash planted it when he came to Bottengoms Farm in 1945. Twenty years earlier he had written and illustrated a book called *Poisonous Plants* and Monkshood, *Aconitum napellus* had a special place in it. Gerard described it as a 'goodly blue flower' which was not to be trusted. Arrows were dipped into its essence. But it did prevent pain although a drip too much might prevent you feeling anything else forever. Bees are working it at the moment, prising their way into it and rocking the slender stems. 'Won't you have a little more of this delicious Monkshood honey?' Alas for the wickedest and most entertaining crimes, the great age of poisoners is past, put to death by forensic experts, but what dramas it generated in a village! Snowdrops sleep in their hundreds under the Monkshood and will erase all evidence of it in February. But it will return, probably for centuries, blue as blue, lovely and treacherous. They called it wolf's bane and Keats advises us not to 'twist/Wolf's-bane, tight-rooted, for its poisonous wine'.

Diana is writing her own funeral and enjoying it no end. She rings up. 'May I have four hymns?' Certainly. 'And the *Te Deum*?' By all means. And bells? Just say the word. She says that she has crossed out 'O Christ our hope, our hearts' desire' and substituted 'Thine be the glory.' But she is having difficulty with the literary claims of Isaiah's holy highway and a favourite poem. Me: 'Is it a very long poem?' Diana, 'rather long.' Me, 'Don't forget the party afterwards.' 'Oh, you should not have reminded me – I won't be there.' Do not be too sure about that, I say, but not into the telephone. More funeral as I peel and halve cookers, dust them with cinnamon and put them into a fireproof dish. Cats wind round my feet, earnestly adoring.

The Mad and the Sane

I am handling Victoria plums, slitting them on the breadboard to let the stones tumble out. It is a plump sexy fruit, nice to touch, firm and soft and juicy. The greengages simply burst on their own account, the blackberries stain everything. The freezer swells. Mr Bradshaw has kindly tamed my tall wild hedge, made it into a come-to-attention straight line, taking care not to lop the lilacs, wielding 'the murderer' skilfully. We have quite forgiven this hedge-trimmer for the wounds it incurs. My only criticism of its use nowadays is that farmers tidy-up too quickly after harvest and forget that they destroy all the hips and haws and other bird foods. Once it was the scythe which was death to the leveller, now it is this crashing knife which slides along the lanes like a cut-throat razor over whiskers. I barrow ash logs into the chimney corner and pile them artistically, leaving the sawn ends showing.

I am working on an essay about the World War One poet Ivor Gurney, the singer of Gloucestershire who, after the horrors of the trenches, like many another poor soldier, ended up in a madhouse, or to be exact Dartford City of London Mental Asylum, a dreadful place. Fourteen years after the Armistice Edward Thomas's widow found him there and gradually 'returned' the shambolic man in pyjamas to who he really was by means of spreading out her husband's maps to the Cotswolds on Gurney's bed. 'I spent the whole time I was with him tracing with our fingers the lanes and byways and villages of which Ivor Gurney knew every step and over which Edward had also walked. He spent that hour (strict visiting times) in revisiting his home . . . he trod, in a way we who were sane could not emulate, the lanes and fields he knew so well, his guide being his finger tracing the way on the map. It was most deeply moving, and I knew that I had hit on the idea that gave him more pleasure than anything else I could have thought of. For he had Edward as companion in this strange perambulation and he was utterly happy.'

When one reads the rules of institutions, prisons, workhouses, asylums, some schools even, certain religious orders, one can only question the sanity of society itself. What of the present culture of the old peoples' home? What will posterity make of that?

To the village to call on Phil and his wife in a garden which is the size of four tablecloths. He is stringing onions, she is tidying-up after the hedgehogs. She feeds them each evening with Phil's fish bait maggots, all four of them as they creep on to the lawn, and she agrees that if it was the seventeenth century Matthew Hopkins, our local witch-finder, would be knocking on her door. Joan also feeds some forty sparrows. Later, Phil brings me two great strings of onions to hang in, first a tree, and then in the larder. Like everything else, they must ripen.

Fordham Wood

It was the kind of weather one reads about more than sees. First an uncanny build-up of meteorological emotion, then the declared helplessness of animals as they sensed it, and then the scramble to collect the garden chairs, the washing, the everything which had been taken outside and left in the sun's safekeeping for what seemed months. It caught me on the last lap, a sheet of rain which soaked me to the skin in one drenching minute. It ran in scallops over the bone-dry earth and rivered its way down the track to where it knew the river was. It churned in the guttering and spouted from rooftops. I let it beat on me, having nothing more to lose and it shot in an arc from my nose. Summer rain *in excelsis*. I had read outside all day and although the sky got lower and lower and the warm breeze stirred into a warm gale, and there was the sound of something or other on the march, still I read on the grass, having just done the watering as usual. The windows were wide as they had been for weeks.

And to think that only two days before the rain I and some of the strongest men the Woodland Trust could muster had nearly killed ourselves planting a dozen oaks in the new wood at Fordham, with a photographer from the local paper capturing our exhaustion. The ground was like concrete. It called for a pick-axe and all we had were beautiful silver spades. So we were reduced to scratching holes for oaklings, and saying sorry to the delicate plants as we introduced them to the home they would have for the following five hundred years. Will they when we are long gone tell each other of their dry starts? The following day about sixty of us walked the wood to be, men, women and children, and assorted dogs, tramping the hot land which is to become Wrens' Wood and listening to Geoff from the Woodland Trust, a Scot, telling us a thousand things we never knew about our own trees. Colchester was a Girtin or Cozens watercolour in the distance. The river on which it stood was a small stream at our feet. Here was a Stone Age farm, here a Roman farm, here the roots of the final wheat to be grown on these acres before a forest reclaimed it.

'Your old population is on its way back. Your barn owls, otters, nightingales, butterflies, wild flowers, your stag beetles, water voles, foxes, plus – Geoff estimates – some

213,000 trees.' I have been made Patron of Wrens' Wood and my pride knows no bounds. The humbling point is, how much of it will I live to see? The downpour will be feeding the ground, my tiny oaks, washing away my scratchings in the sand.

Persian Suffolk

It has been a week of distinctive happenings, each of them closed off in some way from the next and marked. Such as the trip to Boulge – 'Boolj' for non-Suffolk tongues. This is the home of Edward FitzGerald who, trying his hand at learning Persian, produced a masterpiece from a masterpiece, *The Rubáiyát of Omar Khayyám*. I knew it by heart in my teens but now its quatrains tumble about like shedding roses in my head. A blissful line here, a farewell there. It is Fitz's description of being here today and gone tomorrow. We stand around his grave in Boulge churchyard, around which too the late Shah had planted roses from Omar's own tomb at Nishapur. Living nearby at Debach, I was present when they arrived and later took Charles Causley to see where Fitz lay beneath a tilting stone. It was Charles's birthday and we were there at near midnight and a little drunk, and the Shah's roses were black in the blackness. Now they are in unspectacular bloom. There is a defensive line from the *Jubilate* on his grave - 'It is He that hath made us and not we ourselves,' for he was an Irish gentleman out of the ordinary in Victorian Suffolk whose friendships, he said, were more like loves. I call on other buried neighbours, pretty Sue Pirkis, Lady White who picked me flowers, Mr Banthorpe who took all the prizes at the Debach and Boulge Flower Show, and Mr Anderson who was the Scottish shepherd in *Akenfield*. FitzGerald's formidable mother, the friend of Thackeray and who dined off gold plate (they said) lies beside the church in a grand mausoleum. The Rubáiyát sees all bodies as humus for gardens, as dust to feed hyacinths, as blood to colour roses. It was intoxicating stuff for a young man all set to be a poet, with his bike against the rail and his head all over the place.

> Ah, make the most of what we yet may spend,
> Before we too into the Dust descend;
> Dust into Dust, and under Dust to lie,
> Sans Wine, sans Song, sans Singer, and – sans End!

To be accurate, Fitz lies under heavy Suffolk clay, 'loving land' the farmers called it because it clung so and would not let one go. There is a new avenue to Lady White's house but Boulge Wood, where starlings would rest in their thousands, bending the boughs, is in full summer's leaf.

At the Charterhouse

I had to ask the way to the Charterhouse, although how such a London wanderer as myself had need to was bewildering. But there it was, sprawling lavishly near Smithfield, almost as grand as the Grande Chartreuse from which it takes its name. Carthusians were strict and quiet but not austere. How did this monastery-palace-hospital-boys' school-refuge for ageing men manage to retain some of its primal sanctity through so many vicissitudes? Was Carthusian prayer the conqueror in the end? Was it this which finally ousted the royal courts, the view of the plague-pits, the horrors of the Dissolution, Tudor ambition, Stuart profligacy, generations of noisy boys and Hitler's raiders to be as it is now, an acre of refuge behinds the roar of Theobald's Road?

We lunch in what was once the cloister before the Duke of Norfolk roofed it in to make a dry run to the tennis court, and we have tea where Elizabeth I waited for death. Before this there is BCP Holy Communion in what was once the Chapter House, and facing a Giordano altar-piece in which the pregnancy of the Virgin as she meets her cousin Elizabeth could hardly be either more physical or more theological. The Bishop of Lambeth preaches on the prevailing nature of Pharisaism. A Charterhouse brother shows me his rooms. What EC1 bliss and all found. Below, on scattered monuments, is a fame call of Old Carthusians. John Wesley, William Thackeray, Baden-Powell, and in the Chapel itself the quite amazing tomb of the giver of everything, not God but a Mr Sutton. No, a brother may not keep a cat. Back at Bottengoms my cat is sitting on a wall swishing her tail and not best pleased, and a fox is taking a fallen plum into her delicate mouth.

Some alternative set readings for September. Barbara Pym's *Quartet in Autumn*, Elizabeth Bowen's haunting *The Last September* and Ted Hughes' *Seasons' Songs*. Now I must continue where I left off, making hay of the nettles by the stream, yanking them up root and sting, clearing the ground. For soon it will be frozen ground and stalks like wires, then green tips all over again. Nothing ceases. The continuum of plants and soils and weathers must beat us all. Barry, Bernard, Chris and Linda are off in a bus to ring

London bells. They tell me that some of the loveliest peals are in the East End, in those rivery parishes which laid low in marshes and whose towers are now dwarfed by Canary Wharf. But still the estuary birds flock in. What will they ring? 'We'll see when we get there.' They are off, our ringers, the tower captain, another Christopher but still in his teens and with countless towers ahead of him, the ringing women, the ringers' language and craft. 'St John's, Bethnal Green is on our list,' Bernard announces firmly, as though it might escape their attention.

At Discoed

Much gadding about. There are stay-at-home weeks on end, then days away from home, like buses, arrive all at once. In this last September week comes Radnorshire (Powys to the postman) and Westminster, Lambeth Degree holders have been invited to their annual gathering, this time at Westminster Cathedral. After Sung Eucharist at St Matthew's, a church I couldn't at first discover but was eventually led to by the ringing of its bell, we walked through the chilly streets to the Cathedral where all was hospitable, marble, mosaics, cardinals slumbering beneath suspended hats, tea, warmth for Anglicans, lunch, everything.

Then, two days later, it was tiny Discoed, a parish near Presteigne, to join in its poetry festival. Throughout Britain one encounters similar time-lost churches where, in the nature of things, the fire burns low but never quite goes out, where the frontal sags damply and the lectern rocks a bit. Then along comes some inspirer to breathe new life into it – to actively believe in its original purpose. Here at Discoed the inspirer is my old Fenland friend Edward Storey who a few years ago forsook his native flats for the Welsh border. Happening to discover an immensely ancient church more or less in his garden and seeing with a poet's eye the shepherds for whom it was built, he blew on its embers.

I sometimes marvel that so few now come to make a blaze. Villagers will work their socks off for an event to raise funds but are cool and absent when it comes to service, carefully spacing-out their attendance for when they have to read a lesson or carry a bag. Yet there is always the fire burning low and waiting to be blown upon by the spirit.

The autumn is far too lovely to be grumpy. At Discoed the Suffolks are scattered across the Welsh hills like woolly pearls, the clouds bank above the Brecon Beacons and the shadows lengthen. St Michael is in residence in his shrine above the wide open valley. The young rector, who has only got four other churches to care for, presides at Harvest Festival Eucharist and there is a good evening congregation. Also the happy smell of soup heating. I talk about the variable wonders of such places, a wonder taken for granted up and down the land. Here along the Border these wonders follow each other in a wonderfully poetic succession which makes the whole area unique. It is Traherne's country, Kilvert's country, Vaughan's country, Herbert's country and now Storey's country. We drive from poet to poet along empty roads, and to low farms which duck from the wind, and past old battlefields. Tourism, archaeology and a few personal experiences all come together to draw each of our own maps of sacred territory. Once it was a map of cures. Once a way to work. Much-trodden paths could lead to health, to jobs, to marriage and to the eternal. Traherne still tells us that the world is very beautiful and that we are not long in it, so, he says, make the most of it. Adore it even. He possessed it until he was thirty-seven. He was the great appreciator.

October

Islanders - More Wakings - Lifespans - The Leaves Come Down - Living to One's Self - Fire Frost - Diggers - Ilkley Poetry Festival - Crucifixion - Fenland - Swarming in the Nave - A Ploughing Match - Mark Ploughing - Amos the Herdsman - Empire Spa - The Glass Book - St Jude and Harold's Orchard

Islanders

The October calendar says, 'Remember William Tyndale,' but how could we ever forget him, that most wonderful of English translators whose sentences still lie on the tongue of the world? Lying in bed, the light just coming, I can see that Jack Frost hasn't quite got into the room, although he is certainly nipping around outside. I like the way the old house notches up October with isolated chills here and there, their sharp intakes of the breath of stored apples and onions, their cooling passages, their homing rustles in the roof, their suggestion of a mortality which doesn't quite occur. The bedside radio asks, ' Where has heaven gone?' Remotely, my thoughts still half asleep, I recall how death verses in hymns tend to be asterisked, the worst instance of this being St Francis's exquisite and timely, 'And thou, most kind and gentle death,/Waiting to hush our latest breath,/O praise him, Alleleuya!' He was singing to her in his *Canticle of the Sun*.

Later, the Hebridian poet James Knox Whittet arrives. He brings his East Anglian wife with him. We talk about the Scottish islands. His is Islay, population three and half thousand, economy, fishing and whisky. No, alas, I have not visited it but in my youth I did very nearly set up a writer's life on Skye, and I did once descend on George Mackay Brown at Stromness, running into him in his gale-lashed street. I told James how George designed his working day, for writers care for this kind of information. He rose early, made room to write among the breakfast things – and wrote, his back to the window. Then he might go to the pub, after which he definitely stoked up a good coal fire and 'interrogated silence,' as he put it, the ghosts of his Orkney forebears in attendance. Producing tea on my visit, holding up a fragile piece of china, he said, 'Mother's best cups'. Books had tumbled about our ears.

The poet from Islay said that he had entered a remote Hebridian Episcopalian church to discover Evensong in full swing. Just a priest, no one else. I said that I had once had the temerity to sit in R.S. Thomas's empty church to wonder what it could be like to hear him celebrate, preach, look at me. Strangers always make a great showing in country churches and writers tend to stick out a mile.

More Wakings

It is as black as midnight. A furious droning brings me to, or not entirely, because I am in the Malabar caves and about to be compromised by Miss Quested. Gradually I recognise the voice of one of my dear hornets as it bumps against the double glazing. Showing immense courage, I capture it in a glass and carry it out into the garden. Almost wren-size, it zooms fretfully off through falling oak leaves.

Richard Bawden arrives about ten to paint the house. He settles in a cosy spot and assumes the classic posture of the landscape artist, head down out of the wind, eyes roving, watercolours at the ready. Ours is a workaday autumn laced with coffee and visited by cats. We toil on, inside and out, until the commuters come home. I tell Richard about a young Canadian friend who has discovered what to do about all the fragments of talk which mobiles release in railway carriages – pick them up and weave them into plays. Soon, trains will carry warnings - 'You are being dramatised'. Writers are terrible listeners, magpies picking up sentences wherever they can, turning them into confessions, short stories, anything.

It is the twelfth of October 1915 - I am quoting the calendar again - and two in the morning. A middle-aged nurse from a Norfolk rectory is being led out into a yard and shot for not finding patriotism enough to distinguish friend from foe. Visiting a Bavarian hospital shortly before the war, she had given the patients some musical instruments to help them get well, paying for them out of her little private income. Hopelessly kind Edith Cavell, she should have realised that one had to change one's tactics in a war. What would happen if none of us changed our morality?

Lifespans

October, and the first dark as midnight morning, the old farmhouse winter-still. Outside, a bird squawking and the ash-tree hissing, the stream full and rushing to the river. No fading planes steering through the stars to Stanstead, 'a stony place'. It is pleasantly warm but black. Most of the early mornings which Bottengoms has lived, four centuries of them, would have been anything than silent at six-thirty.

Children thundering through the low rooms, labourers feeling their way from beds under the thatch, mothers hollering, the kindling sparking in the newly lit grate. Cats and dogs and pigs and plough horses as hungry as hunters. But now, under its new dispensation of art and writing, it has the silence of the cell. The news or a little music might invade it. I might sing, only this might prove that I have no one until the morning of the weekend to say anything to. Kitty and Dinah are trebly quiet in a corner as they hope to out-sit a mouse. A harvest mouse. It rains steadily, that soft October rain which village people called 'wet'. Wet was the bane of farms like this. From them, in 1917, the previously reserved work-force was called up to die in the unparalleled 'wet' of Flanders.

I think of this as I slide the curtains because the post contains a photostat of Laurence Binyon's manuscript of *For the Fallen*. It lies by the toast as the day lightens, the famous fourth verse as yet un-extracted and unknown except to its author, and with nothing to suggest its official career. The war was well under its mad way when Binyon found words for its mourning. He wrote them as the 1916 summer ended and the heavens opened on the locked armies, drenching the thick clumsy uniforms, holding feet into the earth, drowning guns. Those youngsters who had earlier run off from hated farms had not reckoned to run into their old enemy, the wet, not on such a scale. I stare at Binyon's handwriting as the kettle boils, see his spiky penmanship, the ups and downs of it, the scratchy nib. A huge blot precedes the famous lines:

> They shall grow not old, as we that are left grow old:
> Age shall not weary them, nor the years condemn.
> At the going down of the sun and in the morning
> We will remember them.

Like lines from sacred books, they are said out of context. When at a Remembrance Service I read the whole poem from the pulpit there was a second silence.

> They sit no more at familiar tables of home;
> They have no lot in our labour of the day-time . . .

Breakfast over, the beasts fed, I read some of Seamus Heaney's *Beowulf*. Now here was a soldier who did grow old, who age did wither. His attempt to slay the dragon which threatened his society was the last act of an aged man.

The Leaves Come Down

Autumn for the suburbs. I am walking out of Colchester, striding towards the coast in a wet wind. It is a novelty to be doing this so early in the morning, and against the hoards coming into town, the student army marching on the Sixth Form College, the hurrying shop and office workers, the flood of children humping enormous book-bags, the old women plodding along to where they go on Tuesdays. Flags zip at the mast, cars gridlock, and boys hold out the *Big Issue*. What is ordinary in this world is a novelty to me, a passing show which I cannot miss. Soon I am among the terraces and villas which trickle into the fields and which contain the rooms which the hoards have just left, the tumbled beds and cornflakes, the tellies just switched off after the Breakfast Show, the car-port gardens, the last few flowers, the T-shirts flapping on lines, the waiting cats in the windows, the house agents' boards, the over-all scent of mortgage.

The modesty of these semis and rows and free-standing

bungalows, and kempt and neglected gardens, is here and there interrupted by something big, the barracks, the cemetery, the terrifying walls of St John's Priory as they lean from history into the traffic, and by sedate roads named after the town's celebrities which lead to soaking tennis courts and

A weasel moving its young from loose straw to baled straw and back again

network off into hundreds such places to create a map of residential inconsequence for those who have no address in it. All the same, I often turn off from the sights to explore it. The pavements are messy with trodden leaves and plastic wrappings struggle in hedges. A mangy sun has come out and does wonders for bricks and slates, gives them no end of a going over. Fifty members of the Parachute Regiment are jogging to their barracks in vests and shorts, slapping and puffing along. Here is the Borough Cemetery, Gothic with threatening guard-dogs at dusk for intruders. It is enormous, going on for ever, the tombstones like the sands of the shore uncountable. One or two I know by heart. Here is Christopher James, a little boy who, it says, was 'Born asleep.' Not for him the call-up, the Dissolution of the Monasteries, the Sixth Form College, the girls with their straightened hair, the Building Society, the walk in the sun-rain.

If I walk on I will come to the Strood where the Roman guard keeps watch for the Count of the Saxon Shore. I will arrive on Mersea Island where the Reverend Sabine Baring-Gould wrote 'Now the Day is Over,' where the Colchester natives lie in the oyster-beds, where the North Sea howls. Back home it is post-harvest festival and Gordon and Pam will be emptying the church produce into their car and taking it to St Saviour's, Hoxton, for the London homeless to devour. The sisters there will turn it into meals. A quarter peal was wrung in honour of 'plenty' when all this fruit and veg filled Wormingford church and we went as far as saying the General Thanksgiving altogether. Thank goodness we weren't homeless in Hoxton, thank heavens we weren't farming in Orissa, from where Peter the organist has just returned to tell of unimaginable poverty – and spirituality. After the service I had put out the belfry light and noticed that the incumbents' photos had been hung closer to make way for yet another peal-board, which is only right and proper. I saw too the medieval brasses which had been lifted from the nave floor during the Victorian restoration winking at me. Stiff hands in perpetual prayer, stiff dresses, stiff brass-artists' expressions on their faces. 'We are not where we should be,' they are saying. Perhaps none of us are.

Living to One's Self

'We must cultivate our garden,' said Candide when the world was going mad. He meant no ivory towerism, just doing something sane and delightful which might catch on. Part of my garden is English literature, a handful of country parishes and a spread of friends. Like all such plots it is invaded by what lies around it. At this moment deaths lie around it. So listening to a downpour in bed my thoughts dwell on mourning. The rain crashes through the willows and makes wild music. All night there is no let up. Down it comes. Beethoven on the radio, a novel face down on the bedside table, the curtains wet because the windows are wide, and what sounds like the Psalmist's water-spouts gushing scarcely a foot from my head. Or Thomas Hardy's 'gurgoyle' washing away the plants which Sergeant Troy has planted on poor Fanny's grave.

To St Leonard's, Colchester, to celebrate a clock. It is one of those churches which, although officially redundant, its congregation refuses to let go. It rises in medieval loveliness above the Hythe where the Romans unloaded their ships. Two Tractarian priests had it in their aesthetic grasp for half a century – Fr Newcomen and Canon Carter, good hardworking men who would have fallen foul of today's attitudes. Their parish was large and poverty-stricken, their church was filled with beautiful objects, music and ritual. Known as 'the Divines', they were greatly respected. They wore wide-brimmed Holy Joe hats and soutanes, and Fr Newcomen sported a red wig. Remotely in their history gleamed the spires of Victorian Oxford. Their church is packed to pay homage to the clock, mayor and all. I read George Herbert's poem *Christmas* in which he puts up at an inn, only to discover that Someone has arrived before him. However, there is just room for a late guest.

> All after pleasures as I rid one day,
> My horse and I, both tir'd, bodie and minde,
> With full crie of affections, quite astray;
> I took up in the next inne I could finde.
> There when I came, whom found I but my deare,
> My dearest Lord . . .

The repaired clock tells the time exactly. The Divines' brass and glass glitters, St Leonard, on whose day I was born, peers hazily through Time and Christopher unleashes the organ's power. Nothing certain is known of the hermit Leonard but they say that prisoners called upon him. Colchester was once a clockmaker's hub of the universe. I see them all, these masters of horology, at some long forgotten feast at St Leonard's counting the hours, singing the minutes, their ears fine-tuned to the workings of this very clock. Sick with consumption, Herbert's life would have ticked away at Bemerton quite unbearably had he not understood so well its timeless dimension. 'Listen sweet Dove', he tells the Holy Spirit, 'And spread thy golden wings in me'. He will soon be off to the ultimate Inn. Herbert always sees himself as a guest or a servant timed to be where he should be.

Fire Frost

Bottengoms is a frost pocket. Hard winters make a bee-line to it. It crumps and crunches with cold, and holds on to its frosts even when the sun hits it. Proust once described a Paris frost cutting its way through the walls of his apartment with 'a silver knife' and I too can hear a really great frost doing something to the pintiles which gives me the shivers. And it used to be uncanny how Jack Frost drew his pictures on the inside of the panes, proving that nothing can keep him out. That is, until the central heating arrived. I quite miss his cold art. As children we heard the house being warmed up from scratch every morning, the tinkle of the kindling, the lighting of oil-stoves, the stamping of feet as logs and coals were fetched, and then miraculously porridge steaming in a hot kitchen. Keeping the fire in overnight was an expert business but some managed it. It was an art, the finding the flame, the puffing it into a blaze, the laying of the wood in a kind of wigwam above it and the knowing when to stop. And it was heroic to take off one's pyjamas in the bathroom which was a kind of interior frost pocket especially fitted to our nakedness.

In Suffolk a good man always rose before his wife to make a good fire. But there were good wives who boasted that 'he' never did a hand's turn in the house and who said that 'he' always got out of bed to a good fire, bacon and eggs and a warm shirt. Women at that time were nervous about male domesticity and even where their husbands helped, going so far as doing the washing when babies were born, would brag of their uselessness in the home in order to preserve their masculinity. In winter washing would hang above the frosted grass like crystal boards.

To Essex University to give the third of my seminars. Its grey towers soar above Wivenhoe Park like rookeries for students. My dozen or so drift into our classroom with their stories and poems. Behind the lines being read are the intentions to write. Their ages run from twenty to maybe forty, and their nationalities from here to China. They are each to read me something in their own language. The Jewish girl from Exeter reads something from Exodus in Hebrew, the French student gallops through Rimbaud's *Le Bateau ivre*, the boy from Epping reads me some pages from a novel he is writing about love in Essex. I read them a short story. The evening cold cuts my ears off as I run through the campus to the bus.

Diggers

The sifting, vaguely wandering mists of October, the 'vapours' perhaps of the Psalmist. Below Bottengoms a young man in a digger, all by himself, is fashioning a reservoir out of a red field. The mist alternately hides him and exposes him. The Stour Valley itself is secreted in a fog which an eight o'clock sun still has to reach. My boots are polished by the dag. I would like to talk to the reservoir maker but on and on he digs with not so much as a glance at the gawpers who come to watch him, gathering up a ton of field at a go, and gradually embanking himself in the process. The ghost of a lake is taking shape. Soon there will be acres of shining water where there were acres of corn or beet. My Australian brother, here for a holiday and experienced in earth-movers, watches too, and we talk about the sitting-down business of today's farming. None of the old spade-work. We imagine those digging legions who made the ramparts, the ditches, the railways, the garden lakes, the seven miles of the Devil's Dyke at Burwell, and I remembered the sacked steward in Luke's Gospel who, wondering what will become of him, mutters to himself, 'I cannot dig, to beg I am ashamed'. Most of the digging in Scripture has to do with a pit for oneself to fall into. The last immense European spade-dig was along the Western Front when millions of farmworkers among others dug what in effect were their own graves. The reservoir-digger stops suddenly and there is a great silence. His terrier then dashes from his caravan and rushes to him in an ecstasy of companionship. They whirl in an embrace then the digging goes on, the yellow machine gorging the red soil and tipping it into a bank, the slight figure in the cab ignoring us and half blinded by gulls.

We then drive to Lavenham. When we walked here as boys it was a forgotten, off the map place like a town in a fairy story, all piled up roofs and cobbled streets, plus a palace here and there. We felt that we owned it. We watched the blacksmith and the sparks flew painlessly into a face. We climbed the church tower the better to survey our kingdom, round and round, the dust clinging, an old man calling out below. Now we pay courtesy visits to the men who built the tower, not to mention the whole of Lavenham. There they lie in their screened chantries, wool-merchant Branch and wool-merchant Spring on opposite sides of the nave, their actual tombs inside the glorious fretwork suspiciously smoothed by more than five centuries of choirboys' attentions and suggestive of that 'Foinest bit of sharpening-stone in Hertfordshire'. 'I am Patron of the Friends of Lavenham Church', I inform my brother. He is awed. His wife buys postcards and histories. Tourists still drift through the town and the Market Square where we listened to the Salvation Army band playing on Saturday nights is being photographed. Back in the church we read the exquisitely lettered gravestones on the floor. How young, how young. Here is a gentleman apprentice from Bury St Edmunds, just eighteen. Here is the font with its battered faces in which the babies of the wintering gypsies were baptised. And down the road is the Big Tree bus-stop where we met mother to help carry home the weekly shopping. Only the Big Tree is now a shoot of its once mighty self.

Ilkley Poetry Festival

Stepping from the train one of those ragbag literary reminiscences falls out of my head. This is where Charlotte Bronte, doing the same thing in August 1853, lost her luggage. This very platform. My luggage is sans a bedtime book, which is serious. But here is the Rector of Ilkley, no less, presiding over a sea of old paperbacks to make a bob or two for his church. Skimming the embossed blockbusters I see a tattered treasure, Colette's *Gigi and the Cat* (Penguin), and give the Rector 10p. More he should have had.

Ilkley is surprisingly elegant. I had forgotten that it was a Victorian spa with wide streets and pavements made for promenading and beautiful houses and canopied shops. Everything to satisfy the Leeds bourgeoisie. There is a faint scent of moorland and the roar of unseen spa water.

Dominic the Festival organiser takes me to a grand hotel where the drinking is thunderous and wonderfully cheerful. Large men are making themselves heard in a Priestley kind of way. Some are in full Moss Bros after a wedding. Their women are loud and loquacious and lavishly clothed. Muzak thumps away and barmen fly about. This is life. Soon Beryl Bainbridge, Tom Courtney, Jim Crace, Roy Strong and Roger Deakin will appear. A local reporter interviews me in a corner, holding a microphone to my head. 'What is your favourite book?' Boswell's *Life of Johnson* I answer like a shot because opening it is like walking into a room full of old friends, including of course Oliver Edwards who confessed, 'I have tried in my time to be a philosopher but, I don't know how, cheerfulness was always breaking in'.

Dominic the organiser has been acting in the Mystery plays in York Minster, a six foot St James the Less. There was a scene in which the twelve Apostles have to unroll a long white tablecloth and place their hands above it and their feet below it, a Last Supper à la Leonardo. During the Crucifixion scene Dominic has to look up to heaven only to discover night after night that he locks gaze with a carved face looking down. Could I believe that there was some kind of communication or recognition? He now stares at me to see if I believe him. Without a doubt, I mime, the bar now thundering.

Crucifixion

The Australians take their leave. Amidst brotherly cries of affection I hear a voice from long ago. It is that of old Mrs Buckles standing at her gate at Hoo after I had paid a visit, and holding out new-laid eggs, and saying, 'Come again but not too soon.' The Australians are the concert organist David Kinsela and his lanky cousin, dear guests both. I shall miss David playing Schumann's *Of Strange Countries and People* whilst the dinner cooks, and his cousin accompanying me on long walks to 'see the autumn'. Returning from their vanishing car, an Alfa Romeo which has been looking down its nose all the week at the farm mud, I realise that I must also say goodbye to the fuchsia by the front door before the first frosts blacken it. I cut it two-thirds down and place its last bell-heads in water, where they tremble. More next summer. In my end is my beginning and all that.

Other friends have just come back from Oberammergau. Sitting in my stall before service begins, I turn over the pages of the Passion Play programme and am shocked. 'When I survey the wondrous cross' in church it is more to do with a kind of gently loving respect than horror, and I have often thought how strange it is that the little models of the execution of Christ which we see in church every Sunday fail to appal us. These icons of God in agony made of wood, metal and stone actually lead us away from the tender body itself, maybe because of what the poet said - 'Human kind cannot bear very much reality'. Now, a few minutes before the service, with the introit playing and the choir robing, I look at the Oberammergau Jesus and am stunned. Here is a man who is truly crucified. Here in the glossy photograph is both Isaiah's mutilated Saviour and the savagely killed young Teacher from Galilee, bloody, marred, God-forsaken, naked, dead but still warm. The actor has much to bear – all the mess and pain which the dangling crucifixes cannot show. A filthy business. Pilate washed his hands of it.

Fenland

We are into Luke. Ash-leaves hand themselves down to the tarmac and all the way to Ely ploughmen are blinded by seagulls. The whiteness of the birds and the blackness of the earth turns the flat scene into woodcuts. By taking minor roads we have the scene to ourselves. Three fen men loll against a dredger for elevenses. The levels throw off harsh glints. Unseen yet always present we recognise the Great Ouse. Bunyan's river, the one in which he was both baptised and nearly drowned, and which had to be crossed if one was to get to Heaven. A cathedral which is air and stone floats into view as countless tons of Barnack ridge spin against a puce sky. Ely is subdued and cold. The crushing Church power of the Middle Ages has been converted into holiness in the old streets. The little city smells rivery. We enter the Lady Chapel, that fretted clunch cage for the Virgin, and see the new statue of her. Not the remote Maid or Mother but a passionate Jewish girl, arms aloft, singing Magnificat and causing a stir. The great nave is empty and serene, the summer visitors flown.

The pub is filled with old ladies, scaffolders, men in suits, untidy grandfathers and smart girls whose shoes clatter to the bar and whose voices tease the workmen. The afternoon tells us to see Prickwillow, Forty Foot, Vermuden's Drain, the

Walpoles. Go on, it says, since you are here. Don't miss a thing. And so we do, from level to level, from flatness to flatness, with the villages perched on scarcely perceptible humps and bumps above water, and the landscape going Dutch.

Deciduous trees shed their leaves in order to help them face the winter. It is a kind of sylvan throwing overboard of what can lighten the main structure. The leaves know that they must die, and not the tree itself, and they put on a bravura glory, like French aristocrats on their way to the guillotine, tumbling down in bright colours. Palmate, pinnate, lobed, cordate, ovate, hectic orange, raging yellow, bloody red, they fill my farm track with the mulch of death. As children we kicked them along the lanes, liking their rustle, now cars press all the hiss out of them. The poplars shed my most regretted leaves. Only last month they were still singing to me. Now they are wet and voiceless, caught in the rabbit netting. Humbert Wolfe wrote,

> Listen! the wind is rising,
> And the air is wild with leaves,
> We have had our summer evenings,
> now for October eves!

Swarming in the Nave

We walked to Nayland for supper, carefully picking our way through the sodden grass by the darkening river, and the occasional pockets of trapped heat astonished us. Heifers parted to let us through, sweet-breathed, trusting. I have wet feet. The willow plantation has already lost half its foliage. A boy and a girl and their dog cross our path, strangers, but there is a flurry of good-nights. It is indeed as good a night as St Luke can rustle up. We stopped to take it all in on Wiston Bridge, the full river, the homing rooks, the now impassable banks where the Constables' barge horses softly clumped along, elder branches tucked into their harness to keep the midges off. Leaning over the rail Peter-Paul announces that he will be off to Vienna next week to compose and teach. We have stood on this bridge since we were boys to watch the Stour moving seawards. It smells just like it did then. We push on. The wood is already black and night-filled. It says, 'Watch out! Take nothing for granted'. Its old trees lean out to give us a fright, just as they did long ago.

And here comes Nayland with its hugger-mugger houses which were built for looms but are now prized by retired gentlefolk and young commuters. The latter will be taking off their suits and putting on their jeans and shouting, 'Dinner!' as their children struggle over homework. The ancient streets and courts are blocked with cars. My toes are floating around in my socks. The sensation is private, wicked and perversely enjoyable, so I won't borrow dry ones from Peter-Paul. It is what happens when one arrives the river way.

Whilst preaching on St Luke I catch a faint distraction below, a mild hitting about, and dodging. Of what? If flies have got into the church maybe we should try elder boughs. 'No, no', they explain at the door, 'it's *bees*'. Bees are in the nave and buzzing around. I can see them now, a great many of them, angry creatures zooming through the pointed arches as they seek escape. Who will get them out? Harold, of course. And he does, being a friend of theirs. 'They take their hook', as we say.

Stephen telephones from his Bury St Edmund's bookshop

to tell me that he has sold out of *Korans*. 'Everything Islamic has gone.' Good news. Christians should read the Koran and Muslims should read the *New Testament*. How else can we enter the debate? The editor of my Penguin *Koran* says that it is the earliest and finest work of Arabic prose. It has a whole chapter on The Bee. 'Your Lord inspired the bee, saying, "Make your homes in the mountains, in the trees, and in the hives which men shall build for you. Feed on every kind of fruit, and follow the trodden paths of the Lord." '

A Ploughing Match

World-wide thunder and grumpy rumblings all day. But the sky in Himalayan mood with gorgeous clouds in pile upon pile. Picking blackberries before it pours, I suddenly remember a painting by Harry Hambling of a fat woman doing likewise, her bottom to the lane, her engrossed face buried in the bush. He was an old friend, and Maggi's father. When he retired from the bank she put him to work with a paint box. His pictures contained the hard Suffolk light and his blackberrying woman is a study of absorption. When you pick fruit, particularly wild fruit, you hurry greedily from berry to berry like a child. I have to stamp nettles down to get at the best of them, and there is a flash of lightning. A bird is carrying on alarmingly overhead – I am taking the very bread out of its beak. But the hedges, I tell it, are loaded, and men too must eat. There is still the occasional wild rose in bloom. More sizzles of lightning on the hill like a faulty electricity circuit, jumpy and dangerous. The afternoon is bright, yet at the same time dark like polished iron, and huge spots of rain fall. Then in spite of this overture the approaching storm goes off to Ipswich, leaving me in timid sunshine.

A farmer chats about the autumn ploughing match. We watch the Punches taking to the field once more. Their manes and fetlocks have been given the full beauty treatment. As for their harness, it would do for Bucephalus. They pull the plough-shares through stubble like a silver wire through Cheddar cheese. Almost as well turned-out are their young masters as they totter and lurch towards the markers. They speak loving words to their horses, private endearments which we cannot catch. What a sight. The spectators' faces shine as they take it in. But the seagulls are puzzled. All this flesh and blood in the field instead of that obliging machine which did ten rows to this solitary furrow. It was hardly worthwhile flying from Felixstowe.

Mark Ploughing

I have been hard on Mark, writing him off, rather, in favour of his grandfather and his Punches, walking past his work as though it was not work and merely a skill-less, legend-less business. Mark perched aloft in his cab like a maharajah in a howdah, Mark of the seemingly effortless many shares which slice up the field like butter. Mark with The Who being piped into his ears as he ploughs the Great Field which was once ten fair sized fields before the hedges went. Mark with his red car by the hedge and his holidays in Mexico. However, it is the most lovely autumn day and when I wave he waves, and I see the soil, properly pulverised, falling from each one of his glittering blades 'like meal', just as it would have done when his grandfather was ploughing, and so I recognise Mark's skill. His art even. I give him his due. Suffolks would have ploughed an acre on a good day, Mark thirty. But the gulls would have been the same, wheeling and screaming, and falling on what was turned up like ravenous seraphs. They appear to be besotted by the chance and drama of what might be exposed, and maddened by the odour of earth. Fast food is what they go for, the worms of Shoals, Land Pit Bottom, Holt Lands and all the other ancient fields which have been brought into the Great Field ruled by Mark. And his plough should be added to the list made by a nineteenth century farmer:

> There were wheel-ploughs, and ploughs without wheels,
> ploughs with a foot for sliding over sticky land, and
> swing ploughs that could hold themselves down in heavy
> soil; fen ploughs with disc-coulters and broad-finned
> shares, turn-wrest ploughs for hillsides, light ploughs
> for sandy soils, drag-ploughs for thin ones, trenching
> ploughs for drains, and breast-ploughs for pushing to
> pare off the turf.

And those who worked them would have walked hippity-hop, one foot in the furrow, one on the rise. And he would have ridden one horse back to the farm in mid-afternoon, where his work was far from over. Unharnessing, grooming, loving, feeding, leading the team to water until they lifted their big heads and made the drips fly like diamonds. Mark, when he is done, brakes, jumps down, stretches from cab-cramp, strolls to his Ford and is off. But I have also seen him stop after a few yards, get out and do what ploughmen have done for ever, admire his day's work.

Elisha was ploughing when Elijah made him his heir. He was

ploughing with twelve oxen and walking with the twelfth, thus a skilled farmer. In his radical poem *Piers Plowman* William Langland made Christ a ploughman in a field 'full of folk', made his Church a barn and mankind a crop.

Amos the Herdsman

'They said it would', says my neighbour, 'and it has'. Blow, he means. The oaks thrash about. A handful of us fight our way into St Andrew's for the monthly Evensong. Prestigious Georgian tombs are being polished up good as new by the wild rain. Conkers hurl down. Pity the poor sailors on a night like this. The dead lie neatly in drenched rows and a towering Abies (from *abeo*, 'to rise') which a Victorian parson planted by the porch gives out little woody grunts as the gale hits it. We huddle like sheep in the chancel with the rest of the building in darkness, all eight of us. No organist, just the hooting in the tower and the rattle of window catches. I light two candles, find two hymns, look up four prayers, and we all listen to an excellent tale. A young man being closely questioned retorts, 'Whether he (Jesus) be a sinner or no, I know not: one thing I know, that, whereas I was blind, now I see'.

I talk briefly about Amos, who had the nerve to interrupt the good time being had by all at Bethel, and he not even a registered prophet. But what a writer! If society has to be cracked over the knuckles now and then, let it be by an Amos. His language is like an approaching army. 'The Lord will roar from Zion, and utter his voice from Jerusalem: and the habitations of the shepherds shall mourn, and the top of Carmel shall wither'. Just so. And what had his country done to attract such withering fire from rural Tekos? It had enjoyed itself while its security ebbed away. Amos's fury dies down in chapter nine – played out like a gale. He will help to pick up the pieces after the calamity. He will put his hand to rebuilding the ruins, the re-making the lovely gardens. History is demolition and reconstruction, tempest and fine weather, a reasonable joy after pain. That is how it goes.

The following morning, walking down to Garnons with Yolande, we meet a man riding a bike with a third wheel running along beside him. All three of us are then forced to take shelter among straw bales as a downpour runs along the valley like a curtain, just missing us. The bike and the spare wheel and the puffing rider, who might be fifty. He explains that he is measuring the distance which might disqualify a boy catching the school bus. The spare wheel is a milometer. 'But he might have to walk!' we exclaim. 'He might. How did you get to school, then?' 'Walk', we confess. 'There then.' He bikes off, spinning the school bus mileage, saving the rates, somebody who must surely end up in *Through the Looking-glass*.

Empire Spa

A Sabbath day in Cheltenham. Banners over the classical streets offer the Alpha Course, the Ladies' Health Club and the Literature Festival. The climate is muted, a perfectly English dove-grey, and there is a smither of rain. Glorious trees shed their burnt orange leaves on to glorious architecture, and many young families walk slowly past closed shops. There is the special sound of the pedestrianised town. But Cheltenham was laid out for grand walkers in regimentals and wide skirts, for sauntering carriages, for morning calls, for breathers between adding bits to the Empire. It is unquestionably noble still, even serene. A cruel spiky monument outside my hotel, the Queen's of course, says that it once supported a Crimean gun which was melted down to make armaments for World War Two. In other places the names of Gloucestershire lads cascade down memorials and make me think of Ivor Gurney, the county's shell-shocked voice:

> It is time I should go out to ways older than tales,
> Walk hard, and return
> To write an evening and a night through with so many wills
> Aiding me – little now to learn.

We Festival speakers live above our station in the Queen's Hotel. At breakfast we confront Sir Charles Napier, conqueror of the Sind, full length in glossy oils. His tight uniform hides away his many wounds, his sword drags down and points to carnage in his wake. Napier is imperial bravery personified, a man who expected to fight a battle in bandages. He died from catching cold at Wellington's funeral. Gillian Tindall and I devour bacon and eggs at his feet but he does not reprove us. His fine gaze sweeps over the restaurant, over poets and novelists and critics, just as it swept over the natives, confident in its courage. Then the stroll to the book tent between carpets of winter pansies. Someone lays flowers by a tree planted to commemorate Alderman Smith who helped to lay out Cheltenham's public gardens. The rich dullness of the day is now photograph album sepia. We riffle through first editions, purchase 'slightly foxed' short stories, sign our own books for admirers, feel like footballers, keep an eye on the time. 'When are you on?'

The Glass Book

The summer came to an end when we were at Hengrave Hall. Noonday darkness made a backcloth for the mansion. The temperature plummeted, the rooks swore and a miserable wind played in from the Breckland. All was changed. The boy sweeping up leaves went home and his last pile flew back over the lawn. There was a clatter of attention-seeking hail, short but decided. 'The harvest is past, the summer is ended, and we are not saved.' Quite so.

We have come to see the Oratory Window in this Tudor mercer's palace, Graham being a stained glass man. Contrarily, it faces a blazing sun. A man may look on glass but with some damage to his eye if he isn't careful. By dint of positionings and shadings, and Graham's special opera glasses for viewing stained glass, we make out the enthralling picture-theology of this masterpiece from the Fall to the Redemption. Sir Thomas Kytson the mercer had it made in Troyes during 1525-27. 'In the beginning' has God breathing into the solar system. Big stories are supplemented with marginal stories, scripture with physics, learning with old wives' tales. One could look for ever, as centuries of lords and ladies and their children and servants no doubt did. Borrowing Graham's binoculars, I see that my birth-sign

Scorpio is mercifully fanned by God's breath. His divine puff is zodiacal, inclusive. But what is happening to a house in the right hand corner? I find out in Genesis. It is brimstone burning it up as fire destroys the cities of the plain. Brimstone is sulphur, sulphur is atomic. The exploding city in the window becomes suddenly recognisable. We are reading a glass book which tells a dateless tale.

They say that when Sir Thomas died in 1540 he left warehouses stuffed with cloth of gold, satins, tapestries, velvets, furs, pepper, cloves and madder worth millions. His great Oratory Window illustrates William Tyndale's Bible. I wondered whether he might have read 'The Merchant's Lament' in the Revelation of St John – how they would weep and mourn because the day had come when nobody would buy their gold and silver, linen and silk, ivory and brass, cinnamon, wine, oil, wheat, slaves, and souls of men? If he did he could justly say that no mercer had been more hospitable than he. Had he not made homes for two Catholic saints, scores of musicians and, eventually, for a man who introduced the greengage to England? What more could Sir Thomas have done? And now his beautiful house was prayerfully over-run by a Community of Reconciliation. It seemed to have risen non-judgementally between the old and new faiths and became a shelter for the persecuted and school for the ignorant. His Window must have offered inspiration and distraction by turn, and pleasure all the time.

St Jude and Harold's Orchard

I am planting daffodil bulbs with the potato dib on the feast of St Jude, saint of hopeless causes. This particular flower-bed covers an old flinty path so I have to feel about to make a deep enough hole. I lever up an iron bolt, a nice piece of dinner plate and a horseshoe. Thinking about Jude, I am ashamed to know so little about him other than his frequent

The fields are striped

appearance in the Personal column, so I run inside to look him up. I find nothing to warrant his fame as a solver of problems of a personal nature, instead, a severely-worded warning about those who intrude into a faith which they do not really hold. 'Filthy dreamers,' in his words. 'Murmurers and complainers, speaking great swelling words' – I may have to tone this down a bit in the sermon. Having finished the daffodils, I start on the Rambling Rector rose. Jude goes on about 'clouds without water, trees without fruit withering and twice dead which have to be plucked up by the roots'. But I love his blessing. 'Now unto him that is able to keep you from falling, and to present you faultless before the presence of His glory with exceeding joy . . .'

I take my Poppy Day money up to Harold. He is in the orchard with his ginger Tom and wondering whether he dare climb the ladder to pick Bramleys, and against all medical pleading, he being eighty-six. 'You pick some', he tells me. I pick them with my feet on the ground, his tree hanging to the grass with them. 'But', he says, 'the big 'uns are always at the top'. He gives me a bag of easy-picks. 'Lay 'em out without touching and cover 'em up with newspaper, and leave 'em be.' Leave the high ones, Harold, let them fall. He takes me to the hive where rows of sleepy bees and a hopeful wasp hover. He is much stung, he says, by his bees, and thank God, for he never has as much as a twinge of arthritis. We move on to where he is hardening-off some pansies for his wife's grave. We pass the parade of blackened discs which were his sunflowers, some of them especially grown for the Baptist Chapel harvest festival. They shake wearily when the bullfinches have a go at them. Harold is an unhurried countryman, tiffling about from dawn to dusk in all weathers. He looks longingly at the ladder. He shouldn't have mentioned it to the doctor. The bees, he thinks, are out to get him.

In church I check the names of the dead for All Souls, adding those of my parents and friends. What a roll-call it is. Absent, absent . . . It was once believed that each individual soul was a new creation and destined for a particular body. It was identifiable but not physical. But now, and I quote, 'we tend to consider the doctrine of the soul not *per se*, but in relation to the whole Biblical doctrine of man'. When I read out the All Souls' list I see the neighbours back in their seats, looking for their car keys, hanging up their kneelers, calling out Goodbye.

November

All Souls - The Birthdays - Degradations - Finding Time -
High Ground - Herbert in the November Garden - The Sea
and the Sermon - A South African Poet - More Night Walking
- A Rite - The Cambridge Soldier - The Springwaters - On
Being Heroic - Edmund, Cecilia and the Everlasting Song -
The Caught Moment - Scratchings

All Souls

Reading the ever-growing list of those who have, to quote Henry Vaughan, 'gone into the world of light' I am suddenly struck by the thought of how swiftly they vanish. Here today and gone tomorrow. Why hasn't the village not collapsed as prop after prop is taken away? How does the parish church remain standing when warden, retired general, choirmaster, the inhabitants of 'farmers' pew', the great ladies in the front seats, the gentle figure by the second pillar have all gone?

As I add my parents' names, and those of close friends, to the All Souls roll-call, how is it that tears do not disturb my rationality? The ballpoint scrawls on the lined paper require all my attention. Both morning and evening congregations kneel and listen so as not to miss Aunt Doris and poor John. Here come the priests who helped us out during the frequent interregnums, here is a tower captain, here are the good old regulars, here is a boy. Here are my brief pauses and a mounting silence. But how is it that, churchwise, they have all gone without leaving an unfillable space? Something strange here. Is this what mortality is?

In less rational times people would hang around the church on All Souls' eve, waiting for the year's dead to process across the grass, chatting, engrossed, and apparently not missing the living a bit. Why, the grave-earth hadn't greened, and there they were, not even noticing. St Paul's cheerfulness about his own death must have struck young Timothy and the others as a mite selfish. 'I shall be with Christ, which is far better!' And landing them with the infant Church!

Ancient friends type out their funerals and put them in the post. No fuss. I am to do the committal in church as they don't want me to 'trek all the way to the crem for a couple of sentences'. When, finally, I come to the end of the All Souls list, I say my favourite blessing, the Mosaic one - 'The Lord bless us and keep us, the Lord make his face to shine upon us and give us his peace.' It comes after the laws on 'separation' in Numbers. After which we all creakily resume our seats and find Isaac Watts's 'How bright these glorious spirits shine.'

How golden bright it is outside where the lime leaves fall in their millions – well countlessly anyway. The cars are being carpeted. The air will be delicious, a kind of dying freshness which is full of movement and colour. The Hall trees wave gaudily and the farm hedge will be rattling with birds. We too are deciduous in our way, bursting newly on the scene but ultimately tumbling down like the poor crooked scythe and spade. Then mulching, then living as we never lived before, caught up as we will be in the divine love.

Between services I mow the sopping lawns, anxious on such a blowy leafy day that autumn should not impact them. I scrape mashed cuttings from the blades. The white cat kindly comes outside to watch. The farmer from the Wiston air-strip does his Sunday afternoon Amy Johnson routine, crackling around overhead in a neighbourly fashion. Well-bred gliders look down on him. The clocks having been put back, teatime arrives soon after lunch. I listen to *Poetry Please* on the radio, nursing the cat. They should have read Thomas Hardy's *At Day-close in November* in which

> Beech leaves, that yellow the noon-time,
> Float past like specks in the eye.

The Birthdays

Cambridge at Guy Fawkes. I have bumped here on the country buses for our birthdays, Jane's and mine. This is an ancient custom. We are each other's oldest friends in every sense of the word. She will cook a fine dinner and I will wheel her round the Fitzwilliam Museum, this time to discover where they have put our favourite things after the great refurbishment. Being ninety, Jane will be imperious. Charming young attendants will bring a wheelchair and I will push. I will negotiate the lifts and drive where I am told to, from Breughels to the Freuds, and from the Roman emperors to the armoury. No time to dawdle. No time to catch my face in a bronze mirror as I did long ago. No time to read all the new labels, which is a pity. But time for tea. Back home, pouring the wine, Jane asks, 'Do you believe in heaven - I don't.' She has arranged for 'one of those ecological funerals - you know'.

Before coming home I take one of my November walks round Cambridge. It stays perfect, the grey-gold buildings, the lingering whiff of fireworks, the leaves chasing the sweepers, the undergraduates measuring themselves for gowns in Ryder and Amies, the lingering smell of Reformation in Great St Mary's and the vast familiar glories of the Botanic Garden peeping through its gates. The brave old chaps on bikes, the market stalls, the autumn alleys, the beautiful faces, the peculiar Cambridge cold pushing its way

through the earth. At Bury St Edmunds I make a dash
between buses to sit in my canon's stall in the cathedral for a
few minutes. There is a new cushion embroidered with a
quill pen, not a computer. It is the feast of St Leonard, my
patron saint. He was a French hermit whose official life is
'historically worthless' - says the dictionary. They said that
prisoners called on him. So I like to think that he did his best
to 'Open the blind eyes, to bring out the prisoners from the
prison-house'. Leonardo was named after him. So was the
country hospital in which my father died. Leonard was a
hermit from Noblac, near Limoges during the sixth century,
they say, a November liberator. Only do not take anyone's
word for it. Let him be free of biography.

Degradations

The Reformation was Word over Image, printing having
been invented. Now, the camera having been discovered, it
is image over word and we look with horror. These
unimaginable images clog our heads. We look at a
continuation of that scene in the guardroom when the
prisoner is stripped naked and mocked, arrayed in fancy
dress, spat on, whipped, jeered, all his modesty gone. Asked
why, the American guards explain that they are only obeying
orders. The night garden is as black as the photos. Gradually
it starts to offer its spatial solitude, owls cry by the river, the
Stanstead planes deal in further stars and the cold air drives
through my shirt. The poets mock the justification for what

we are capable of. I think of the child's persistent questioning of Old Kaspar in Robert Southey's *Battle of Blenheim* - 'But what good came of it at last?'

Yesterday a retired American airman called. He and his wife had been to look up a name on the old airfield memorial, a twenty-six year lieutenant named Kenneth Kitt, shot down in France in 1944. He would have walked past my farmhouse, probably with a girl, visited the Crown, gone to the pictures, danced in the village hall, all the time thinking of Ohio. They showed me his photo. The new face looked out at me. The cousins took more photos, catching the lieutenant up in my fields - although never quite. Sixty years on is quite a handicap. But at least he is now in view.

Finding Time

The other morning I was shocked to find myself listening to the News thrice in succession as I did the chores. Thrice was the poor wounded man shot in the mosque, three times I heard this particular day's menu of disaster, feeding on it less at each repetition. But it ran on. And after supper would come the hectoring newscasters, though not I discovered in the house of a poet friend. 'I hear the headlines before breakfast, and that is that.' From then on he would read, write, walk, hear music and see those he loved. He was no longer young and would now challenge the News imperative - its round the clock necessity or norm. Emulating him to some extent, for I am a poor soon-breaker of self-imposed rules, I have discovered a kind of elongation of the day, plus a sharpened view of the entire News business. And plus a refreshment. William Hazlitt wrote an essay called 'On Living to One's Self' in which he saw himself as 'a silent spectator of the mighty scene of things' - and his contemporaries saw him as a ruthless observer of the world's evils and foibles. To get away from his 'News' he would go on long walks in the countryside, careful not to take a companion with him, for this would invalidate the journey. 'I like to go by myself. I can enjoy society in a room (not quite true) but out of doors, nature is enough for me. I am then never less alone than when alone.' He would add, 'I cannot see the wit of walking and talking at the same time', and there is something in this.

Walking-talking crocodiles of children in town and grown-ups in the village chatter by, and although I am Hazlittian in my preference to walk alone, I am struck by their happy sounds at being released from the cage, for this is what it appears. On Saturday a local naturalist showed me wonders on my doorstep which I had never seen before and talked eagerly for miles, leaving me as night fell with a new map of the few miles which I thought I knew like the back of my hand. Had we tramped the green lanes, woods and meadows with respect for each other's silence, that is all they still would be - a wildish few acres down the road. But David has to take friends 'into my world' and the only way to achieve this is to add a companionable commentary all the way. During the course of this he confessed to being a loner - the kind of solitary walker who has a genius for encounters en-route. People, flowers and birds, skies, water, his spaniel Joe, the Shetland sheep in the orchid meadow which he has virtually single-handedly put back from scrub, just tell him things. David has actually not got time for the News and hasn't much idea of what is going on in this sense. Where I am concerned he is the spirit of the Essex Wildlife Trust, its very articulate soul, but one born in solitariness. 'They all speak to me' - he means those who are fortunate enough to run into him on one of his walks. We call on the great apple-grower - over two hundred species - and buy some Coxes. We see where in 1855 they pulled down a medieval church, carting it to where the parishioners lived and putting it up again, and taking the tombstones but not the bodies. David said that we knew different things, he and I. We certainly were differently alone. I suppose we all are one way and another. 'And He departed again into a mountain, Himself alone.'

High Ground

At the P.C.C. in my neighbour's farmhouse I wander away from the agenda and think of all the similar meetings I have attended in rectories, vicarages, parish rooms, sports pavilions, summer gardens, barns, sheds, manors and bungalow lounges, and of all the bureaucratic saints who hold country churches together. The agenda is essentially unchanged. Quotas jostle with faculties, liturgies with bells, pews with grave space, any other business with the hope that we will soon be saying the Grace and be home before ten. Tonight the house is cosy and I am able to watch a moon the size of a dinner-plate roll across the uncurtained window. Next year's Family Purse sets us reeling. We discuss the incumbent's pension. 'Pension never enriched young man,' said George Herbert in his thirties, adding, 'Living well is the best revenge'. I imagine him at the Bemerton vestry asking, 'Is it your wish that I should sign this' before looking around for his lute.

Six the following morning. A heap of breathing fur on the dresser unwinds and becomes two young cats who dance about the second they hear the larder door swing open. Greedy-guts eyes, whirling tails and flattering rubs against my bare legs. They are into the larder and tiptoeing through the laid out Bramleys before I can stop them. Whiskas and saucers of milk are served. My mind is on higher matters. On my lecture on John Constable in Cumberland. In 1806 his uncle David Pyke Watts thought that a trip to the Lakes would do wonders for his thirty year-old nephew, would show him what scenery really was – not common ploughland in the Stour Valley. Uncle David was by now a fierce critic of what he considered to be the young artist's slapdash style. 'Paint a blackbird on your easel, John,' sighing, 'Finish, finish!' The family agreed. John's pictures, so rough and strange. Who would want them hanging in their parlour? It was autumn in the Lakes. Constable did watercolours and drawings from dawn to dusk, after which he attended musical evenings with hospitable North Country friends, met Wordsworth and took huge walks. He was tall and good-looking and women stared at him. But it was not the right time of the year for him . . . 'I never did admire the autumn tints, I love the exhilarating freshness of spring'. Seven weeks among the mountains were enough for him and he returned to East Anglia, but with a folio of work which belied his indifference to this landscape, although he never went north again. Before I set off to Keswick I read more of Richard Holmes' *Coleridge*, a masterpiece.

Roger Deakin arrives and we set off on Constable's

journey. The M6 is a knotty rope of container traffic criss-crossed by armies of starlings. What are they up to? 'Nothing,' says Roger. 'Creatures are not necessarily doing something in our terms.' He has actually watched butterflies sunbathing. We turn off to Derwent Water. It is a great moment. I see Constable's coach lumbering along and then the tottering finger-post 'Derwent Water' and the young

A hedge in November

painter hoping that he hasn't forgot his *Lyrical Ballads*. Seven years earlier Coleridge was being shown around his friend Wordsworth's home country by the great poet himself and observed 'Vortices of flies'. The dreaded lake clegs, maybe. Clegs, midges, they all do it, rotate dizzily, spiral, dance madly in a vertiginous mass, and why? 'Because they are glad to be alive', says Roger. We are now vertiginous ourselves, part of late year tourism, of cars and walkers and climbers, of B & B seekers, of sightseers and followers in the footsteps of the Romantic Movement. But of course, like everyone else, we deplore this invasion of the sacred scene. Grasmere itself is a busy hive of zipped-up folk in big boots exercising their walking-sticks. There in the churchyard lie the modest memorials, there by the side of the peering lane lies Dove Cottage. Writing to Dorothy Wordsworth from Keswick Coleridge told her, 'How deeply I have been impressed by a world of scenery absolutely new to me . . . a vision of a fair country'.

Roger believes that it is not too late for swimming and persuades a lady novelist to plunge into an icy lakelet with him. I wake up as early as I can to see the mountains discard their layers of mist and stand naked and craggy for miles and miles. Roger emerges from the hotel pool and we have breakfast, glancing at our lecture notes and the one by one appearances of our Literature Festival colleagues. A thousand boys and girls appear, but not for most of us. Their hero is Nick Butterworth the children's writer and they swarm around him for autographs. I buy two of his books and am transfixed, the world of children's literature being as little known to me as that of the City – those smooth magazines which worried-looking young commuters devour on the train. More children's writers arrive and they are not like us. How can they be so famous? They take the stage like gods and hold court like kings. Cumberland's entire education system has been closed down in order that its pupils can meet them in the flesh. They are diffident and shy for the most part, youthful themselves and gently smiling, and probably loving their writing more than their readers, and perhaps not 'being good with children' except on the page. 'Tell us a story', shout the boys and girls. That is better. Nick Butterworth reads, looks up, reads, glances over the rows and rows of devoted heads, and goes on reading. Never stops. Soon he will have to descend from Olympus and just sign, for this is the pattern of literature festivals.

Roger and I drive home with bonfires all the way, for it is Guy Fawkes night and Britain is lurid.

Herbert in the November Garden

The dead russet apple is to be cut down. There was no lingering in its demise, no withering here and there. Two springs ago it was its usual world of blossom (though no fruit later), then it died. It was a grand member of the orchard which John Nash planted after his demob as an official war artist in 1945. When it was really alive its russets rained down, so many that we would beg the postman, the passing children, the passing anyone, to take twenty, fifty, all you can manage. But tomorrow the saw, Joachim on the ladder, Ian and I below to haul away its heaviness, for newly lifeless boughs weigh a ton. A bow-saw will make them manageable, will provide food for the fire and apple-wood for Stephen the carver, twigs for kindling and a ten-foot trunk to grow a Rambling Rector up. So today it is clearing the ground before we make a start. I feel like the barber of the Bastille clearing aristocratic necks for the blade.

It is an exquisite November day, very still, very subdued and with heart-catching colouring. Various creatures come out to observe these austere preliminaries, robins, chaffinches, a late bee or two, a nice dog. The earth is still dark with the final russet leaves and I can hear the critical chock-chock of pheasants. So many rooks fly over that they darken the sky. 'Try this russet,' we used to say, 'take some home'. I think of the unkempt trees in William Dyce's *George Herbert in his Garden*, the dead branches poking from the ivy and the cassocked poet beneath them, one hand holding a book, the other raised in praise or a gesture of farewell. There is fishing tackle to remind one that Izaak Walton was Herbert's first biographer and in the distance the pale spire of Salisbury Cathedral to point to the poet's weekly walk to sing in the choir. And between Bemerton and the city, the River Nadder, chilly and uninviting. All this in 1861. All of Herbert's physical existence over by 1633. Vikram Seth bought his rectory in 2003 and will be swimming in the river when it is inviting. A housekeeper led me to it just before he arrived, and just before nightfall, and I forgot to see if the trees were pruned. Herbert believed that gardens should be medicine-chests as well as pleasances, utilities and dreams. The rose itself cannot escape:

> What is fairer than a rose?
> What is sweeter? yet it purgeth.

The Sea and the Sermon

Advent and its thrillingly expectant hymns – and its thrilling accusations from Amos, that urgent lay voice, that ceaselessly longing plea for light in contrast to the bright lights. For Amos nature itself cries to nature as it brings God into his creation. That young herdsman of Tekoa, that mere dresser of sycamore figs, apologises for daring to interrupt the silence caused by those who are qualified to prophesy but who haven't been doing their official task for ages, but he says he has to speak. Even had they spoken, their voices would have sounded pretty conventional and dull after being so long out of practise but his, which had only previously been heard in orchards and pastures, was at least fresh. Some people listening would have added, 'impertinent yet beautiful'. Like Jeremiah, Amos, alas, was dismissed as a sweet talker. Nations prefer national speakers, qualified messages of salvation from the horse's mouth, not from some rural poet cum-visionary. 'Seek him that maketh the seven stars (the Pleiades) and Orion, and turneth the shadow of death into the morning . . . the Lord is his name.' What kind of warning is that?

The coming of Christ into our history brings happiness and fear. How are we to address him? The old hymnists offer enchanting titles. Choose one, accept them all, Dayspring (my favourite), Adonai, Emmanuel, Great Judge, Light of All, Bridegroom, Incarnate Word, Lord of David's Key, Desire of Nations, The Lamb, Redeemer of the Earth, Shepherd, King, Saviour, Little Child of Bethlehem, the sacred nomenclature hangs like tapestry in the Advent aisles. Outside, it whistles along the tumultuous Suffolk shore where I am tramping with Ian, a gale in my face, this how-to-address Jesus list of options or completion. Unguarded fishing-rods shake against the bulwarks of Southwold pier and black seas crash around. Staring north we imagine that we can see Lowestoft, and south, Sizewell. The nuclear domes usually become pearly and Indian after dark. The waves join hands and rush towards us to make a terrific battery, dragging up shingle and weed like refuse and hurling them at the concrete. Victorian terraces run on and on, and summer's bunting hangs in rags. Later, having read David Taylor's *George Orwell*, I walk round Southwold to find him. Here at thirty-six High Street is his parents' house from which passers-by would have heard his typewriter rattling, and here was the Copper Kettle, his sister's teashop. This was the age of 'slender means' and class distinctions as subtle as those at Versailles. I sit in St Edmund's church for the hundredth time. It is a holy palace of glass and flint fit for Adonai-Dayspring-Light of All, though Amos would have preferred the stars above it. On the tower wall hangs a little carving made by a boy who had been set to watch for the Spanish Armada. For natives like myself, local seaside towns and interior villages are cupboards where we expect to find what we are looking for.

A South African Poet

Mid-autumn. The countryside is a dull gold, like neglected brass, and very quiet after the harvest. The tumble of the first leaves provides a small commotion. Little noises which take place all the year but are hidden by machines and winds, are clearly heard. I listen to them as I pull up inedible leftovers in the kitchen garden, flocky radishes, rattling runner beans, bolting this or that. I am thinking of a poet's funeral. What to say, what to do.

The first writer-friends in a writer's life remain so influential that when they 'go' they are apt to leave one strangely unprotected. I imagine that my old friend Ralph

Currey must have felt like this when T.S. Eliot died all those years ago. I went to Eliot's memorial service at the Abbey and afterwards watched Ezra Pound making an uncertain way to a traffic island. Valerie Eliot told me that Pound kept on saying, 'I am sorry, I am so sorry . . .' But not telling her what for. Eliot had been wonderfully kind to my friend R.N. Currey, calling him one of the best poets of the Second World War, which indeed he is. But, as with the fate of much-anthologised poets, comparatively few had read the 'full' Currey, only these excellent representative verses, so this is what I would talk about at his funeral, the Ralph of South Africa and East Anglia, the English Master at the Grammar School, the blind nonagenarian, the companion who, when I started to write, accepted me. His own poems showed nothing of his years and were curiously youthful throughout. Neither did poetry show in his face, which remained that of a gunner-officer of the Forties. There was nothing in it to say that he wrote. He was a calm widower feeling his way round the tall townhouse for cups or glasses or books which had to be read to him, including his own when we persuaded him to edit his *Collected Poems*. Boys from the school would find his MSS, read out punctuation, put it together. And soon I will be in the Great Hall after the cremation and the boys and masters will be reading aloud, and the youthful poems written by an old man as well as by a young Major will be listened to without any discernable time-break. His mother had cared for the victims of the concentration camps which we built during the South African War, his father was a Methodist minister, always on the move. His wife was Stella Martin Currey the novelist. Their son James Currey was one of the great anti-apartheid publishers. What poor fragments of what we were blow about our funerals.

More Night Walking

We praise darkness in the Benedicite and cast away its works in the Advent collect. In one darkness we praise the Lord for ever and in the other we regret its use as cover for our misbehaviour. Darkness in Wormingford is now at a premium, though not at Bottengoms Farm I am glad to say. Here and there the village is ablaze with vast wattage and the pub is like a fairground, alight from end to end. The Benedicite sees darkness as one of the handiworks of God and not as a void. Religion sees it as the symbol of unenlightenment and demonises it. I have always loved it and do not have to go far to find it, just out of the front door at the right hour. So devoted am I to it that I never carry a torch or anything which could affront it. The countryside at night graduates from having light enough to read by, as they say, to pitch black. Plants tell an unbotanical tale in the dark. They become Oberon's flora – Oberon, King of Shadows.

I remember the ambiguities of darkness when I preach on Nicodemus, that furtive seeker of Christ. Here he comes, stumbling through the Eastern city at night, head in cloak, reputation to look after, the high court judge who is fascinated by the teachings of an unofficial prophet and healer. His usually ordered thoughts are in a whirl. So far he has not emerged from the dark sheltering womb of his official existence. Then into it, disturbing it, comes this young rabbi. He keeps to the wall, scared of identification, hoping not to wake the dogs, the watchman. Here is the door and the relief when he is inside it. Very soon this skulking figure of respectability would come out, would be quite reckless, would himself carry a large amount of myrrh and aloes for the burial of the person who had told him that 'God so loved the world that he gave his only begotten Son, that whosoever believed in him should not die but have everlasting life'. But now he would be assisting the burial party to stave off the smell of death with spices, and to seal the poor ruined flesh in darkness.

It is pretty black when, cramped by television, I walk through the lane to take soundings of the night. Coleridge and the Wordsworths had a government spy set upon them for doing as much. It had been rumoured that they were signalling Napoleon's ships, why else would such obvious left-wingers be wandering about the Quantocks at midnight? They were all in the late twenties and were continually writing things down – the revolutionary poems of *Lyrical Ballads* to be exact. Late in the afternoon of 13th November, just as the sun was setting, the three of them set off from Quantoxhead for Watchet just to see sunlight become moonlight on the sea because it was the moment of greatest darkness, and as they strolled along *The Rime of the Ancient Mariner* began to keep in step in Sam Coleridge's head. In time he would walk the entire poem. Darkness has its own fertility. And of course I haven't walked very far from the illuminated house when it isn't very dark at all. In spite of this the familiar daytime landscape has become another country, a realm of uncertainties and foreign shapes.

A Rite

Bottengoms Farm, dawn. Kitty, full of breakfast, takes up her observation post at the window, being by nature a watcher and a holy one. Her tail waves around, her fur fluffs out. Her jade gaze swivels from east to west to follow the flight of birds and falling leaves. In another manifestation she would be in an opera-box or at Wimbledon, never missing a note or a serve. I drink tea and now and then say a little prayer which is unworthy of God's ear. Soon, the sun jumps up from behind the hill and sparkles wildly over the barn. In the absolute morning quiet I hear the voices of farm children from long ago getting ready for school and the boots of labourers as they slope off for a smoke before harnessing-up. 'Rise and shine!' mother would be shouting up the ladder which led to the servants' attics. The farm dogs would be hurtling around, everybody's friend. Dogs seem to like getting up. All those centuries of early mornings, all those saints coming round season by season, it made one giddy. You had to hang on for all you were worth for a full lifetime of them.

I am not hanging on to anything at the moment. I read a few pages of the life of C.F. Cavafy, the Alexandrian poet famously described by his friend E.M. Forster as 'a Greek gentleman in a straw hat, standing absolutely motionless at a slight angle to the universe.' The farmer's wife would not have allowed a book on her breakfast table. But there it is, places of toil fall into idle hands. Children find their way to the village churchyard, farmers' voices become tangled in the trees, beasts cease to be. But the birds are routinely the same as they ever were, rivers of rooks in the late afternoons, chevrons of geese, hooping and hawking, in the half light. And the big square room continues to be sheltering.

And writers sit about when one should be 'getting on'. The Alexandrian poet would not have known about these things, being street-wise. His streets belonged to a classical world which had piled up, period by period, civilization by civilization, whereas an English village is a surface which is annually combed by generation after generation. Cavafy combed his Alexandria for what could not happen there again, as writers do. For a particular moment at a particular spot.

> I never found them again – so quickly lost
> Those poetical eyes, that face
> Pale . . . in the darkness of the street.

Tom Liston has arrived for Remembrance Sunday all the way from Florida. He must speak, of course. He is in his eighties and commanded a group on our World War Two aerodrome, Colonel Liston from long ago. No runways left, only the service roads leading to cornfields now. There is a special quietness up there, the kind of silence which allows dog walkers and young gliders, and the man on the combine to hear snatches of big band music and bombers limping home. Not even larks can deafen these sounds.

As I begin the service at the back of the church I say, 'Please will you stand and face the war memorial' and so the familiar elegiacs fall into place. They began with an armistice – *sistere* – stand still. Colonel Easten then reads the names and afterwards Phyllida tells me that she must be the only person present who could put faces to them. At Bulmer they have a little book of biographies below their war memorial, photos, occupations, village addresses, jobs, some words and pictures to warm the marble above.

Patriotism was often low on the list of reasons for the Great War men to leave their villages. Agriculture was in the doldrums and rural poverty as bad as bad could be. To get off the hated land was a dream which the war made true. How could they have known that they would soon perish in mud? Reading once more Wilfred Owen's *The Send-off* I hear as I always do the sub-text. A few survivors 'May creep back, silent, to still village wells/up half-known roads'. There is a chilly understanding of the labourers' lot.

We once drove along the half-known road to Passchendaele on a drizzly afternoon, our car taking the same route as all those tramping feet which would never return. For such a great destination one would expect a great sign, some heroic pointer to where one must turn off from the highway. Instead, so minimal was the signpost that we almost drove past it. The mud in the cemetery was silver-grey, the war graves white as snow as they drifted across the slight rise. We read in a great book like that in Revelation a few names from the Artists' Rifles and looked across Flanders. I bent down and touched the silvery mud. Then we returned to Ypres to sit in a teashop in that beautiful brick square. They brought us twelve different tea-bags and hot water. Englishmen, do it yourself. You understand its mysteries. Boys at the next table laugh. One says, 'I'll be mother' and pours out. And I hear, as I hear in church, a ploughman explaining,

> We are the Dead, Short days ago
> We lived, felt dawn, saw sunset glow,
> Loved and were loved, and now we lie
>   In Flanders fields.

There is little point in raking up the leaves at Bottengoms before the twelve great oaks have shed. They will take their time – November is too good to miss. Only a hard frost will bring them down and even then they will be too leathery to mulch. They will stick together on the ground for weeks to come. The moon looms through these oaks and there is no wind to stir them. Girls' voices now and then filter through their branches as horses are cosseted. Their roots are in a running stream and their tops in moody skies.

The Cambridge Soldier

The 'remembrance' continues to float from the village to wherever I happen to be, the silence too. At home it was silence upon the silence like Krishnamurti's 'The silence of the mind is the true religious mind, and the silence of the gods is the silence of the earth. The meditative mind flows in this silence, and love is the way of this mind.' It certainly is quiet along the Backs. Dahlias and rudbeckia lean wearily against their stakes in the fellows' gardens and rooks waver between architecture and tall trees. A kind of punt-upping is taking place on the cold water, the empty boats rocking about in groups. I walk through the college canyons, through brick alleys, past muted gardens and eventually to the station, with a nod to the hero soldier on his plinth. They say that he is holding-up the traffic and might have to be moved. He has just come home after beating the Hun and has a laurel wreath dangling from his rifle, and he has been striding into Cambridge since 1922. They talk of him being marginalized, of marching out of the Botanical Garden, maybe. I remember thinking of him when I was at Passchendaele in the spring, in the way which images have of striding in the 'real thing', as it were. The daughter of the boy who had modelled for him had written to me about the suggestion to shift him from his traffic island. I said that he should continue to hold up the cars and containers, the bikes and the buses, for this is what statues are for, to put a brake on lesser matters.

The Springwaters

'Let's go to the Springwaters!' we would cry. They were not far, just a mile or two towards where grandmother lived, though well off the road and invisible. Even we children, who knew them so well, remained surprised when they suddenly revealed themselves in the humpy meadow. We did them the honour of lying flat on our stomachs to watch their perpetual activity, the sand spiralling in their depths but never clouding them. We would let the springs jet between our toes, paddle about a bit, and then the water did grow dark, only to clear again in minutes once we had stepped out. We cupped it in our hands and drank it, sieving out the stray stickleback or beetle, worshipping its purity. It ran through the grass in a series of ditches and ponds, breaking cover here and there, and was to us unstoppable. A business park now obliterates it, but does it block the flow? I like to believe that concrete is no more than a brief check to it, then when the business park cracks and granulates and gets blown away, the Springwaters will surface again and be once more a visible fraction of the mighty water table of our land.

A St Martin's sun swims about in a colourless sky as I clean out the springs at Bottengoms. They are identical to the

Springwaters, everlastingly whirling up and clarifying their beds. But they have to be raked of leaves and sticks and hay. It is about to rain but doesn't until I have finished, then it roars down for hours. I remember Matthew Paris writing about a St Martin's flood in 1236 - 'Then on the morrow of St Martin (November 12th) and within an octave of the same there burst in astonishing floods of the sea . . . and a most mighty wind resounded, with great an unusual sea and river floods together.' He would have been awed by the sound of rain on corrugated iron. Sheltering in the shed, I revel in the deafening clatter.

On being Heroic

On the Saturday afternoon screen heroes are doing what only heroes can do and the watchers are ecstatic. Hardly knowing the rules of any game, I am merely interested in people being so happy. Heroes were rarities but now they trot out to the field every weekend for their adoration. In ancient times they wore a crown of wild olive which, when they joined the immortals, hung upon their gravestones. Once the hero sang the tribe's heroic deeds then he became the person in the song. Christ was anti-heroic, St Paul quite classically heroic. Jesus stood heroic values on their heads, Paul cleansed and reused them, knowing that the Church would need them if it was to survive. Two of Christ's temptations in the wilderness were about the old heroism. He could be a king-god like

Zeus and descend on Caesar's throne, routing doubt as to
his divine claims. He could take as his divine right all
earthly power. It is significant that his friends never saw
him in heroic terms, not even those whose privilege it was
to witness his transfiguration. And his failure to be heroic
on the Cross bewildered them. The closest he came to

Young man with dogs

heroism in their eyes was on Palm Sunday, and if only he
had ridden on! If one had to name the typical heroic and
anti-heroic followers of Christ they would be St George
and St Francis, and the Christian world has used them
broadly as ideals and opposites.

The history of twentieth century heroism and anti-heroism, of leaders and those who led by other means could not be more contrasting. Hitler's rallies and Mussolini's balcony (he was too short to be a hero and had to stand on a concealed box) were heroics which would now be laughed off the political stage, nor would Churchill's oratory move us, noble though it would be. He remains perhaps the last acceptable hero in the classic mould. Football stadia, our bloodless Colosseum, contain these aspects of our heroics. Charles Kingsley's *The Heroes* (1856) taught me classical attitudes. I read it when I was twelve but even then I noted that marble men were modelling for what flesh and blood had achieved. Now I read Seamus Heaney's *Beowulf*:

> They sang then and played to please the hero,
> words and music for their warrior prince,
> harp tunes and tales of adventure . . .

Alternatively, I think about Dietrich Bonhoeffer and the night before they hanged him, when he was thinking about Gethsemane. No hero worthy of the name would have gone to his death with words like these, but Jesus did. Which is why Bonhoeffer wrote, 'In me there is no bitterness, but with you there is patience; I do not understand your ways, but you know the way for me . . . Lord, whatever this day may bring, your name be praised'.

Edmund, Cecilia and the Everlasting Song

It is said that Bach's eyes faded when he copied his brother's collection of organ music by moonlight. House lights are beginning to defeat moonlight in the village. There is a glaring where there once were shades of darkening. We see this all the way to Bury St Edmunds to hear the B. Minor Mass. We hiss through miniature lakes. Windscreen wipers fling away the rain with metronomic screeches. It is the eve of Edmund and Cecilia – the 'woman who sang to God in her heart'. Bach never heard a complete performance of the B. Minor Mass. I imagine the monks in their vast abbey on a November night holding out their white feet to a bit of a blaze in the warming-room, thankfully repeating, *Deum de Deo, lumen de Lumine*. We park in a side street under a plane tree. Christmas lights, not yet switched on, rock in the wind. A few steps away lies poor young Edmund, 'kyng, martyr and virgyne', lying beyond our knowledge, our East Anglian saint. He was a German prince who had been willed our crown and who, they said, picked up our language from an Englished Psalter. Raiders shot him full of arrows when he was thirty and made him our Sebastian. They built a tremendous abbey over him where all the kings of England knelt at his shrine, as did the barons before riding off to Runnymede to enforce our law. On St Edmund's Day, November 20th, we read from Proverbs: 'Mercy and truth preserve the King: and his throne is upholden by mercy. The glory of young men is their strength: and the beauty of old men is the grey head.'

As the Mass reaches its mighty climax of *Pleni sunt coeli et terra gloria ejus*, I think of Edmund's bones below the municipal flower beds more fittingly covered now than with jewels, and of him and Cecilia singing away still, for as we know the songs which saints sing have no ending. In his poem *Church-Musick* George Herbert writes,

> Now I in you without a bodie move,
>   Rising and falling with your wings:
> We both together sweetly live and love,
>   Yet say sometimes, God help poore Kings.

The Caught Moment

Listening to Samuel West reading *Ode on a Grecian Urn*, I play around with the notion of the arrested moment. Both John Keats and the urn maker would have spent many hours creating that arrested moment which is the subject of both the potter and the poet. And what a long time it would have taken Vermeer to paint the moment when the milk poured from the jug and Chardin that when the apple-peel fell from the knife. By being able to paint the moment when these ordinary things happened an artist can arouse in us a greater interest than we might have for a battle scene or a shipwreck.

Then arrived the camera and a shutter which fell faster than the guillotine, cutting off death and time in order to produce an arrested moment. As I pore over the old photo album and look deeply into faces, I can say, 'What men or gods are these?' knowing that nobody can tell me. In these Box Brownie snaps, 'what maidens loth' are hanging around Felixstowe pier? What wet dog, what bare young man with his towel, what large woman in pearls, what rushing children, what aeroplane buzzing around in the Thirties' sky, what youth trying his luck on the sands? And

here in a frame is my teenage father off to Gallipoli, fresh
as a daisy in Mr Emeny's studio where soldier after soldier
clasped his cheese-cutter hat as he 'watched the birdie'.
Here is a kilted boy hugging the bagpipes and grinning. '
Heard melodies are sweet, but those unheard/Are
sweeter;/therefore ye soft pipes, play on'. He is dead, that
much I do know. Here am I in Cornwall long ago.

Here is the map of the not so long ago –
The one we spread on the spur of the moment,
Although the road to Lanivet seems to have fallen through a tear
Which was only a crease when we first unfolded it.
Spurred on by it, we reached Bodmin Moor and
Its human sites, its huts and tors, its house of monks.
Look! a corner-full of sea has spilt from the sheet.

There were five of us then and here are the
Photographs to prove it, still as immaculate as those
Words we shouted up by the Cheesewring,
And not one of us older than we would like to look now.

Admire how well the film holds each of us in shape.
Praise its blue day, its technical brightness. Look,
No shadows! How lucky we were to be fixed by that
Solution in the dark room, and so prove how often
We walked on the high ground, looking, talking, loving.

We'll admit some loss of breath, though not of face,
When we stood on Hawks Tor, Rough Tor, or in the
Lea of that farm made out with the lens where we
Spoke of pre-history. Did the hut men's eyes
Widen like ours? Were their naked feet warm to the
Granite? Did their women, like ours, sing them
Down to food by an ancient hearth-stone?

How those old home circles drew us to the Moor.
How we stared where others had stared before.
There they were, just like us, naked in the sun,
Bruised by rocks, pointing to Devon or whatever they
Called it, though innocent of trigs and contours,
Taking-in the ocean and all their realm.

And here we are, all five of us and each with miles to go.
The two of dust smile as they make ready for the descent,
Their faces defining an exact position on this map.

Scratchings

A long walk to the village on the last day of November. Willows, horse-chestnuts and ashes have dropped their leaves, but oaks and sycamores burn with colour and are putting on a show. Rossetti's gold bar of heaven blocks the way to Bures. Children burst from school into cars and are whirled off to hot rooms when they should be shushing their way home through fallen leaves and yelling like freed slaves. The churchyard wall tips towards the lane, though can never fall, it having been locked in this position for as long as anyone can remember. 'The dead are having a stretch', is what they used to say.

I pay calls on the dead. Here is Mrs Constable, John's aunt, aged twenty-eight. Here are the Everards and Nottidges and a better class of people than some I could mention. Here are Mr and Mrs Green who died in 1742, just missing the first performance of Handel's *Messiah*. And here are neighbours who have hurried ahead and who I would have passed on a nice autumn day like this. Their modest memorials lack religious confidence but observe to a T *The Churchyards Handbook*. The church strikes cold and is making its usual noises, clicks and clunks and little sighs. The new *Common Worship* books gleam by the font. Here on a pillar, well-scratched, are the names of T. Scarlett and G. Scarlett who in 1673 decided to be immortal. Further up the aisle a Tudor hand has carved an antler and what looks like a poem or love-letter. And here is a pentagon to keep the Wormingford witches away. There is Jabez on the war memorial. His name means pain.

December

All that Matters - 'A Beckon of Farewell' - The Creation of the Creator - Wisdom Week - Winter at the Window - Theodora - The Truths of Fiction - To Console - On the Shortest Day - The Night Painter - Being Very Old - Christmas Afternoon

All that Matters

It suddenly struck me that the straight line of twelve oaks which lead to Bottengoms and which mark the parish boundary would have been planted when oaks were scarce due to the huge felling caused by Nelson's navy. Entire forests went to sea during the Napoleonic wars. My c.1800 trees shed their leaves with aggravating slowness so that there can be no complete rake-up before Christmas. And then, wonderfully beautiful and youthful though they are in full dress, stripped naked they reveal the pitiful lacerations of the great 1987 gale. Broken boughs, hang-limbs, wounds like those under the bright uniforms of naval officers, are bared for all to see. Every year I wait and hope for the winter winds to bring them down, but still they swing high up against the sky.

I am planting bulbs, dibbing them in swiftly with a robin to help. Tipped with green, they say, hurry, hurry, hurry. Then to a redundant church to buy cards. Stalls for other goods have crept in and the tall grey aisle along which the snowy choir processed with cross and banner is now a little market. Tractarian angels stare down. 'It doesn't seem right', say the ladies taking my cheque. A golden reredos catches the early afternoon sun. A tape plays carols below the fine organ. I note Gainsborough's uncle, the one who sent him off to London to be trained as an artist, is half-way down the Incumbents' Board, the Reverend Humphrey Burrough M.A., his mother's brother. The boy was thirteen and returned home, they said, well versed in petticoats. Shopping in sacred buildings, a bit of business in the holy place, has a long history. Never mind. D.H. Lawrence wrote:

> All that matters is to be one with the Living God,
> To be a creature in the house of the God of Life.
> Like a cat asleep on a chair
> at peace, at peace
> And at one with the master of the house . . .
> feeling the presence of the living God
> like a great reassurance . . .

The small Suffolk market-town of my childhood sparkles with Christmas in every way it can. The pubs are cosy and decorated. The sun goes down below the roofs with a gory crash leaving behind an insipid moon. Country buses squeeze through old streets saying, 'sorry, sorry' as they lumber along. We like to think that poetry is bred on mountains and fields, but it frequently comes from pavements. W.B. Yeats was a 'solitary man', in a crowded London shop when

> While on the shop and street I gazed
> My body of a sudden blazed;
> And twenty minutes more or less
> It seemed, so great my happiness,
> That I was blessed and could bless.

It is Advent and Isaiah and Amos thunder and sing to us in turn, the Official and the self-confessed unofficial prophets, entrancing speakers both. It was actually Isaiah who followed Amos's inspired outbursts, the theme of which was the need of their nation to have a higher concept of God than that which prevailed in the Temple services. So they sang his glory, Isaiah in the process reaching those heights of Messianic prediction which echo in our Advent hymns. As with pregnancy, Advent is more disturbing than the actual birth. It is full of fear and dread. Advent – God's adventure is entering his own creation. Its language is unsparing, its consequence incalculable. It follows me into the bank, into Marks and Spencer's, into the Library, and makes severe argument with the pleasant trash of the season.

'A Beckon of Farewell'

The rain stops and a disconcerting silence follows. Only the swollen stream's voice can be heard. My feet wring water at every step but are not cold. Blackbirds suddenly sing and feed, making a meal out of nothing. The sun makes a brief, gaudy appearance like some old diva on the brink of retirement, casting weak rays over the played-out meadows.

Jean has died. It is most unreasonable of her at her age. I will walk as usual to the village shop and she will not be there en-route to pass the time of day with. I have known her all her life. No Jean in Magdalene Cottage finding something for dinner in her stamp-size garden. No Jean riding her mother's old bike through the alarming cars, no Jean sitting with a neighbour in the field outside making holly wreaths, or being pert with the bus-driver. Him: 'Colchester?' Her: 'Yes – unless you know somewhere more interesting'. So she has left Magdalene Cottage for ever, that precariously sited dwelling by the main road which belonged to her grandparents and which as children we called the Lemonade Shop. There we parked our bikes against the little porch to buy with a penny a glass of water and a spoonful of lemonade crystals. Mrs

Christiana Thompson, Jean's Gran, would wait patiently as we swigged it all.

They were Chapel people, independent folk with a bit of wit, a bit of land, a bit of everything. They went on living at Chapel Corner ages after their green corrugated-iron shrine gave way to a smart bungalow. It had been built with farm labourers' pennies in 1898 and it had bred a distinctive East Anglian spirit. I didn't know that Jean's Gran's name was

The river

Christiana until I took her funeral. Christiana of Magdalene Cottage – how close to John Bunyan these old nonconformists had stayed. Right up until now. We still remember that when Christian died that 'the trumpets sounded for him on the other side' but we have forgotten what happened to his wife. Bunyan's description of the death of a country-woman is exquisite.

'Now the day drew on that Christiana must be gone. So the road was full of people to see her take that journey . . . So she came forth and entered the River with a beckon of farewell . . . So she went and called and entered in at that

Gate with all the ceremonies of joy . . .' These old Stour-dwelling Baptists saw a local Jordan all their lives. Michael the vicar and the Baptist pastor, between them, saw Jean across it in the parish church, as did the entire village. How odd to find her gone, and no age at all, they said.

Advent with its delights and terrors, the birth, the judgement. I see in my mind's eye the crowned Being of the Easter Rite and the mosaic of his two-fingered blessing in the apse. Our painted windows are black inside and coloured in the churchyard. Who names this Child? The hymns are filled with answers. Dayspring, Desire of Nations, Light of All. The medieval knight and his two wives, their hands amputated, lie in wooden prayer. ' Wake, O wake!' we sing.

The Creation of the Creator

It is doubtful if the farmers who lived at Bottengoms do as I do at six a.m., take up a watching position by the stove, tea in mug, cats on knee, silence on the radio, in order to see in the morning. They would have rolled out of bed into the yard whilst their wives lit fires and their children did their chores and their dogs went wild, and their men made sullen appearances. Sit – at six! However, sit I do, often for an hour or more, looking out at blackness, then streaky dawns. At first the window frames a void, then a picture. I could see Nayland if it wasn't for the hill. I can certainly see catkin stubs already. What shall I do today? Later, bathed and fed, I read a chapter or two of Angela Carter's *Wise Children*, a not entirely suitable novel at such an hour. The first Christmas cards, like the first swallows, wing in from abroad, my sister's covered with all the concerts which she has attended in Sydney. One from Africa laments the passing of the years since we last met. Stage coaches gallop along snowy lanes on each of them. I think of sitting in the Opera House with my sister and the shipping in the harbour passing and re-passing so near, but not hearing a note of music, and of the heat outside. The morning gets on its way but taking its time. I write, getting quite a lot done. The telephone is a white mute.

Choosing Sunday's hymns at midday makes a break. Maybe Fred Pratt-Green's 'Long ago, prophets knew', a hymn about pregnancy. He once collected me from Norwich station in his little car to take me to the Literary Society – wise old friend. Or 'Wake O Wake' in which Jesus is long past birth, being a Bridegroom on his way and 'in sight' so that the 'wedding song swells loud and strong'. St John of the Cross is the greatest of the 'epithalamium' poets, seeing himself so absolutely and without question Christ's bride:

> O night that joined the lover
> To the beloved bride
> Transfiguring them each into the other.

Philip Doddridge in 'Ye servants of the Lord' meets the Bridegroom less ecstatically. Advent hymns alternate between the frightening and the blissful, but our choir's commonsense won't let them get out of hand.

Wisdom Week

December gales and everything bends to the winds. I am buffeted to Bury St Edmunds to give a talk to the Sudbury Archdeaconry Retired Clergy Association. We meet in the telling stillness of a retirement home from which weather of every kind is excluded. There is the silence of those who have said all they had to say. Present are parish priests, an archdeacon, a bishop, some canons, all of whom had at some time or other drifted into Suffolk, preached, retired and stayed. I imagine that I am able to read missionary and empire and village lives in their faces. I talk about books, soliciting their reading and chatting about mine. Questions expose scholars and more complexity than might have been assumed. I realise that they know quite a lot about each other and are dryly amused by what they know. How good they are, I think.

It is Wisdom Week – O Sapientia – the feast, if you can call it that, which the Church first celebrated in the Eighth century. St Paul saw Christ as one 'in whom all the treasures of wisdom and knowledge are hidden'. We have to dig for such rewards, they are not to be picked up on the surface. They do not blow across religion like curling leaves which attract a brief attention. As well as O Sapientia we are to remember Dr Johnson, who would have been astonished and even dismayed to have found himself in the Church Calendar. He was a man who was too hard on himself. His kindness was of that rare sort which allows a person to go to great inconvenience in order to help a fellow creature. In his case, a lasting inconvenience which made no sense to his friends. His guiltiness about so many things would have been funny had it not made him so unhappy. He couldn't get up in the morning, he liked a drink but not clean linen, and he loved ladies. Looking at himself, he concluded that his 'was not a life to which Heaven is promised'. But it was.

Winter at the Window

The day is barely light and has been pencilled in. The sheep can only be detected by their movements in the wet grass, the rooks wear their best black and the oaks are stripped at last. The local Adult Community College arrives at the church for a talk, then a walk. O'Connor stained glass (1869) is as rich as fruit-cake and contrasts with the grey outside. My class sits in the frigid pews, the vicar introduces me and then vanishes to snugger climes, and we settle to candle stubs and icy wall tablets, a glimmering reredos and the clunk of the tower clock. I tell them about quoins and bellfounders, place-names and farming, nightingales and knights, dragons in meres and spandrels, the 1870 Education Act, set-aside and the River Stour whose ford gave us birth, and no one blows on their fingers.

We walk to see the churning millrace, and there is Neil laying a hedge, so cameras out. His plants are five year-old maple. He makes a long, daring slash in each stem, slants it over and ties it. A friend assists. They wear helmets and these apart the pair of them might have come straight out of 'December' in a fourteenth century missal. They are standing where Wormingford began. In the warm pub, drinking coffee I suddenly think again of the wall tablets, of their harsh whiteness and arctic surface, especially the one to a young man who failed to come back from the Raj. Tennyson, grief stricken by the death of his friend Arthur Hallam who died abroad and who had a similar memorial put up to him in his West Country church, wrote, 'There comes a glory on the walls.'

> Thy marble bright in dark appears,
>   As slowly steals a silver flame
> Along the letters of thy name,
>   And o'er the number of thy years.

Theodora

Having felled the dead apple-tree I stand aghast. What a space, what wreckage. What a stump. Passing walkers stare at the mad axeman. Then all is changed. Tony Venison arrives suddenly, surveys the scene and says, 'A Rambling Rector rose.' The late and much mourned Geoff Hamilton used to tell us that this unruly and cover-all Moschata hybrid was worth growing for its name alone. Rambling Rectors have risen to wayward heights in English gardens ever since the Reformation, covering old trees with huge hanks of white flowers. ' Prepare the bed,' orders Tony and goes off to buy me one. In doing so I excavate a barrow-load of broken bricks, a pottery jam-jar and somebody's abandoned straw nest. The soil is rich and friable and tied together by nettle roots.

At Little Horkesley Theodora accepts her Anglican-Greek baptism without a murmur. 'She is not to be called Thea' commands an Athenian cousin 'because it means "aunt"'. Silent, and delicately beautiful, Theodora lies in her grandmother's shawl in Michael's arms, oblivious to her rite of passage, the mopping of her brow, the sugared almonds, the silver crosses which the Greek relations are now pinning

to our lapels, the choir's 'I sing of a maiden' and my Orthodox
prayer, discovered in an old book:

> Blessed is God, who desires that all men should be saved and
> come to the knowledge of the truth,
> Blessed is God, who gives light and sanctification to every
> man that comes into the world.
> Blessed are they whose transgressions are forgiven and whose
> sins are covered.
> Blessed is the man to whom the Lord imputeth no sin, and in
> whose mouth there is no deceit.
> O Christ our God, rich in mercy, who clotheth thyself with
> light as with a garment, grant unto us a robe that is radiant
> with light.
> Grant unto Theodore this robe of light, Amen.

From the christening feast in the old barn we look down on
uphill and a-dale farmland, and devour honeyed biscuits
served on lemon-tree leaves brought from Athens, and
Theodore is handed around from woman to woman,
sleeping, sleeping.

The Truths of Fiction

I have gone to purchase my Christmas cards in the church
where, as a boy, I went to Evensong. I sit on a stack-chair and
look around half expecting to see the long dead crouching in
the invisible pews. But it smells the same as it did, and this is
a comfort. And G.F. Bodley's golden reredos shines just the
same. But the fine organ which the immortal Mr Vinnicombe

played for half a century is silent. He taught my brother Gerald music, dropping a book on his fingers when the sounds became unbearable. Working my way along the Charity Cards stall, hearing the river-long choir sweep up the aisle to 'Hark, the glad sound, the Saviour comes!', I see him rolling on the organ-stool in the candle-light, rotund, perfectionist, thinking of a visit to the Four Swans after the service. Yes, the Charity Cards' lady is willing to take a cheque. Yes, Robert Cardinall's paintings of Moses and Aaron are still in place. They had been the altarpiece when Thomas Gainsborough was a child here and he would have seen them. Outside the west door the market traders pack up their stalls and call it a day. Villagers pile into muddy buses. Back home I read 'The Adoration of the Magi' on one side of my cards and Alzheimers on the other.

Early morning and there is a wisp of dawn over Duncan's farm. The radio rattles along with things which do not penetrate, then, like a blow, it says that Malcolm Bradbury has died. Malcolm my friend, Malcolm who taught Ian McEwan, Rose Tremain, Kazuo Ishiguro, who told them, 'You are a storyteller'. Malcolm who understood better than most the importance of the novel as a teller of the truth – dead, alas. Fiction can contain and reveal aspects of reality which are beyond other forms of expression.

Christ's friends were made uneasy now and then by their great teacher's descent into storytelling. Surely a master should leave that kind of thing to the entertainer by the hearth or in the market place. But Christianity was taught in a series of excellent tales, as well as in sermons. In Waterstone's I search for suitable presents. The tables tremble under the diaries of politicians and the lives of footballers. But here are the novels, shelves and shelves of the truth. Malcolm would have approved to see his students there in force. He has made the day different – his going, that is. When friends are not very well for quite a long time one expects them to live for ever.

To Console

The view from on high – i.e. my study window from which centuries of farmers would have woke up to find snow. The window too from which John Nash, a snowophile, would sometimes paint the white garden. What he particularly liked were moderate falls which allowed the brown winter grass to poke through. His first great winter picture was 'Over the Top' in which a group of heavily clad soldiers scrambled out of their trench, their khaki and the snow creating the colour mood which the artist looked for all his life. He once told me that he had given one of the soldiers the face of a singer he had heard at the Queen's Hall just before he joined up in 1916 'to show the death of civilization'.

Helmeted riders jog past just as I am looking out and give little nods. Blackbirds scuttle under the Butcher's Broom (*Ruscus aculeatus*), a glossy Mediterranean shrub much admired by Virgil. A surprisingly hot sun then enters the smeary glass. The radio can't keep up with snow chaos, as it calls it. Ian telephones from Edinburgh to tell me that the city is an enchantment and that he too cannot cease staring at it from his Prince's Street eyrie and 'O that we were there!' I make do with the Stour Valley, stopping every few yards to regain breath, the cold snatching it from me. Lapwings have arrived, snow or no snow, and are parked with their customary neatness across the levels. Soon the 'lapping' of their wings will precede courtship. At the moment they are standing stockstill, crested and bright, and all turned to the west.

I am reading Kazuo Ishiguru's novel *The Unconsoled* just as Bishop Harries talks of consolation on 'Thought for the Day'. He speaks of the failures of consolation and about Iris Murdoch pronouncing it a fake. There are moments when

Four guinea fowl 1983

one must not attempt to console, when the word must not be uttered to the parents of murdered children. When one should keep one's mouth shut. 'In Rama was there a voice heard, lamentation, and weeping, and great mourning, Rachel weeping for her children, and would not be comforted, because they are not.' Yet consolation is among the Church's gifts and many Christians found it best expressed in an ancient book called *The Consolation of Philosophy* by a writer who was thought not to be a Christian, Boethius. He wrote it in prison during the sixth century. King Alfred, Geoffrey Chaucer and Elizabeth I, each translated it, and the whole of Europe read it, for there has always been a need to be consoled. Boethius was a wise statesman who spoke up for a friend who was wrongly accused of treason, and who was executed. To be without a philosophy, to lack a philosophical language in religion, would certainly make me disconsolate. Cast down. To be acceptable, consolation must be pushed past kindly platitudes and could take the shape of a silence in which an immense sorrow can begin to heal.

A tramp to the village school where the World War Two air-raid shelter has been turned into an office for our Headteacher Mags. The Bishop of Chelmsford is here to bless it. St Andrew's School itself is of ecclesiastical flint and cut stone and is redolent of the 1870 Education Act. We talk of epic snowfalls such as that in 1947 when the bus slithered through arctic canyons below Sandy Hill. The thing about snow is that it is not very interesting except at the local level, when it is enthralling. The air-raid shelter has in turn been loos then a store for defunct desks and now a carpeted and computered den for Mags. The newest pupil cuts the ribbon to declare it open yet again. Never throw away an air-raid shelter, it is sure to come in handy.

On the Shortest Day

This is a date which held for my father some portent he was unable to explain. He had to announce it without fail, 'This is the shortest day!' Looking at the tall bare may-hedge and the colourless sky, this time it is certainly one of those English under-stated days, the kind which Thomas Hardy found dismally to his taste, to his inspiration even. Job once admitted to having said things which he did not understand - 'things too wonderful for me, which I knew not'. And Coleridge confessed to suffering a similar dilemma. 'Did I say that?'

They are saying that a quarter of our farmers have left the land these last two years – plus their men of course. It is like a re-run of that 'flight from the land' before the First World War when the great agricultural depression spelt ruin for master and man alike. It was set in motion by endless rain and by the huge grain imports from the prairie farms of North America and Canada. We in East Anglia called it 'the coming down time' as the old family farms collapsed. What a slide into the abyss it was. The government asked the Norfolk farmer-novelist Henry Rider Haggard to make an inventory of the disaster, this in 1900. It sits on my shelf, this village by village account of the fields being deserted and the people fled. Rider Haggard quoted Judges on the title-page - 'The highways were unoccupied . . . the inhabitants of the villages ceased'. Looking at the A12 and at Wormingford, one could hardly say this now, but looking at our fields you would be lucky to see anyone at work in them. The countryside now has a new kind of resident who is neither rural nor urban, or suburban, but is as yet unspecified. In certain circumstances it is not possible to say who or what we are, only time will tell us this.

This shortest day is mild and still. Primroses are in bloom. So is the brave *minimus narcissus*. A few of them trumpet goldenly on my desk, an early Christmas present. In the half-light I cut out brambles and rake up black leaves. Towards evening I join the army of shoppers in the High Street, our swollen plastic bags shining like huge pearls under the festive lights. Young families with beautiful faces pass. Plaguing children tug at hands. Worn to shreds taped carols go on and on. A kind of human goodness passes and re-passes. People seem to retain a serious thought in their heads as they buy foolish things, reminding me of what the Irish poet W.R. Rodgers wrote:

> To welcome gravity, and to forego fun
> Is still their fate who seek the heavenly One
> And choose the Star.

The Night Painter

It is Huneker the Jewish feast of light. Joachim will be leaving his Berlin flat for the synagogue, probably on his motorbike to dodge the neo-Nazi yobbos. He has been busy designing the gardens for the Museum of the Wall. I think of him and his light, and his intellectual face, and his work, as I am taken to David and Elaine's for a contemplation of light and darkness. 'Dovecots for sale' says a sign at their gate. Their river is the Colne and it slinks along by their white house. Twelve of us are sitting in a ring in a candle-lit barn and although it is midday I find myself thinking of the painters of night, Rembrandt particularly. In his study of the artist's domesticity, *Rembrandt's House* Anthony Bailey describes how he acknowledges light and darkness being part of earth and air, and how in the paintings and drawings the viewer is forced to search for the source of whatever light there is. Elaine, speaking for light, hands each one of us a postcard of a Rembrandt nativity and we gaze, not on 'the great judge and king of all', but on a little Dutch boy who is all light and who looks out from what looks like a Wormingford barn, big black house that it is. The boy glows in the rustic gloom - Saskia's baby? Rembrandt's last painting, discovered on the easel after his death, was *Simeon in the Temple*. An old man now holds the little Dutch boy, addressing him as a light to lighten the Gentiles. The Temple is sparsely illuminated, as all interiors were before electricity. Walking home down the black track, the floodlit tower of Stoke-by-Nayland church blazes five miles away. Frost threatens, so I find a Waitrose bag to cover a stem of yucca blossom – yuccas have no idea of the seasons and will bloom at dead of winter or midsummer. Back in the farmhouse I stand by the light-switch, savouring the darkness of an ancient interior, attempting to see what Rembrandt saw, the furniture shapes, the rooms running into each other without end, the absence of definition.

Being Very Old

Harold rides his bike to the Beehive at eighty-five, Flo walks into church for Evensong at a hundred-and-one, and wearing silver shoes, and Helen, now a centenarian, waits for Gordon and me to have coffee with her after Matins. Spread on the chenille tablecloth will be her latest quiz, simmering on the Aga will be her lunch, in her sitting-room flames will be leaping from a good coal fire. Although she knows that the world is divided between those who can do word puzzles and those who go to pieces at the mere sight of an anagram, she says, 'I have saved the literary ones for you'. And I think, 'I have known you most of my life, dear cruel old friend, and it is no good saying I have forgotten my glasses' because Gordon will say try his.

I first came to Helen's when her front room was the Post Office, her garden was a kennels, and the slight scarcely altered figure pouring the coffee was walking onto the village hall stage in an Agatha Christie play. Helen no longer comes to church after sixty years in the choir - 'Let it come to me'. Fair enough. Very old people are young in their own rooms but not as young outside them. Michael arrives with the Sacraments and we all sit round reading our cards. When we leave, she watches us from where she believes she is hidden, but where we can trace her shape. It is where the Post Office counter was and she waits by it, quite still, very pale. She has no truck with theological questions and is among our cradle nonconformists who sing, 'Blessed assurance, Jesus is mine!' And that is that.

Christmas Afternoon

Home from Little Horkesley church and a turmoil of children to a roaring fire and a blizzard of cards. I have said farewell to the medieval wooden knight and his ladies and seen that they are stuck with holly, and to Jane Austen's ancestor in the sanctuary, and to the cheery mob, and now the feast is my own. I will eat chicken and drink port and read a life of John Winthrop and answer telephone calls from Sydney. They will begin with banter about the weather, their heat, my cold. Their beach, my snow-laden house. Except it is not un-springlike, a nippy wind notwithstanding.

John Winthrop lived a few miles from Wormingford. The entire area was known as the Godly people of the Stour Valley, Puritans all and determined to be the Godly people of Massachusetts Bay. As a boy I used to imagine them setting out in their wagons for the coast and turning at the crossroads to watch their farmhouses vanishing from sight, this house maybe. I thought of their first Christmas in 1630, an abolished feast, and some lurking hankering for a revel. Winthrop, the new Governor of this fraction of Massachusetts, and as such the ancestor of the White House, wrote in his journal: 'The wind comes from the northwest very strong and some snow' and that it was 'so cold as some had their fingers frozen and in some danger to be lost'. On Christmas Day they ate clams, mussels, ground nuts and acorns, and made such big fires to keep warm that they burnt some of the houses down. Hezekiah Woodward said that Christmas was 'the old Heathens' Fasting Day, in honour to Saturn their Idol-God, the Papists' Massing Day, and the Profane Man's Ranting Day, the Superstitious Man's Idol Day, the Multitude's Idle Day, Satan's – that Adversary's – Working Day and the True Christian's Fasting Day' and that he was persuaded 'no one thing more hindreth the Gospel – than Christmas'. So Scrooge was right after all. Curiously, the new Governor allowed some Valentine customs. He had been married three times and wrote exquisite letters to his second wife. 'Thou must be my Valentine, for none hath challenged me'.

And then I remember Christmases in Cornwall. Though

not as far as Massachusetts they are now remote. How we walked along Constantine Bay, how we - all the post-dinner walkers – were spread out in such faraway groups that there could only be passing shouts. How the tide hissed in and out and the gulls wailed. How my Cornish friends boasted about the Cornish warmth, as compared with the Suffolk climate, and how wrong they were, although I was too polite to say so. All this is now pictures in the fire. The cats rise from the hearth and stroll through the cards, toppling them over, and there is enough food in the old brick larder to feed the five thousand without a miracle. Television on Christmas Day is forbidden and CDs play holy music, and the pages turn.

There is, many have 'heard' it, a birthday singing in the air. Poets have orchestrated it, so it must be true. It is like the everlasting rise and fall of the Cornish sea or the oceanic voice in shells. The Godly folk at Massachusetts Bay might have cut out the romps – including ball games in the muddy street, but would they not have talked so much about Scripture that their tongues drowned out the angels' song? God must have a special earplug for Christmas so that he can listen to such words as the Eastern Orthodox Church kept by them for this annual happiness.

'Christ is born, give glory, Christ comes from heaven, meet him. Christ is on earth, be exalted. O all the earth, sing unto the Lord, and sing praises in gladness, O all ye people, for he has been glorified.'

But now we have two Bethlehems, the 'little town' of the carol, like the Child lying so still, and that concrete city on the screen with the tanks blundering through Manger Square, and yet they remain one and the same Birthplace. And so the year ends once more, profoundly among the pretty litter, the log ash and the soft rain.